CAMBRIDGE
UNIVERSITY PRESS

Cambridge Lower Secondary

Computing

LEARNER'S BOOK 7

Victoria Ellis & Sarah Lawrey

CAMBRIDGE
UNIVERSITY PRESS

Shaftesbury Road, Cambridge CB2 8EA, United Kingdom

One Liberty Plaza, 20th Floor, New York, NY 10006, USA

477 Williamstown Road, Port Melbourne, VIC 3207, Australia

314–321, 3rd Floor, Plot 3, Splendor Forum, Jasola District Centre, New Delhi – 110025, India

103 Penang Road, #05–06/07, Visioncrest Commercial, Singapore 238467

Cambridge University Press is part of the University of Cambridge.

It furthers the University's mission by disseminating knowledge in the pursuit of education, learning and research at the highest international levels of excellence.

www.cambridge.org
Information on this title: www.cambridge.org/9781009297059

20 19 18 17 16 15 14 13 12 11 10 9 8 7 6

Printed in Malaysia by Vivar Printing

A catalogue record for this publication is available from the British Library

ISBN 978-1-009-29705-9 Paperback with Digital Access (1 Year)
ISBN 978-1-009-29703-5 Digital Learner's Book (1 Year)
ISBN 978-1-009-29702-8 eBook

Additional resources for this publication at www.cambridge.org/go

Endorsement statement

Endorsement indicates that a resource has passed Cambridge International's rigorous quality-assurance process and is suitable to support the delivery of a Cambridge International curriculum framework. However, endorsed resources are not the only suitable materials available to support teaching and learning, and are not essential to be used to achieve the qualification. Resource lists found on the Cambridge International website will include this resource and other endorsed resources.

Any example answers to questions taken from past question papers, practice questions, accompanying marks and mark schemes included in this resource have been written by the authors and are for guidance only. They do not replicate examination papers. In examinations the way marks are awarded may be different. Any references to assessment and/or assessment preparation are the publisher's interpretation of the Cambridge International curriculum framework requirements. Examiners will not use endorsed resources as a source of material for any assessment set by Cambridge International.

While the publishers have made every attempt to ensure that advice on the qualification and its assessment is accurate, the official curriculum framework, specimen assessment materials and any associated assessment guidance materials produced by the awarding body are the only authoritative source of information and should always be referred to for definitive guidance. Cambridge International recommends that teachers consider using a range of teaching and learning resources based on their own professional judgement of their students' needs.

Cambridge International has not paid for the production of this resource, nor does Cambridge International receive any royalties from its sale. For more information about the endorsement process, please visit www.cambridgeinternational.org/endorsed-resources

Third-party websites and resources referred to in this publication have not been endorsed by Cambridge Assessment International Education.

Introduction

Welcome to Stage 7 of Cambridge Lower Secondary Computing!

Computers and technology play an important role in our lives and are all around us. Learning about technology will help you understand the world you live in.

In this book, you will:

- develop your computational thinking skills and create programs in Python
- discover how data can be used to plan and help us in real-life situations
- learn all about different types of networks and how data allows us to access websites
- think critically about devices and systems and how useful they are for a certain purpose, such as asking yourself, 'What does the internet allow us to do?'

...and much more!

Computer scientists work with lots of different people when developing computer programs. Like a computer scientist, you will have lots of opportunities to work with a partner or a group in the activities throughout this book. Sharing your ideas with other people helps you learn more about how computers and technology are used. You can always learn new skills from working with others!

Some of the activities will be done away from a computer. These activities will develop your computing knowledge, and activities on the computer will develop your computing skills.

There is also a project for you to complete at the end of each unit. These give you the chance to be creative and will help you develop your understanding.

We hope you find learning more about computers and technology exciting, and that you enjoy discovering how the modern world works.

Victoria Ellis and Sarah Lawrey

Contents

Note for teachers: Throughout the resource there is a symbol to indicate where additional digital only content is required. This content can be accessed through the Digital Learner's Book on Cambridge GO. It can be launched either from the Media tab or directly from the page.

The symbol that denotes additional digital content is:

The source files can also be downloaded from the Source files tab on Cambridge GO. In addition, this tab contains a teacher guidance document which supports the delivery of digital activities and programming tasks in this Learner's Book.

How to use this book

This book contains lots of different features that will help your learning. These are explained below.

This list sets out what you will learn in each topic. You can use these points to identify the important topics for the lesson.

In this topic you will:

- understand the structure of a flowchart
- know how to follow a flowchart
- learn how to edit a flowchart
- learn how to correct a flowchart
- create a flowchart to solve a problem.

This contains questions or activities to help find out what you know already about this topic.

Getting started

What do you already know?

- You should have seen flowcharts, or other types of diagram, where you follow the arrows from one box to another.
- You should be able to follow a sequence of instructions, or an algorithm.
- You should have experience of creating and editing algorithms. For example, you might have created programs using Scratch.

Important words are highlighted in the text when they first appear in the book. You will find an explanation of the meaning of these words in the text. You will also find definitions of all these words in the Glossary and Index at the back of this book.

Key words

data flow
flowchart
input
output
process
variable

You will have the opportunity to practise and develop the new skills and knowledge that you learn in each topic. Activities will involve answering questions or completing tasks by using a computer. Some activities don't require a computer. These are called unplugged activities, and they help you understand important ideas about computing.

Unplugged activity 1.5

You will need: a pen and paper

An algorithm needs to take the number of hours from the input, and then output the number of minutes in those hours, and the number of seconds.

The flowchart pieces are shown in a random order. On a piece of paper, rearrange the flowchart symbols and draw the lines to join them together.

minutes = hours * 24

Start

OUTPUT minutes & "minutes"

seconds = minutes * 60

OUTPUT seconds & "seconds"

Stop

INPUT hours

OUTPUT "input the

Peer-assessment questions help you evaluate the work of your peers.

Unplugged activity 1.7

You will need: a pen and paper

Write a list of questions that make use of the comparison operators – for example, 'Is 2 < 1'? Make sure that you have at least one question for each operator.

Swap your questions with a partner.

Write an answer to each of your partner's questions.

Swap the answers back.

Peer-assessment

Check your partner's answers. Give them a tick if they are correct. Add the number of ticks and give your partner a final mark.

If your partner has any incorrect answers, explain to them why their answer was incorrect, and make sure they understand the reasons.

These tasks help you to practise what you have learnt in a topic.

Programming tasks are in Unit 1

Programming task 1.1: Investigate

Investigate:

Read through this flowchart by yourself and identify its purpose.

Join with a partner and explain to your partner what the flowchart does.

Identify the variable and what it will store.

Use your own name as input and tell your partner what the output is.

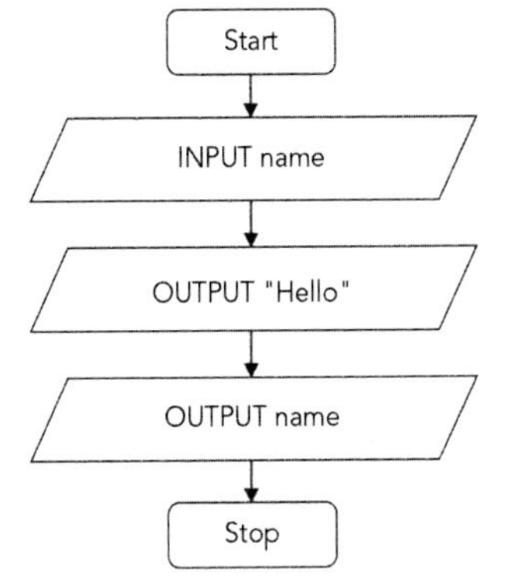

Figure 1.11: Flowchart for programming task

Practical tasks are in Unit 2

Practical task 2.6

You will need: a desktop computer, laptop or tablet with source file **2.3_computer_games.accdb**

Open the file 2.3_computer_games.accdb. You are going to create a query to find out which games in the database have an age rating for children over 10 years of age. The criteria that you will need to create this query is '>10' for the Age rating field.

Use the instructions given above to create a query.

1 Make all the fields appear in the query.
2 Add the criteria to the Age rating field.
3 View the results of the query.

Self-assessment

Look at the answer section or ask your teacher to tell you what the query results should be.

- Did you get the same result from your query?
- If you did, why do you think these are the only records that appear?
- If you didn't, can you see where you may have done something incorrect? Follow the instructions again carefully to check your query design is correct. Make sure that you have put the correct criteria in the criteria row.

Self-assessment questions help you think about your work and how you learn.

When you see this icon, you are going to do a digital activity using a source file or website link. This content can be found on Cambridge GO. Your teacher will help you to get started.

These questions help you to practise what you have just learnt.

Questions 1.3
1 What is a selection statement?
2 What shape is selection in a flowchart?
3 How many arrows come from a selection box in a flowchart, and what is written on each?
4 What are the three parts of a selection statement?

Important safety tips to remember when using a computer and going online.

Stay safe!

Remember to always make sure that any website you use will encrypt your personal data before you send

These tell you interesting facts connected to the topic.

Did you know?

Flowcharts are used in all sorts of industries and professions, not just computer science. You are just as likely to see a flowchart in science, geography, history or even

This contains questions that ask you to look back at what you have covered and encourages you to think about your learning.

Next time you write a program, what will you do differently? Will you do more planning before you start? Or revisit some of your past programs to help you identify what to do?

This list summarises the important material that you have learnt in the topic.

Summary checklist

- [ ] I can identify the flowchart shapes for input/output, process and start/stop.
- [ ] I can follow a flowchart.
- [ ] I can test a flowchart using input data and checking the output.
- [ ] I can find an error in a flowchart and correct it.
- [ ] I can make a change to a flowchart.
- [ ] I can create a flowchart to solve a problem.

At the end of each unit, there is a project that you might carry out by yourself or with other learners. This will involve using some of the knowledge that you developed during the unit. Your project might involve creating or producing something, or you might solve a problem.

Project 1: micro:bit bird

You need to develop an interactive bird using the micro:bit.

This bird needs to be visual; that is, an image.

Users need to be able to interact with the bird. For example, they might feed it, let it fly or put it in a tree.

You will need to work in pairs to do the following.

- Create a design for the bird and give it a suitable name.
- Decide how the user will interact with the bird. There must be at least two actions they can do.
- Decide what the input for each action will be, and the output. How will the user know what they have done?
- Produce evidence of testing your program.

These questions look back at some of the content you learnt in each unit. If you can answer these, you are ready to move on to the next unit.

Check your progress 3

1 State the name of the text-based address for a website. [1]

2 Which of the following would help keep data safe when it is transmitted from one device to another? Select the correct answer. [1]

A Crosstalk

B Decryption

C Encryption

1 Computational thinking and programming

1.1 Flowcharts

In this topic you will:

- understand the structure of a flowchart
- know how to follow a flowchart
- learn how to edit a flowchart
- learn how to correct a flowchart
- create a flowchart to solve a problem.

Key words

data flow
flowchart
input
output
process
variable

Getting started

What do you already know?

- You should have seen flowcharts, or other types of diagram, where you follow the arrows from one box to another.
- You should be able to follow a sequence of instructions, or an algorithm.
- You should have experience of creating and editing algorithms. For example, you might have created programs using Scratch.

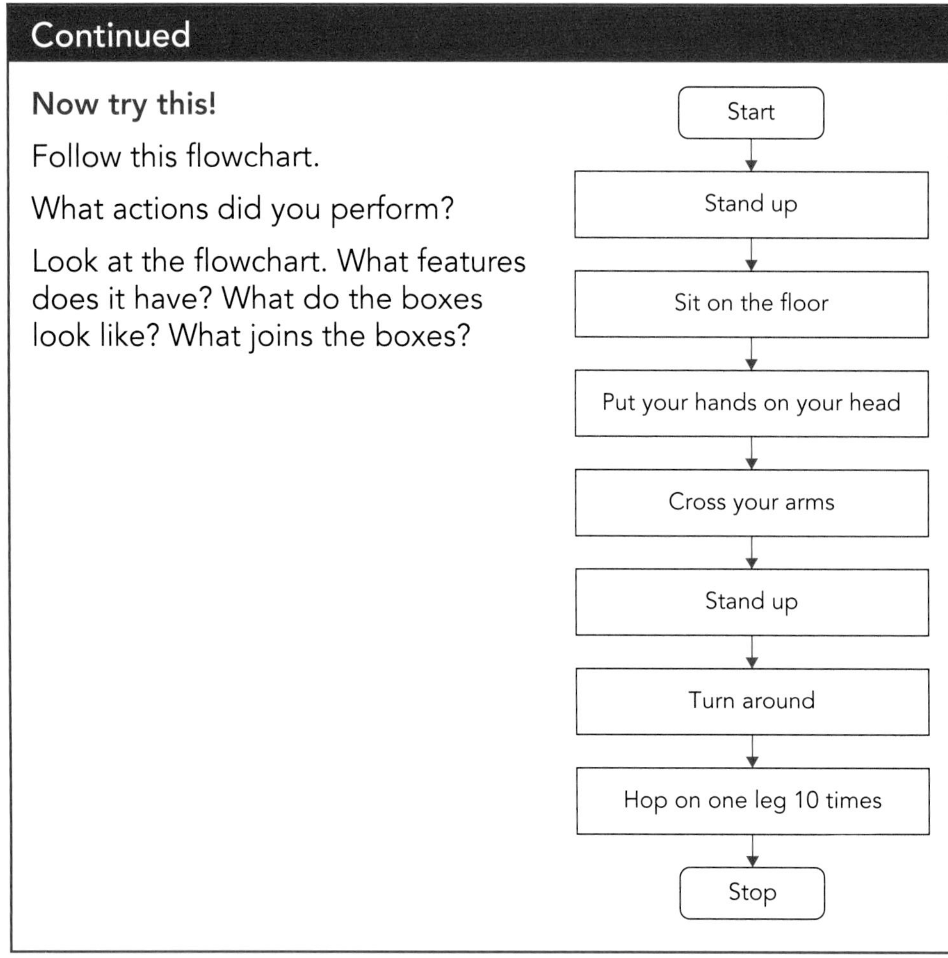

Following flowcharts

A **flowchart** is a diagram that shows a sequence of steps that should be followed. The diagram could ask you to do practical activities, like the one in the Now try this! task, or it could represent the steps that a computer program will follow.

Both types of flowchart will have the same features, so we will look at both.

A flowchart has to follow set rules. These rules include:

- specific shapes for different purposes:
    - **input** – for the user to enter data
    - **process** – to do a calculation or action
    - **output** – to display words and numbers to the user
- a start and a stop (sometimes these might be labelled 'begin' and 'end')
- **data flows** (the arrows that show you how to move through the flowchart).

This table shows the flowchart shapes and their purpose.

Shape	Description	Example
	Start or stop Start: this is the first box in a flowchart. It has an arrow to the first box to run. Stop: this is the last box in a flowchart. It has an arrow from the last box to run.	Start Stop
	Input or output Input: this takes a value from the user and stores it somewhere. Output: this displays a message, or makes a sound.	Shout "Hello" OUTPUT "Hello"
	Process This is an action. It tells something to change.	Stand up Number = number + 1

Table 1.1: Shapes used in flowcharts and their meanings

Data flow

A data flow is an arrow. The arrows show you which box to move to next.

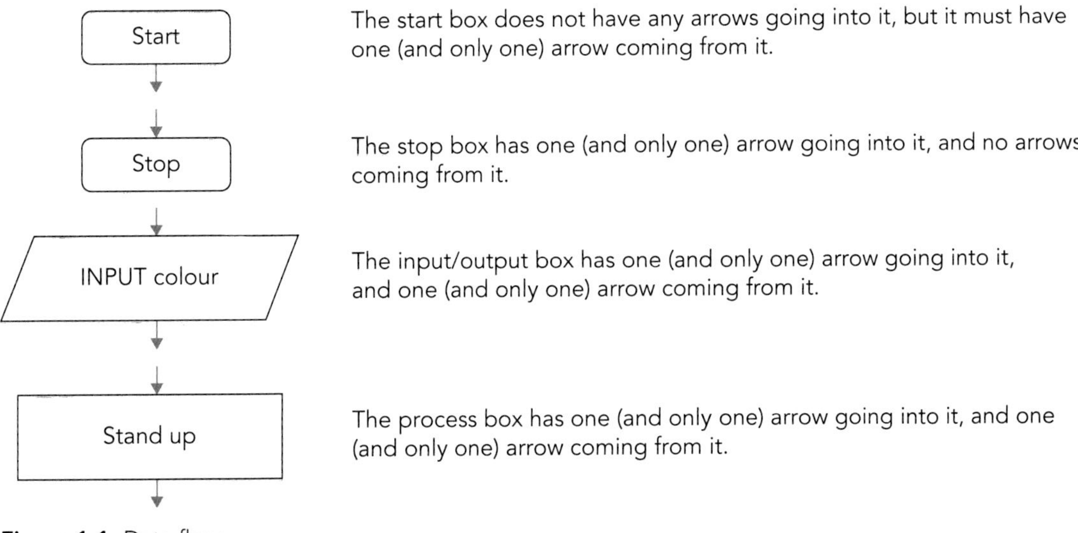

Figure 1.1: Data flow

Questions 1.1

1 What is the shape of the output box?

2 What is the shape of the process box?

3 How many data flows go into a start box?

4 How many data flows go into a stop box?

Following a flowchart

To follow a flowchart:

- find the start box
- follow the arrow from start to the next shape
- perform the action in each shape
- continue until you reach the stop box.

Unplugged activity 1.1

Follow this flowchart and perform each of the actions.
Compare what you did with a classmate.
Did you do anything differently?

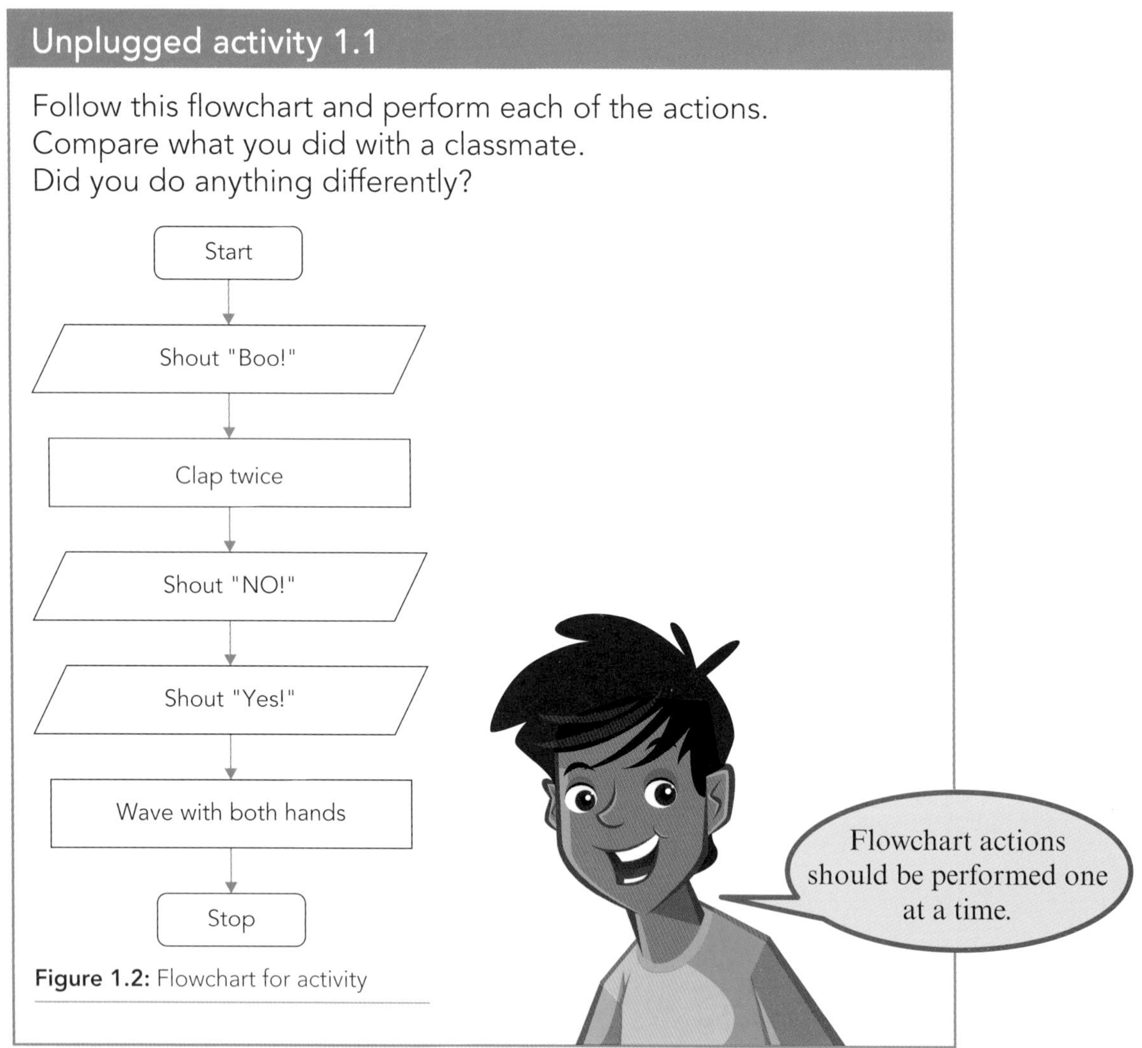

Figure 1.2: Flowchart for activity

Storing data

Read this flowchart:

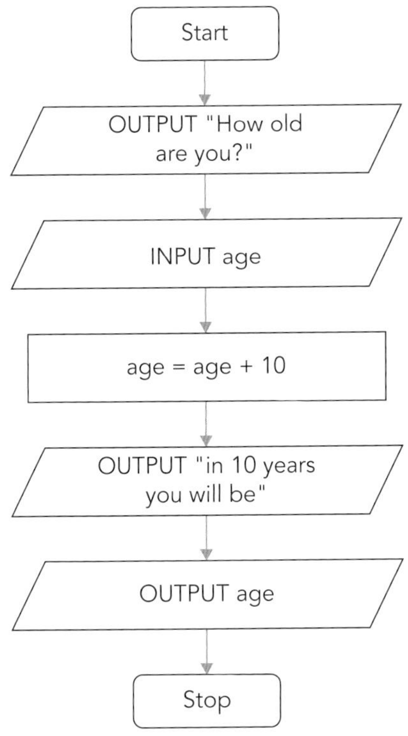

Figure 1.3: Flowchart

This flowchart uses a **variable**. A variable is a named storage location where you can store data. The data value can change in a variable. In this flowchart, the variable is `age`.

The flowchart can put data into `age`, for example:

INPUT age

Figure 1.4: Input box

The data the user enters will be stored in `age`.

The flowchart can change the data in `age`, for example:

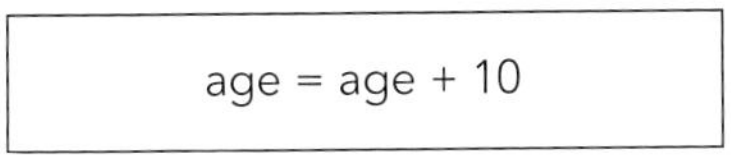

age = age + 10

Figure 1.5: Process box changing data

This adds 10 to `age` and then stores the result.

The flowchart can access the data in `age`, for example:

This will output the contents of `age`.

OUTPUT age

Figure 1.6: Output box

Unplugged activity 1.2

You will need: an empty box, a sticker, pieces of paper and some pens

Get into groups of three and number yourselves 1, 2 and 3.

Someone in the group should write `'number'` on a sticker and put it on the box. The box is going to act as the variable.

Figure 1.7: The 'variable'

Put a value into `number`:

- Person 1 writes 23 on a piece of paper
- That person then opens the box and puts the piece of paper in the box

`number` now stores 23.

Figure 1.8: Storing a number in the 'variable'

Continued

Add 10 to `number`. Person 2 performs these actions.

- Open the box and take the piece of paper out.
- Add 10 to the number on the paper.
- Write this value on a new piece of paper.
- Put the new piece of paper in the box.

`number` should now store 33.

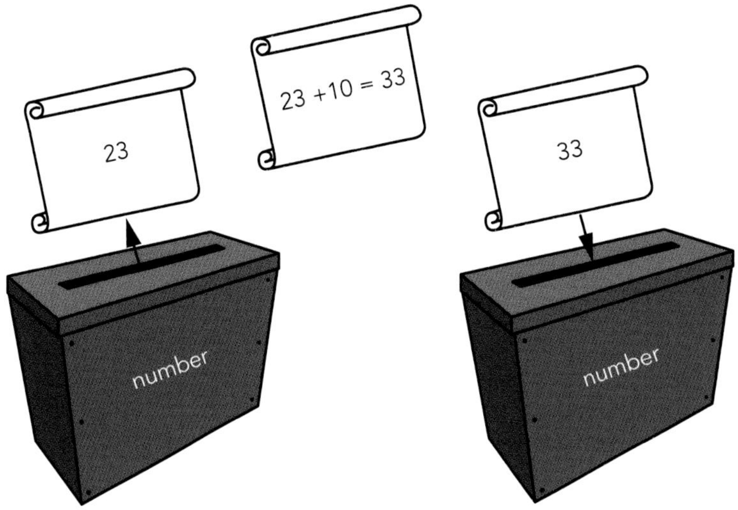

Figure 1.9: Changing the number in the 'variable'

Outputting `number`.

- Person 3 should open the box and take the piece of paper out.
- Read out what is on the piece of paper.
- Put the same piece of paper back in the box.

33 should have been output.

Take it in turns to give the other members of your group instructions to either put a value into `number`, change the content of `number` or output the content of `number`.

Everyone should follow the instructions to make sure they are run correctly.

Figure 1.10: The output

Programming task 1.1: Investigate

Investigate:

Read through this flowchart by yourself and identify its purpose.

Join with a partner and explain to your partner what the flowchart does.

Identify the variable and what it will store.

Use your own name as input and tell your partner what the output is.

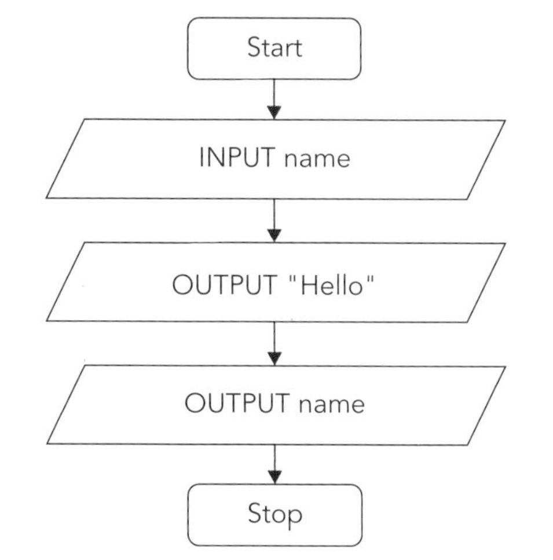

Figure 1.11: Flowchart for programming task

Did you know?

Flowcharts are used in all sorts of industries and professions, not just computer science. You are just as likely to see a flowchart in science, geography, history or even philosophy.

Programming task 1.2: Predict and Run

Predict: Discuss the purpose of this flowchart with a partner. Explain to each other what the flowchart will do.

Run: Test your program. The first time, input the number 10. The second time, input the number 20.

- What is the total?
- Were you correct?

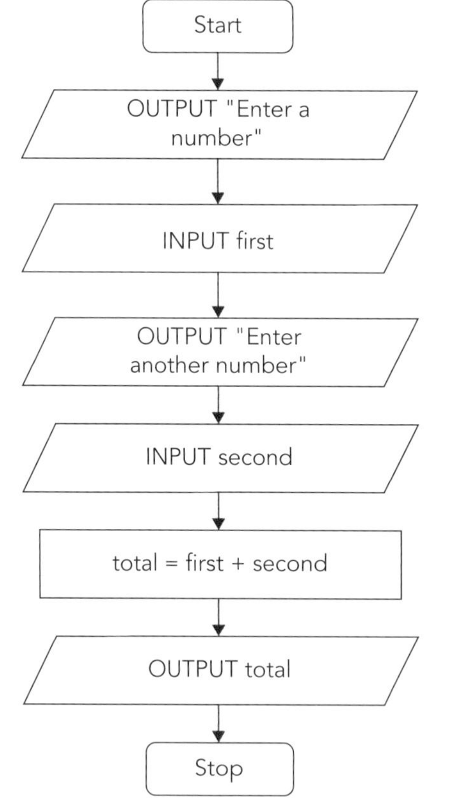

Figure 1.12: Flowchart for programming task

Editing and correcting flowcharts

You may be given a flowchart that does not work – it doesn't do what it is supposed to do. Or you could be given a flowchart that needs to be changed to do something new, or to do something extra.

Before you do either of these, you first need to trace the algorithm yourself. You need to walk through the flowchart one step at a time to find out what it does.

Correcting errors

If you need to correct an error, compare what the flowchart does to what it should do. For example, the number 20 is output instead of the number 10. You need to find out why and then make the change.

Common errors may include:

- using the wrong mathematical operator (+, -, *, /)
- using the wrong values in a calculation
- not taking the correct value as input from the user
- outputting an incorrect value.

You need to test the flowchart before you look for the error, and then test it again with the same data after to make sure it now works.

Unplugged activity 1.3

This flowchart should add together three numbers that are input by the user and output the result.

There is an error in the flowchart.

Work in pairs to walk through the flowchart and find out what it does.

Input some numbers – for example, 1, 2, 3 – and see whether it outputs the correct value (6).

Did the flowchart give the correct result?

Discuss with your partner where the error is and change the flowchart. Test your flowchart with the same data and see if it gives the correct result.

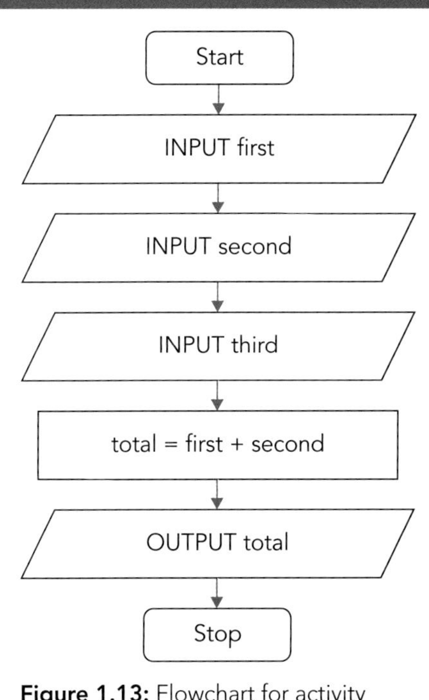

Figure 1.13: Flowchart for activity

Programming task 1.3: Predict, Run and Investigate

You will need: a pen and paper

This flowchart should:

- take a number from the user
- multiply the number by 2 and output it in a message
- multiply the number by 4 and output it in a message.

Predict: Identify a number to be input.
Write down what the output should be.

Run: Test the flowchart with the number you have identified and write down the output.

Investigate:

1 Identify where there is a difference between what you predicted, and the result.

2 Identify the error, or multiple errors, and change the flowchart.

3 Re-test the flowchart with the same number. Write down the output.

Repeat until the flowchart works.

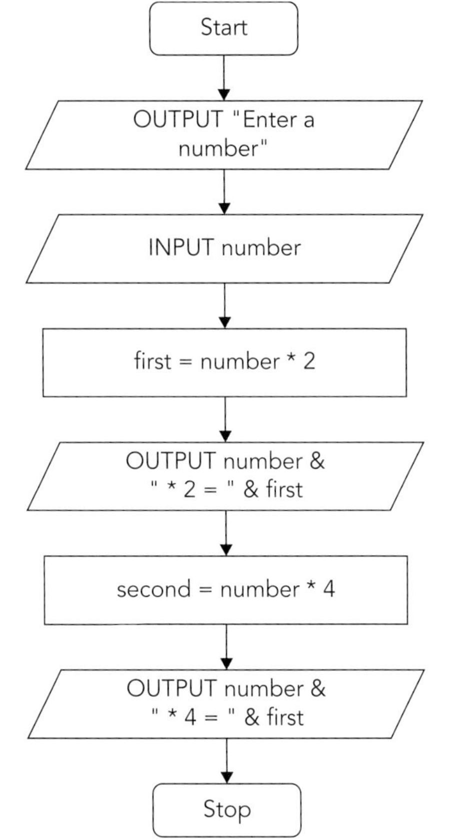

Figure 1.14: Flowchart for programming task

Changes

If you are changing a flowchart, you first need to work out what the flowchart does now. Then identify what it needs to do, and the difference between these. Change the flowchart and test it to see if it now works.

Common changes may include:

- performing a different mathematical calculation
- changing the output
- including an additional input or output
- inserting an extra calculation.

Unplugged activity 1.4

You will need: a pen and paper

This flowchart calculates the number of years (approximately) that someone has been alive.

Test the flowchart with a partner. Take it in turns to input the data and calculate the result.

The flowchart needs to be changed to also output the number of months in that many years. For example, in 10 years there are 120 months.

There are four different additions below but only one will perform the change required. Work out with your partner which is the correct addition.

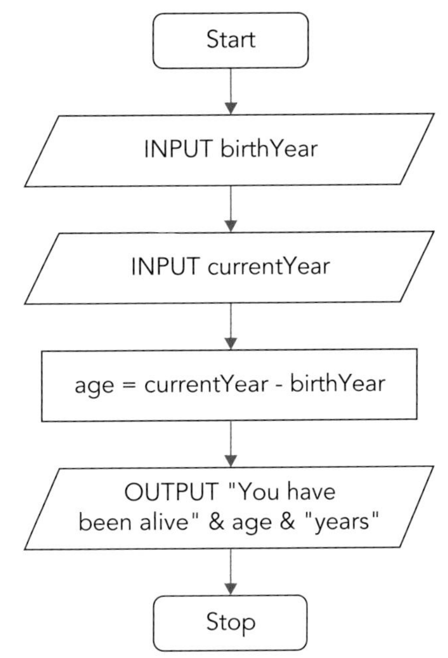

Figure 1.15: Flowchart for activity

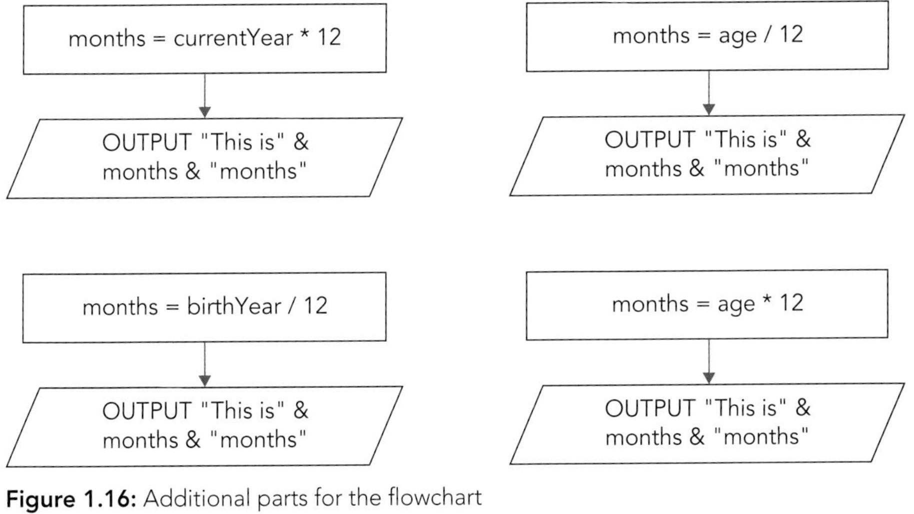

Figure 1.16: Additional parts for the flowchart

Redraw the flowchart with your selected addition.

Test your flowchart and make sure it works.

Programming task 1.4: Predict, Run and Modify

You will need: a pen and paper

Read this flowchart:

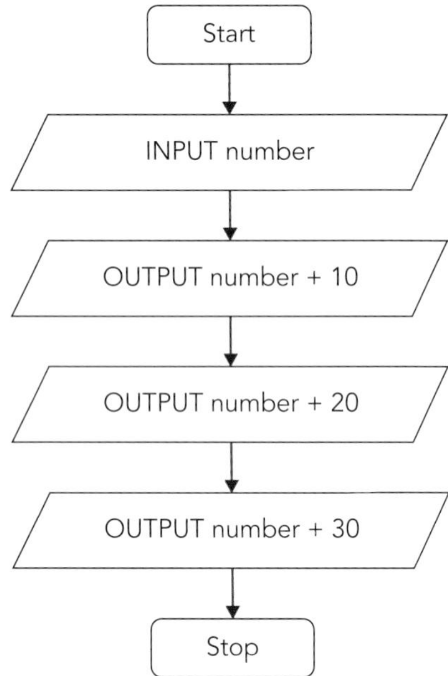

Figure 1.17: Flowchart for programming task

Predict: Identify a number to input and write down what you think will be output.

Run: Test the flowchart by inputting your number and writing down the output. Compare the output to your prediction.

Modify 1: The flowchart needs to also output the result of the number input + 40:

- Identify the flowchart shape that this calculation will be put into.
- Identify the position in the flowchart for this to be put.
- Redraw the flowchart with your addition.

Swap your flowchart with a partner. Predict and run your partner's flowchart. Did it give the correct answer? If not, tell your partner what the difference was, so they can find and correct the error.

Continued

Modify 2: The flowchart needs to output a message with each value, for example, "10 + 10 = 20".

- Identify how a message can also be output.
- Identify the places in the flowchart that this change will be placed.
- Redraw the flowchart with your addition.

Swap your flowchart with a partner. Predict and run your partner's flowchart. Did it give the correct answer? If not, tell your partner what the difference was, so they can find and correct the error.

Modify 3: The flowchart needs to ask the user to input their name at the start, and then a message that says "Goodbye" followed by their name.

- Identify how the name will be input, and how the message will be output.
- Identify the place in the flowchart where the input will go.
- Identify the place in the flowchart where the output will go.
- Redraw the flowchart with your addition.

Swap your flowchart with a partner. Predict and run your partner's flowchart. Did it give the correct answer? If not, tell your partner what the difference was, so they can find and correct the error.

Create a flowchart

You have learnt the symbols for flowcharts, you have followed flowcharts, and you have changed and corrected flowcharts. Now it is time to create your own flowcharts.

When you create a flowchart for an algorithm, it is a good idea to start by writing down the steps of the algorithm.

Example:

A flowchart needs to take a user's name and their favourite food as input, and then output a message telling them that you don't like the food they have chosen.

Split this long sentence into short statements, each statement should only do one action:

1 Take user's name as input.
2 Take favourite food as input.
3 Output message saying "I don't like" food entered.

From this you can start to draw your flowchart.

1 Always start with start!

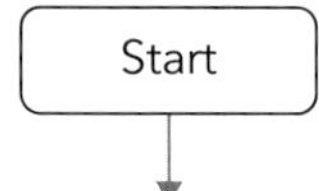

Figure 1.18: Start box

2 The first action is 'Take user's name as input'. Draw an input box. Write a statement to input the name. Because the name will be stored, it needs a variable.

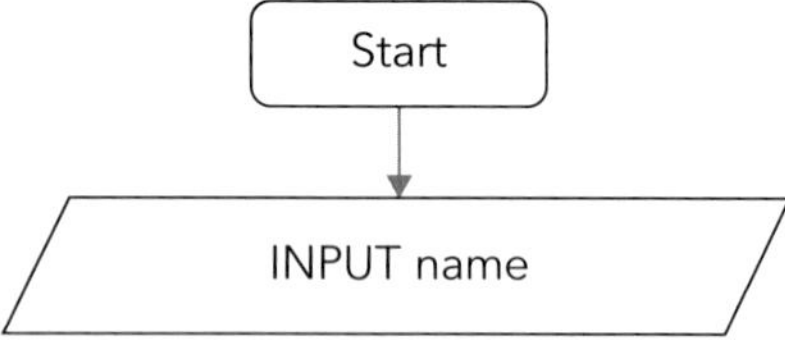

Figure 1.19: Input 'Take user's name as input'

3 The second action is 'Take favourite food as input'. Draw an input box and write the statement to input the favourite food. It will need a variable.

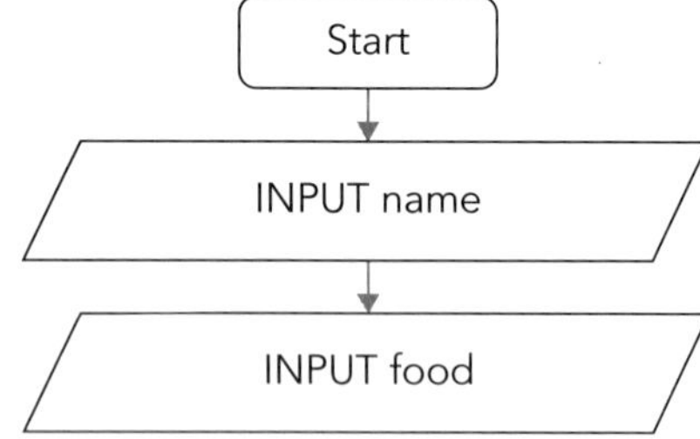

Figure 1.20: Input 'Take favourite food as input'

4 The third action is 'Output message saying "I don't like" food entered'. The food entered will be stored in the variable `food`.

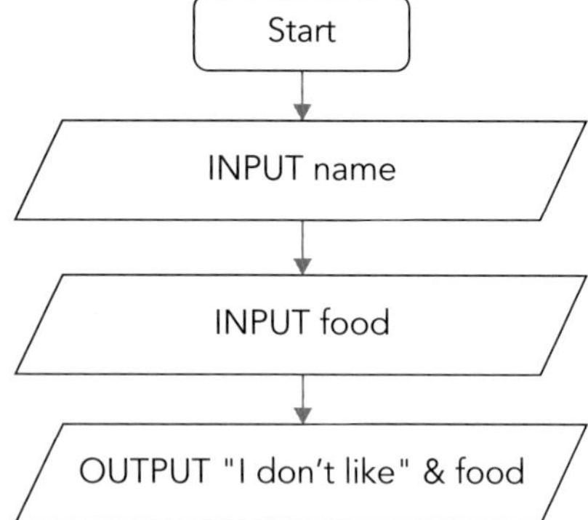

Figure 1.21: Output message 'I don't like food'

5 Always end with a stop.

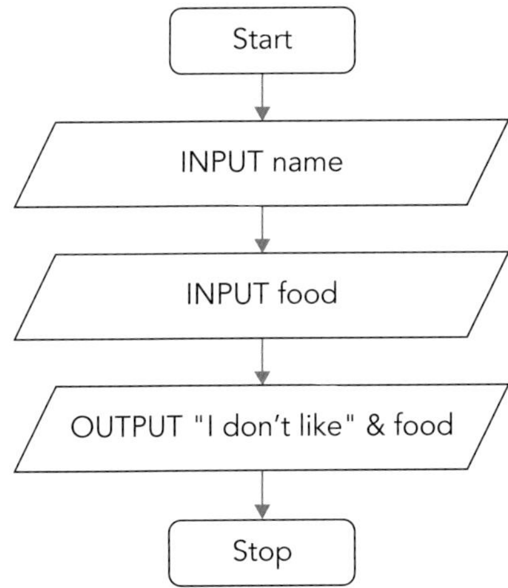

Figure 1.22: Flowchart with stop box

When you have drawn your flowchart, use this checklist to make sure you have met flowchart requirements:

Requirements checklist	✓
Is there a start and a stop?	☐
Are all inputs and outputs in the correct shape?	☐
Are all processes in the correct shape?	☐
Does each input, output and process have **one** data flow arrow going in, and **one** data flow arrow going out?	☐
Do all the boxes lead to another box?	☐
If you have used a variable, have you used the same name consistently?	☐
Have you used the correct mathematical symbols (+, -, *, /)?	☐

Table 1.2: Flowchart requirements checklist

Did you know?

It is OK for your algorithms to not work first time. All programmers make errors, even professionals who write programs all day. Have you heard of patches being downloaded for software? This is where an error is found and it needs to be fixed.

If these are all met, then it's time to test your flowchart.

Predict what the output should be, then **Run** the flowchart to see if it works correctly.

If it does, then great!

If it doesn't, that's OK. Look at the output you got and the output you expected. What is the difference? Then find the error.

Unplugged activity 1.5

You will need: a pen and paper

An algorithm needs to take the number of hours from the input, and then output the number of minutes in those hours, and the number of seconds.

The flowchart pieces are shown in a random order. On a piece of paper, rearrange the flowchart symbols and draw the lines to join them together.

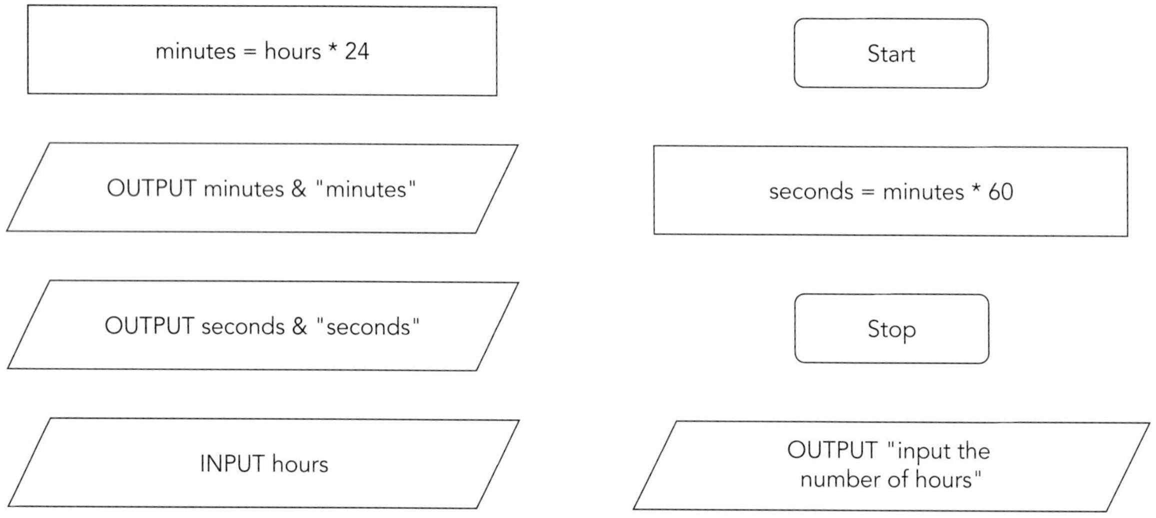

minutes = hours * 24

Start

OUTPUT minutes & "minutes"

seconds = minutes * 60

OUTPUT seconds & "seconds"

Stop

INPUT hours

OUTPUT "input the number of hours"

Figure 1.23: Flowchart pieces for unplugged activity

Programming task 1.5: Make and Predict

You will need: a pen and paper

Make: The perimeter (the length of all the sides added together) of a square is the length of one side multiplied by 4.

The area of a square is the length of one side squared.

Draw a flowchart to take the length of one side of a square as input, and then output the perimeter and area.

When you have drawn your flowchart, compare it to the flowchart checklist.

Predict and Modify: Predict the outcome and run your flowchart to make sure it works. If it doesn't, then modify it until it does.

Swap your flowchart with a partner. Predict and run their flowchart to make sure it works.

Continued

Peer-assessment

Compare the two flowcharts: yours and your partner's.

- Are they exactly the same?
- What are the differences?
- Do the differences change how the algorithm works?

Questions 1.2

1 Create a flowchart to output the chorus of a song, one line at a time.

2 Create a flowchart to take a number as input, divide the number by 2 and output the result.

3 Create a flowchart to take a distance in miles, convert it to kilometres and output the result.

4 Create a flowchart to take a number as input, then output the first 12 multiples for that number. For example, if 2 is input, then the flowchart should output:

$2 \times 1 = 2$

$2 \times 2 = 4$

$2 \times 3 = 6$

$2 \times 4 = 8$

...

$2 \times 11 = 22$

$2 \times 12 = 24$

Summary checklist

- [ ] I can identify the flowchart shapes for input/output, process and start/stop.
- [ ] I can follow a flowchart.
- [ ] I can test a flowchart using input data and checking the output.
- [ ] I can find an error in a flowchart and correct it.
- [ ] I can make a change to a flowchart.
- [ ] I can create a flowchart to solve a problem.

> 1.2 Selection and logic in flowcharts

In this topic you will:

- understand how to use selection statements in a flowchart
- follow flowcharts that use selection and predict the result
- follow flowcharts and algorithms that use IF THEN ELSE
- select and use <, >, <=, >=, == and !=
- use the Boolean operators AND, OR and NOT in selection.

Key words

AND

Boolean condition

Boolean logic

comparison operator

condition

IF, THEN, ELSE

NOT

OR

selection statement

Getting started

What do you already know?

- What you do next will depend on what your decision is:
  - If I have toast, then I need to put the bread in the toaster.
  - If I have fruit, I need to cut it into smaller pieces.

  The same thing happens when you are designing a computer program.
- You have probably used branching algorithms, most likely in Scratch. A branching statement has a condition – this is a question that only has two possible answers, true (yes) or false (no).

Continued

Here's an example:

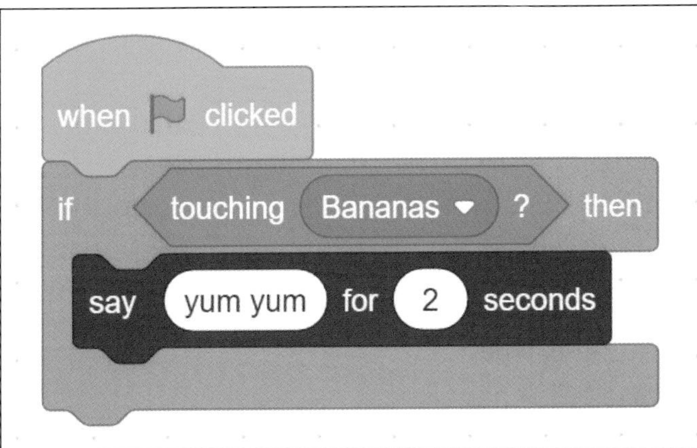

When the cat touches the Bananas sprite, it will say 'yum yum'.

- You might have used comparison operators in your mathematics lessons. You might have even used them in Scratch.

  Comparison operators are: = > < >= <=

  You use a comparison operator to compare the numbers on either side of it. For example, are two numbers the same? Is one number greater than another number? Is one number less than another number? Check what you already know by answering these questions:

  Is 10 > 3?
  Is 20 = 19?
  Is 100 < 50?

Now try this!

Read these statements and perform each action. You can do this on your own or with a partner.

- If you like the colour red better than the colour blue, stand up, otherwise sit on the floor.
- If you like fruit better than pizza, put your right hand on your head, otherwise put your left hand on your head.
- If you like maths better than science, laugh, otherwise say 'shhhhhh'.

Now look around at everyone else. Is anyone doing the same actions as you? Why are people doing different things? Why are some people sitting down?

You have just been running selection statements.

Selection statements

A **selection statement** is used when a decision needs to be made in an algorithm. It has a **condition**. This is a statement that will be either true or false.

- If the result is true, then one action will take place.
- If the result is false, then a different action will take place.

Selection statements often have the key commands **IF**, **THEN** and **ELSE**. Selection statements have three parts:

1. condition: The condition (can only be true or false).
2. true: The action that happens if the condition is true.
3. false: The action that happens if the condition is false.

This statement can then be written as

IF (condition) THEN (true) ELSE (false)

Did you know?

Computers cannot make decisions without being told to. Almost all of the decisions that computers make are programmed using selection statements.

Unplugged activity 1.6

You will need: a pen, paper and scissors

In pairs, take a piece of paper and cut it into 10 different pieces.

Write a different number on each piece of paper. Write any numbers you like, not just 1 to 10.

Put all the pieces of paper face down on the table, so that you cannot see the numbers.

Each of you pick a number, then follow this statement:

IF you have a higher number than your friend THEN you win a point, ELSE you lose a point.

Keep playing until one of you reaches 10 points.

Congratulations, you just ran a selection statement!
You executed the three parts of a selection statement:

- The condition (is your number higher than your friend's number?)
- The action if it is true (you win a point)
- The action if it is false (you lose a point)

Selection in flowcharts

Selection uses the diamond symbol in a flowchart:

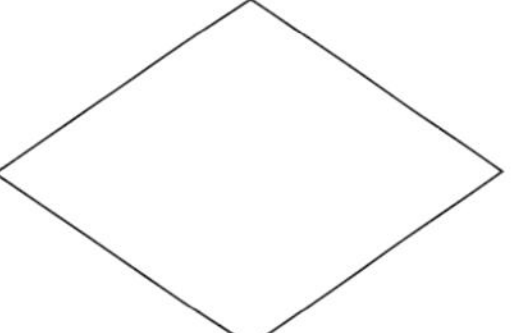

Figure 1.24: The selection symbol

Inside the diamond, you write the condition. For example,

IF colour chosen = blue

Note: In a flowchart the 'equals to' symbol can be = or ==.

Keep in mind that the word IS can be used instead of IF in a flowchart.

The diamond then has *two* arrows that come from it. One arrow is followed when the condition is True (or yes). The second is followed when the condition is False (or no). True and False need to be written on the arrows so we know which is which.

Here's an example of both ways this can be shown:

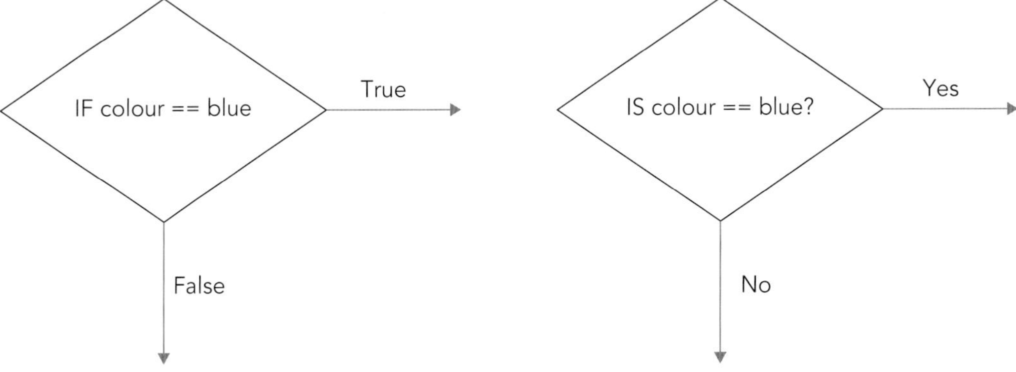

Figure 1.25: Examples of a selection statement

This format matches the selection statement format IF, THEN, ELSE we looked at earlier. It has the three parts:

- IF: The condition (that can only be true or false) within the diamond.
- THEN: The action that happens if the condition is true, follow the True or Yes arrow.
- ELSE: The action that happens if the condition is false, follow the False or No arrow.

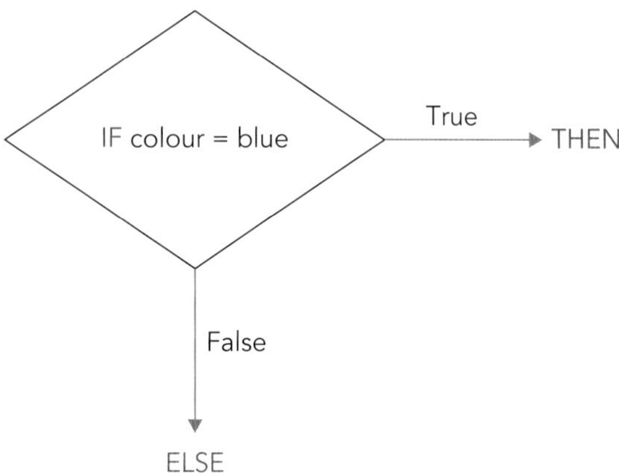

Figure 1.26: Examples of a selection statement using IF, THEN, ELSE

Programming task 1.6: Investigate

You will need: a pen and paper

Read this flowchart with a partner.

Investigate: Discuss these questions with a partner. Point to the different parts of the flowchart and write your answers to the questions.

1. Where is the selection box in the flowchart?
2. What is the condition in the flowchart?
3. What happens if the condition is true?
4. What happens if the condition is false?

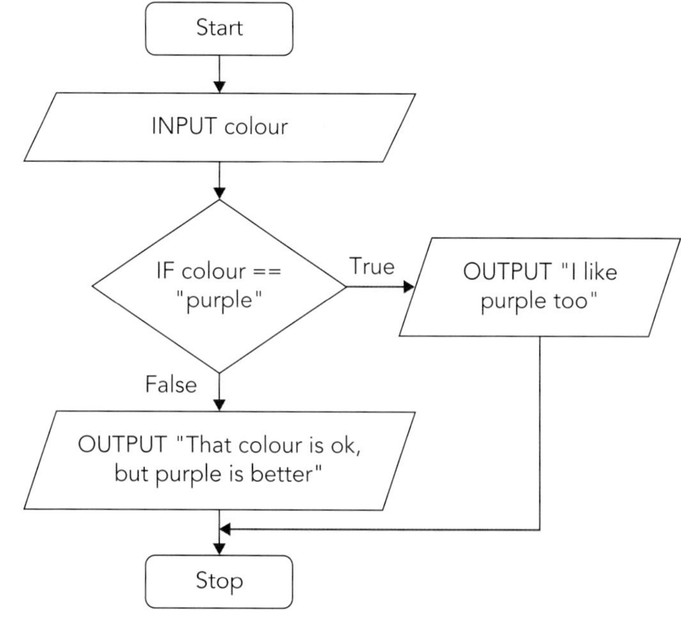

Figure 1.27: Flowchart for programming task

Self-assessment

How did you follow the flowchart? Did you miss out some of the boxes, or did you read each box one at a time in order?

Did you help your partner? Or did your partner help you? How did you decide on the correct answer to each question between you?

Programming task 1.7: Predict

Predict: Work with a partner and follow this algorithm. Predict what will happen if:

- the number 4 is input into the algorithm?
- the contents of the two output boxes are swapped around (although the arrows stay in the same place)?
- there is no INPUT answer box?
- the decision changes to IF answer >= 4?
- the 'True' and 'False' are removed from above the data flow arrows?

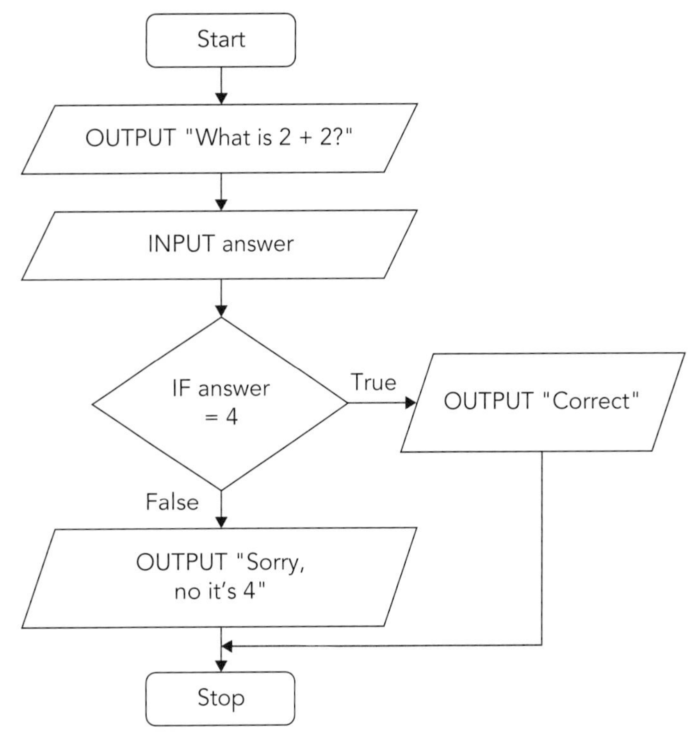

Figure 1.28: Flowchart for programming task

Questions 1.3

1. What is a selection statement?
2. What shape is selection in a flowchart?
3. How many arrows come from a selection box in a flowchart, and what is written on each?
4. What are the three parts of a selection statement?

Comparison operators

Do these symbols look familiar from mathematics?

> < >= <=

These are called **comparison operators** and we include them in statements in algorithms. We use them to perform comparisons between different values.

The different operators are shown in this table:

Operator	Description	Examples
>	greater than	10 > 2 20 > 19 200 > 0
<	less than	100 < 200 1 < 2 0 < 10
>=	greater than or equal to	100 >= 100 120 >= 99 22 >= 1
<=	less than or equal to	100 <= 100 82 <= 99 1 <= 3
==	equal to	100 == 100 20 == 20 1 == 1
!=	not equal to	2 != 1 100 != 99 0 != 10

Table 1.3: Comparison operators

Did you know?

These operators might be different depending on the language you use. Especially the symbols for 'equal to' and 'not equal to'.

For example, in the language Visual Basic, 'equal to' is = and 'not equal to' is <>.

These are the symbols that are used in the programming language Python, which you will be using later in this unit.

You can put one of these operators in a selection condition, and the result will be either True or False.

Let's look at an example:

Is 10 > 2?

This is asking whether the number 10 is greater than 2.

- If 10 is greater than 2, the result is True.
- If 10 is not greater than 2, the result is False.

What is the result? True.

Unplugged activity 1.7

You will need: a pen and paper

Write a list of questions that make use of the comparison operators – for example, 'Is 2 < 1'? Make sure that you have at least one question for each operator.

Swap your questions with a partner.

Write an answer to each of your partner's questions.

Swap the answers back.

Peer-assessment

Check your partner's answers. Give them a tick if they are correct. Add the number of ticks and give your partner a final mark.

If your partner has any incorrect answers, explain to them why their answer was incorrect, and make sure they understand the reasons.

Boolean logic

The conditions in the flowcharts above can only be answered by True or False. These are called **Boolean conditions**. Boolean means that there are only *two* options. These could be:

- True / False
- Yes / No
- 1 / 0
- Positive / Negative

There is no 'maybe' answer.

Unplugged activity 1.8

You will need: a pen and paper

Work with a partner. Write down three questions that can only have two possible answers: true or false. Ask your partner your questions, and they will ask you their questions. When answering, try and work out if there is a possible third answer. For example, do you prefer apples or kiwi? Your partner might not like either!

Continued

Self-assessment

How many of your questions only had two possible answers?

Were you able to find more answers to your partner's questions?

How did you change your questions to try and make them have only two answers?

Figure 1.29: George Boole

Did you know?

George Boole was a mathematician who lived in the 1800s. He developed Boolean logic, which computers (and humans) still use today. **Boolean logic** is named after him.

There are different Boolean operators. The three basic operators are **AND**, **OR** and **NOT**. The operators are used when you need to check more than one condition.

AND

This statement has one condition on either side. If both conditions are true, the result is true. Otherwise, the result is false.

Is *Condition 1 true* AND *Condition 2 true*?

Condition 1 result	Condition 2 result	AND result
true	true	true
true	false	false
false	true	false
false	false	false

Table 1.4: All outcomes for the AND operator

Let's look at an example:

Is 10 > 2 AND 20 > 5?

- Condition 1: is 10 > 2? This is true
- Condition 2: is 20 > 5? This is true
- Boolean operator: AND

Both are true so the result is true.

Let's look at another example:

Is 2 > 10 AND 1 > 0?

- Condition 1: is 2 > 10? This is false
- Condition 2: is 1 > 0? This is true
- Boolean operator: AND

One is false so the result is false.

OR

This statement has one condition on either side. If one or both conditions are true, the result is true. It is false only when both conditions are false.

Is *Condition 1 true* OR *Condition 2 true*?

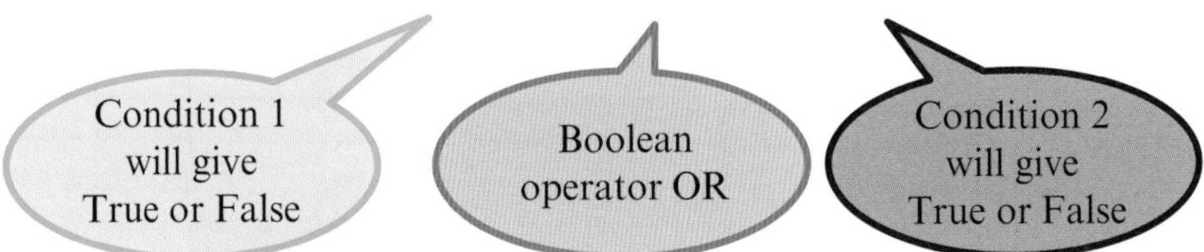

Condition 1 result	Condition 2 result	OR result
true	true	true
true	false	true
false	true	true
false	false	false

Table 1.5: All outcomes for the OR operator

Let's look at an example:

Is 10 > 2 OR 20 > 5?

- Condition 1: is 10 > 2? This is true
- Condition 2: is 20 > 5? This is true
- Boolean operator: OR

Both are true so the result is true.

When you use NOT, the outcome is the opposite to the condition. If the condition is TRUE, the outcome will be FALSE.

Let's look at another example:

Is 2 > 10 OR 1 > 0?

- Condition 1: is 2 > 10? This is false
- Condition 2: is 1 > 0? This is true
- Boolean operator: OR

One is true so the result is true.

NOT

The Not statement has only one condition. If the condition is true, it makes it false. If the condition is false, it makes it true.

Is NOT *Condition 1*?

Boolean operator NOT

Condition 1 will give True or False

Condition result	NOT result
true	false
false	true

Table 1.6: All outcomes for the NOT operator

Let's look at an example:

Is NOT 10 > 2?

- Condition: is 10 > 2? This is true
- Boolean operator: NOT

NOT reverses the true to give false.

Let's look at another example:

Is NOT 2 > 10?

- Condition: is 2 > 10? This is false
- Boolean operator: NOT

NOT reverses the false to give true.

Unplugged activity 1.9

You will need: a pen, paper and scissors

In groups, cut out 15 pieces of paper. On each piece of paper write a number from 1 to 5, and a colour from purple, red, green, yellow, orange. Each piece of paper should have a number and a colour written on it. For example:

3, green

Place these pieces of paper face down on the table.

Each person in your group then writes a selection statement that uses Boolean AND, OR or NOT on another piece of paper.

For example:

- If your card is orange AND is less than 2, sing a song.
- If your card is 1 OR 5, sit on the floor, otherwise put your hands on your head.

Fold these statements in half and put them in the middle of the table.

Pick one statement from the middle of the table and read it out.

Each person in the group then picks a card and tests the statement, performing the required action.

Peer-assessment

Check which action each person in your group is performing. Say 'yes' if they are doing the correct action. If they are not, give them a hint such as 'your card is orange' to help them.

Did you know?

Not everything related to computers relies on Boolean values. Some mathematics and computer science looks at something called fuzzy logic. This allows values between 0 (false) and 1 (true).

Fuzzy logic is used when a result has more possibilities. For example, the temperature can be hot or cold, but it can also be:

very hot
warm
OK
chilly
quite cold
very cold

There are not just two possibilities.

Programming task 1.8: Run and Modify

You will need: a card from Unplugged activity 1.9

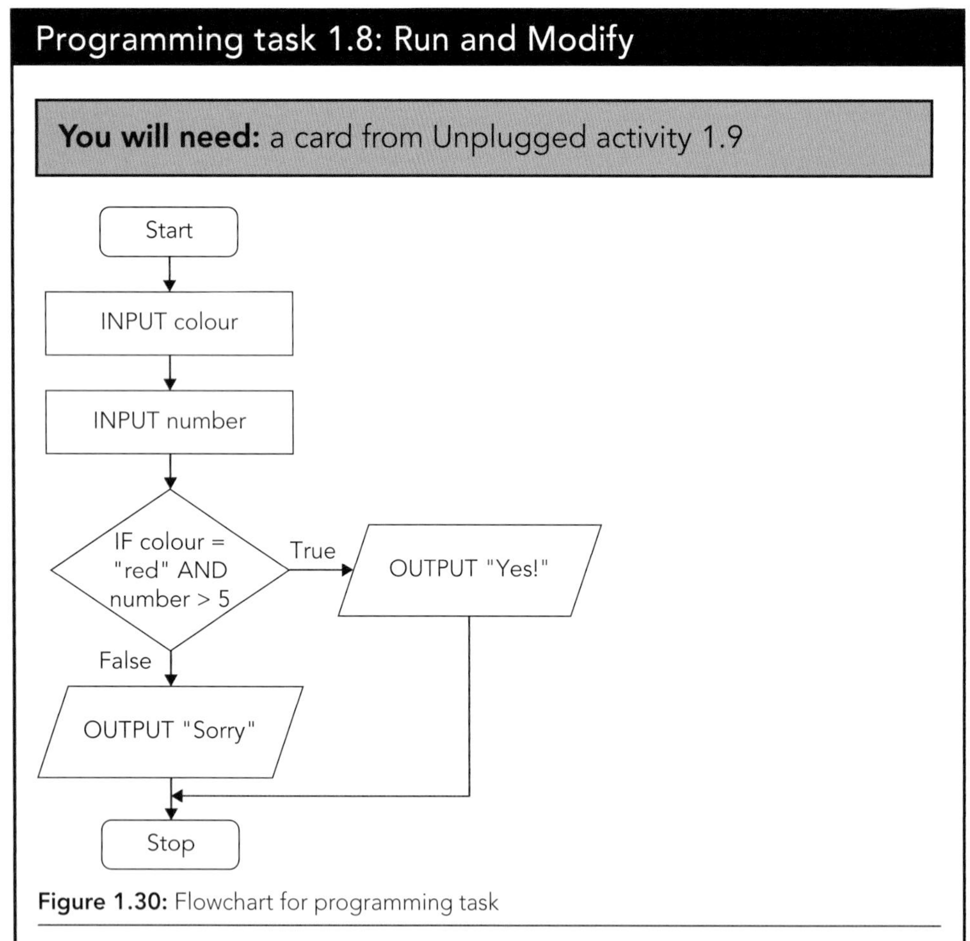

Figure 1.30: Flowchart for programming task

Continued

Run: Pick a card with a number and colour from the Unplugged activity and run the flowchart. What will your card output?

Put your card back and pick another. Run the flowchart again. Was the result different? Keep picking cards until you have output both 'Yes!' and 'Sorry'.

Modify: The flowchart needs to be changed. If the colour is red or blue then 'Yes!' should be output. Discuss with a partner how you would change the flowchart.

Questions 1.4

1 What are the two Boolean values?
2 What is the result of True AND True?
3 When will a Boolean OR condition give False?
4 What does a Boolean NOT do?
5 When will a Boolean AND condition not give True?

Summary checklist

- [ ] I can describe the purpose of a selection statement.
- [ ] I can identify the three parts of a selection statement.
- [ ] I can follow selection statements in a flowchart.
- [ ] I can predict the outcome of a flowchart that uses selection.
- [ ] I can identify that Boolean value can only be True or False.
- [ ] I can describe the function of AND, OR and NOT.
- [ ] I can follow algorithms that use AND, OR and NOT.

1.3 Pattern recognition and sub-routines in flowcharts

In this topic you will:

- understand what is meant by pattern recognition
- understand the reasons why pattern recognition is used when designing solutions to tasks
- understand how sub-routines are designed in flowcharts
- understand how to follow flowcharts that use sub-routines
- understand how to change flowcharts that use sub-routines.

Key words

call (a sub-routine)

efficient

identifier

pattern

pattern recognition

return (from a sub-routine)

sub-routine

Getting started

What do you already know?

- Patterns are everywhere in our everyday life. You will have seen them at home, in the park and in school subjects. Patterns you come across in school could be:
  - What is the pattern in these numbers?
    1, 2, 3, 4, 5, 6
  - What is the pattern in these shapes?

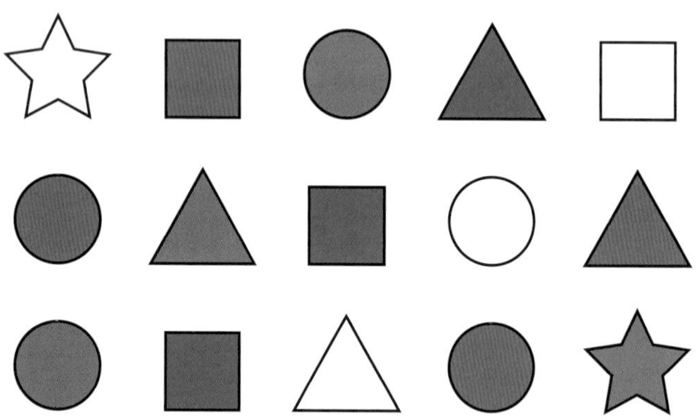

Continued

- The symbol for a sub-routine in a flowchart is:

- A sub-routine is a program that can be used multiple times in an algorithm. It can also be used by different algorithms.

Now try this!

Read this list of colours.

violet	**purple**	**blue**	**red**	**green**	**orange**
green	**yellow**	**blue**	**violet**	**violet**	**purple**
blue	**red**	**green**	**orange**	**green**	**yellow**
blue	**violet**	**violet**	**violet**	**purple**	**blue**
red	**green**	**orange**	**green**	**yellow**	**blue**
violet	**purple**	**blue**	**red**	**green**	**orange**
green	**yellow**	**blue**	**violet**	**purple**	**blue**

Can you identify any patterns in this list of colours?

How many different patterns can you find?

Compare your patterns with a partner's. Did you both find the same patterns? Or different patterns?

Is there a right answer to how many patterns there are?

Pattern recognition

A **pattern** is a repeated design or sequence. You probably see lots of patterns every day without even realising they are there. When you look at something and identify a pattern, this is called **pattern recognition**.

Did you know?

Patterns occur naturally in plants and animals. People can find mathematical rules that describe these patterns. Next time you walk past a plant look for a pattern in its flowers or leaves.

Patterns can be identified when developing computer programs. The patterns could be:

- features in a program that will appear several times
- the same action being performed several times
- the same background or images used
- the same decisions being made
- the same inputs and outputs being made
- the same calculations being performed.

And many others.

Activity 1.1

You will need: a computer game with patterns in it

Find the patterns in the game.

Open a computer game, for example Pac-Man or Tetris, or another game that your teacher tells you to use. Play the game on your own.

In a group of three, write down any patterns (or repeated elements) in the game.

As a hint, in Pac-Man, each level has the same layout. In Tetris, each shape can move left or right.

Share the patterns you have identified with the rest of the class.

How many different patterns did you identify?

Self-assessment

Give yourself a rating based on the number of patterns you identified. Were they all about the design, or were some about the data, processes and outputs?

Orange = I identified at least one pattern.

Blue = I identified more than one pattern but they were all the same type.

Purple = I identified more than two patterns and there were at least two different types of patterns.

Pattern recognition is important when writing algorithms and programs for many reasons.

- Instead of writing the same piece of code several times, you could write it just once and then use it several times.
- Patterns can save you time when writing the program. If you use the same code several times then you only need to test it once. If it works once, it will (hopefully) work every time.
- Patterns can also make your program more **efficient**. This means that it could run faster or use less memory, because instead of having a lot of individual elements all working on their own, you could just have one that appears several times.

Which would you prefer to do?

1 Write the same piece of code 20 times.

Or

2 Write the code once and then copy it 19 times.

Questions 1.5

1 What is a pattern?

2 What is an example pattern in a computer program?

3 Why is it important to identify patterns when designing an algorithm?

Sub-routines

A **sub-routine** is a self-contained algorithm. It has an **identifier**, which is the name of the sub-routine. By using this identifier you can **call** the sub-routine from other code. Calling the sub-routine means that:

- the algorithm in the main code stops where it is
- the sub-routine runs
- at the end of the sub-routine, the algorithm **returns** to where it stopped in the main code.

Unplugged activity 1.10

You will need: a pen and paper

Here is a sub-routine:

Identifier: Dance

Stand up

Turn around once

Wave hands in air twice

Turn around once

Sit down

Each time **Dance** is written, the steps in the sub-routine are run.

Run this algorithm by yourself and perform the actions:

Dance

Dance

Dance

How many times did you stand up? How many times did you turn around?

Compare your answers with a partner's. Did you both stand up the same number of times? If not, run the algorithm again and see who was correct.

Continued

Write your own sub-routine with the identifier **Dance2**. Include a series of actions for a partner to perform. Make sure that these are safe in your classroom environment. If you are not sure, check with your teacher.

Write an algorithm that calls both Dance and Dance2 multiple times. Swap your algorithm with a partner and run each other's algorithms.

Sub-routines in flowcharts

The symbol for a sub-routine in a flowchart is:

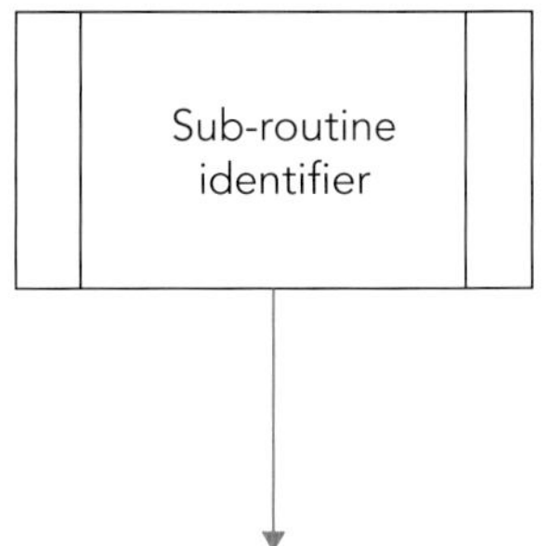

Figure 1.31: Symbol for a sub-routine in a flowchart

This is used to start the sub-routine and to call it from another flowchart. The identifier (name) of the sub-routine is written in the shape.

The sub-routine has one arrow coming from it in the actual sub-routine.

Where it is used to call the sub-routine, it will have one arrow going in and one arrow going out.

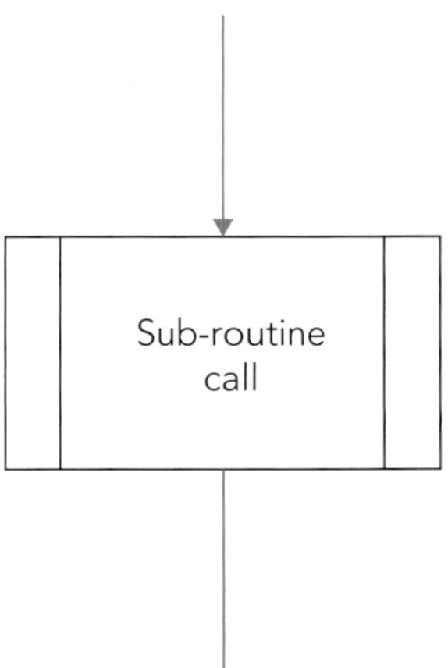

Figure 1.32: Symbol to call the sub-routine in a flowchart

A sub-routine needs an identifier (name). This could be anything! However, identifiers should be appropriate and meaningful.
For example, a bad name for a sub-routine that outputs a story is `mathsQuestions`.

The identifier can be two words in a flowchart, but in these examples, we will use programming-style identifiers. These will be one word (`'addNumbers'` instead of `'add numbers'`). They will also have brackets () after the name: `addNumbers()`. This is because these brackets will be needed when programming sub-routines, and it makes it clear that the identifier refers to a sub-routine instead of anything else.

Here's an example of a sub-routine declaration.

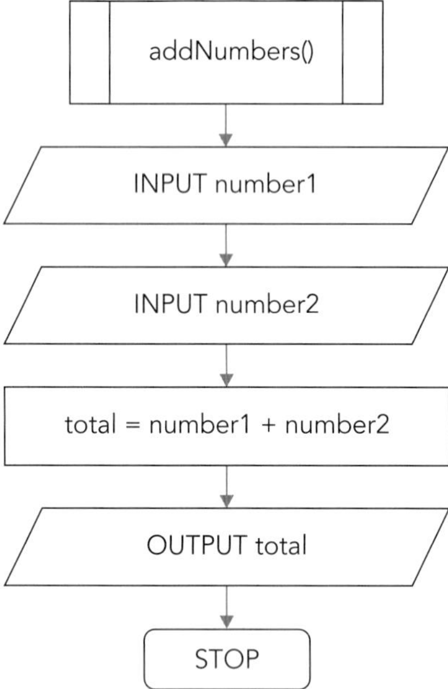

Figure 1.33: Example of a sub-routine declaration

Sometimes the STOP in the flowchart might say RETURN instead.

Questions 1.6

1 What is the identifier of this sub-routine?
2 What data is input into this sub-routine?
3 What process takes place in this sub-routine?
4 What is output in this sub-routine?
5 What happens when STOP is reached in this sub-routine?

Here is an example of this sub-routine being called from Sofia's flowchart. It is called by using the same symbol and the sub-routine's identifier.

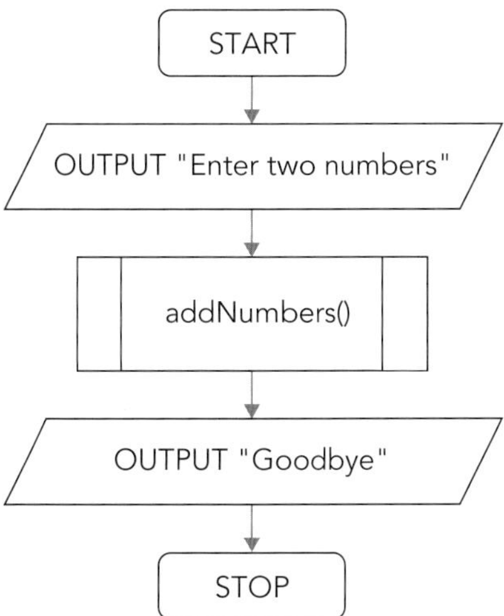

Figure 1.34: Example of a sub-routine being called from a different flowchart

Let's trace Sofia's flowchart with the input values **1** and **9**, and see what the output is.

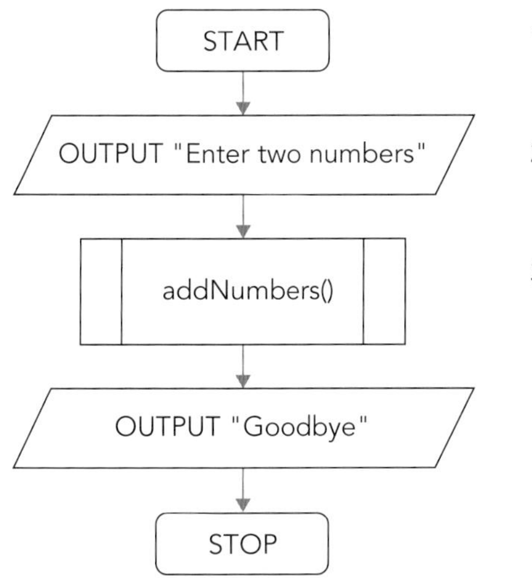

1 Begin at "Start".

2 "Enter two numbers" is output.

3 The sub-routine `addNumbers()` is called. At this stage we jump to the flowchart for `addNumbers()`.

Figure 1.35: Flowchart to trace

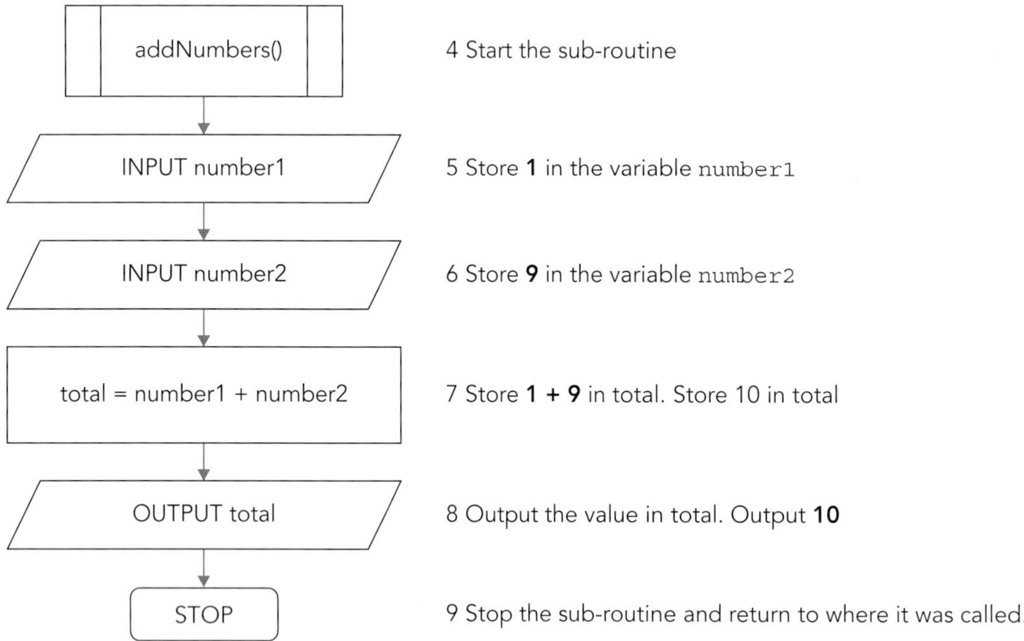

Figure 1.36: Sub-routine AddNumbers

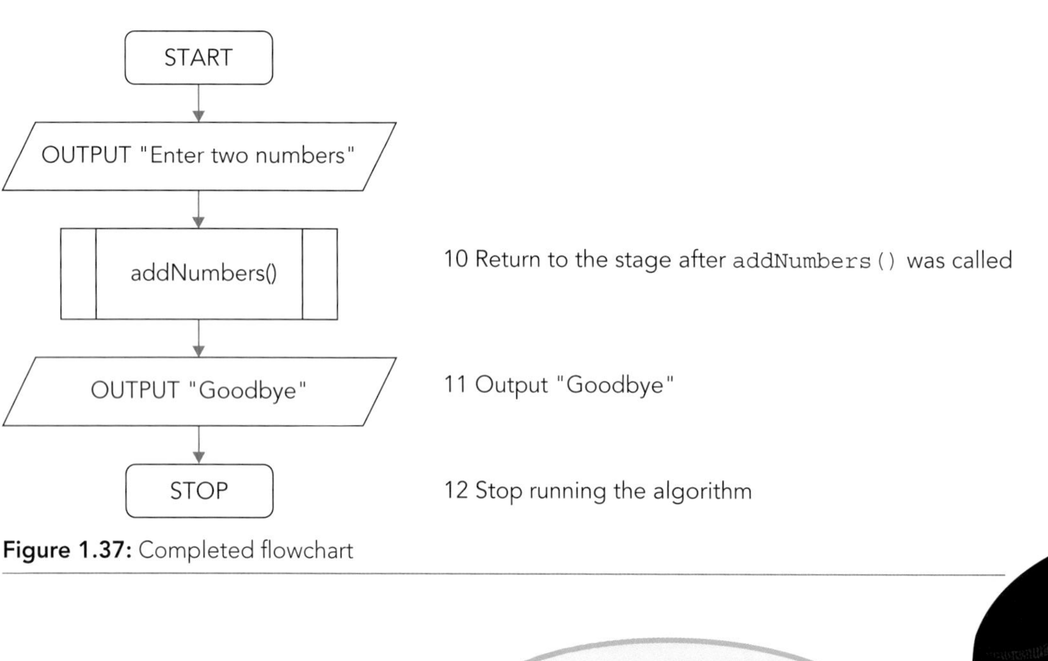

Figure 1.37: Completed flowchart

Do you understand how sub-routines in flowcharts work?

Programming task 1.9: Run, Investigate and Modify

You will need: a pencil and paper

Read these flowcharts on your own first.

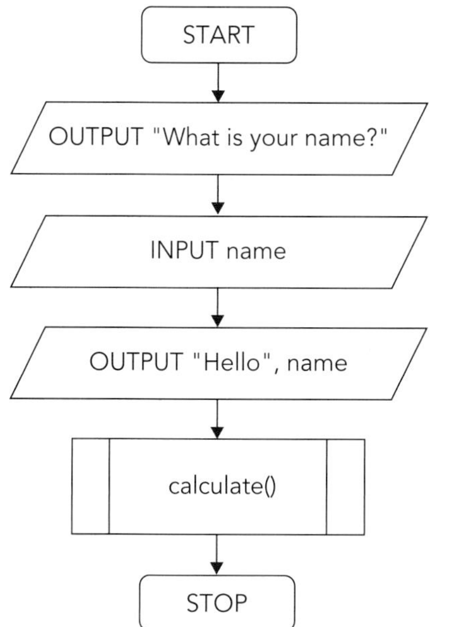

Figure 1.38: Flowchart for programming task

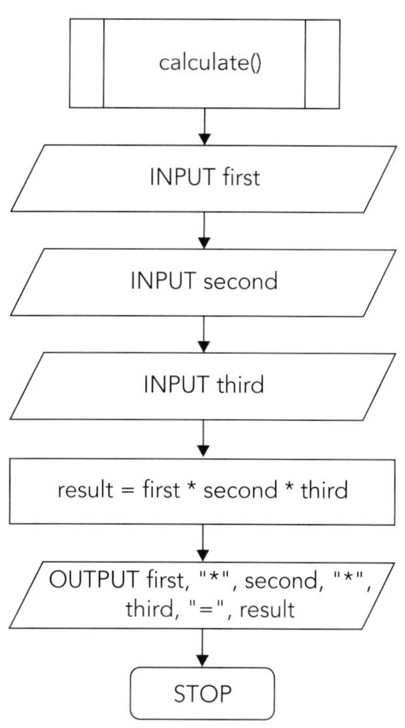

Figure 1.39: Sub-routine for programming task

Run: Trace each flowchart and write down the output. When asked for an input, first enter 1, then 2, then 3.

Investigate: Join with a partner. Show your partner the order that each shape in each flowchart will run. You could read each statement, or copy the flowcharts and use a pencil to draw a line between the flowcharts.

Explain to your partner when the sub-routine is called and what happens when the sub-routine reaches its STOP box.

Modify: Work with a partner to make these changes to the flowcharts.

1. In the main flowchart, once the sub-routine has run, output "Thank you for running this flowchart".
2. In the main flowchart, call the sub-routine a second time, before the "Hello" message is output.
3. Change the identifier of the sub-routine to `multiply()`.
4. Change the sub-routine to add the first two numbers and then divide this total by the third number.

Make sure you test each of your solutions. Select suitable data to input into each flowchart. Make sure they give the correct output.

An algorithm can have several sub-routines. A sub-routine can even call another sub-routine.

Programming task 1.10: Investigate, Predict, Run and Modify

You will need: a pen and paper

Read these four flowcharts by yourself.

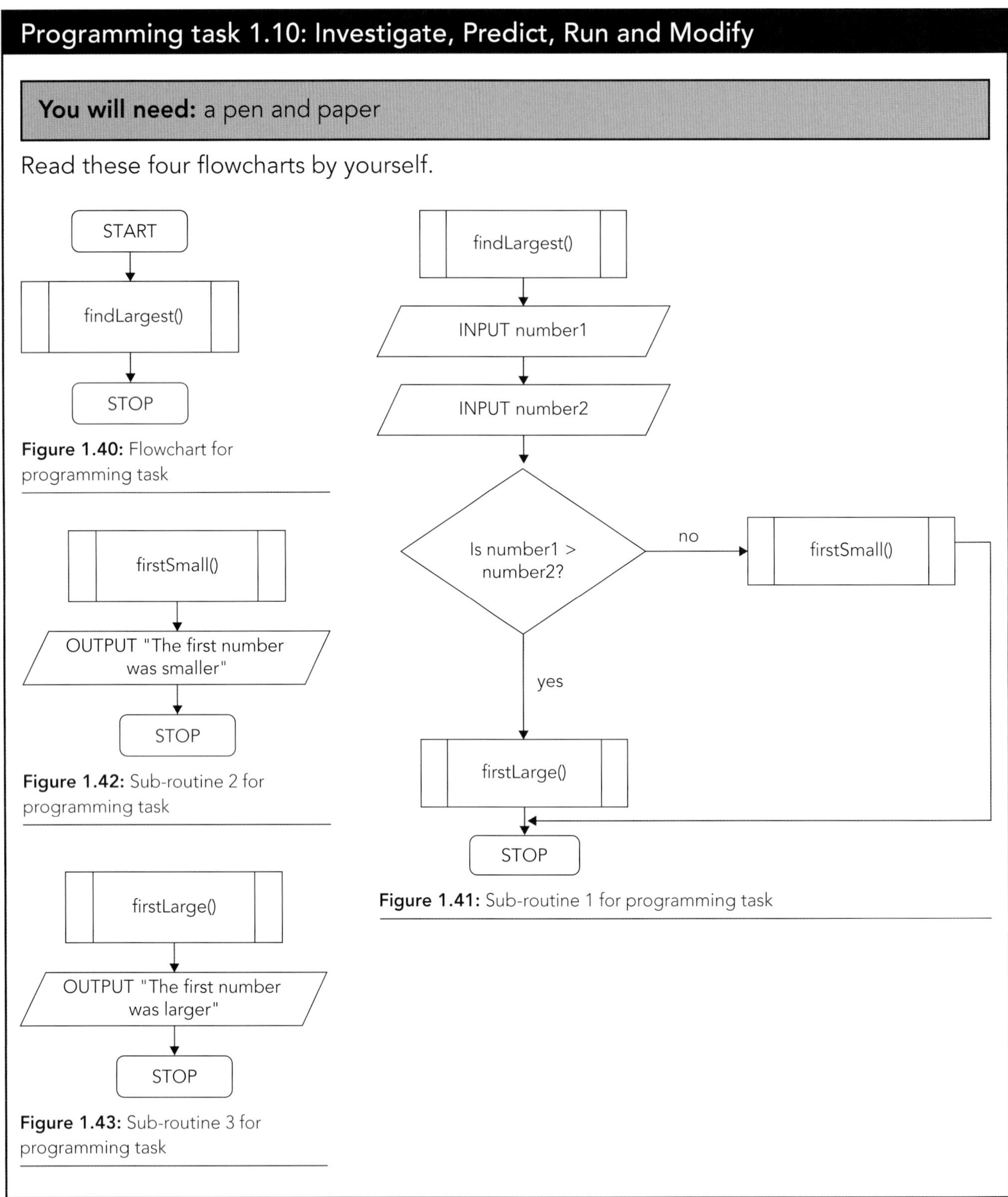

Figure 1.40: Flowchart for programming task

Figure 1.42: Sub-routine 2 for programming task

Figure 1.43: Sub-routine 3 for programming task

Figure 1.41: Sub-routine 1 for programming task

Continued

Investigate: Write three questions about the structure of these flowcharts for a partner to answer. For example: What are the identifiers of the sub-routines? How many sub-routines are there? Where are the sub-routines called from?

Work with a partner. Ask each other your questions and discuss whether the answers given are correct.

Swap partners and ask your new partner the same questions. Discuss whether their answers are correct.

Predict: Work with a new partner.

Give your partner two numbers. Ask your partner to predict what they think the output of the flowchart will be.

Run: Check your partner's answer by inputting the numbers you gave them. Check if their prediction matches the result. Explain to your partner why they are correct. If you do not get the same answer, work through the flowchart together.

Modify: Join with a group of three other people, including people you have not worked with on this flowchart.

Work as a group to change the flowchart(s) to meet these new tasks. You may need to redraw one, or more, flowcharts.

1 Change the message output in the sub-routine called if the first number is smaller to "The second number was larger".
2 Change the identifier of the sub-routine `findLargest()` to `compareValues()`.
3 Change the flowchart that runs first to output a sensible message before and after the sub-routine is called.
4 Change your latest flowchart to output "The numbers are the same" if the two numbers input are the same.

Errors in sub-routines

You might see a flowchart that has sub-routines, but it does not work properly. There could be an error.

Here's a reminder of some common errors from Topic 1:

- using the wrong mathematical operator (+, -, *, /)
- using the wrong values in a calculation
- not taking the correct value as input from the user
- outputting an incorrect value.

There are some common errors that appear in selection statements and sub-routines. These include:

- using the wrong comparison operators: > < > = < =
- using the wrong identifier to call the sub-routine
- putting the symbol to call the sub-routine in the wrong place in the flowchart
- trying to use data in the sub-routine that exists in a different flowchart or sub-routine.

To find and correct the error:

1 Test the flowchart with some data to see what the difference is between what it should do and what it does do.
2 Change part of the flowchart.
3 Test the flowchart with the same data again to see if it works.
4 Repeat until it works.

Programming task 1.11: Predict, Run and Modify

You will need: a pen and paper

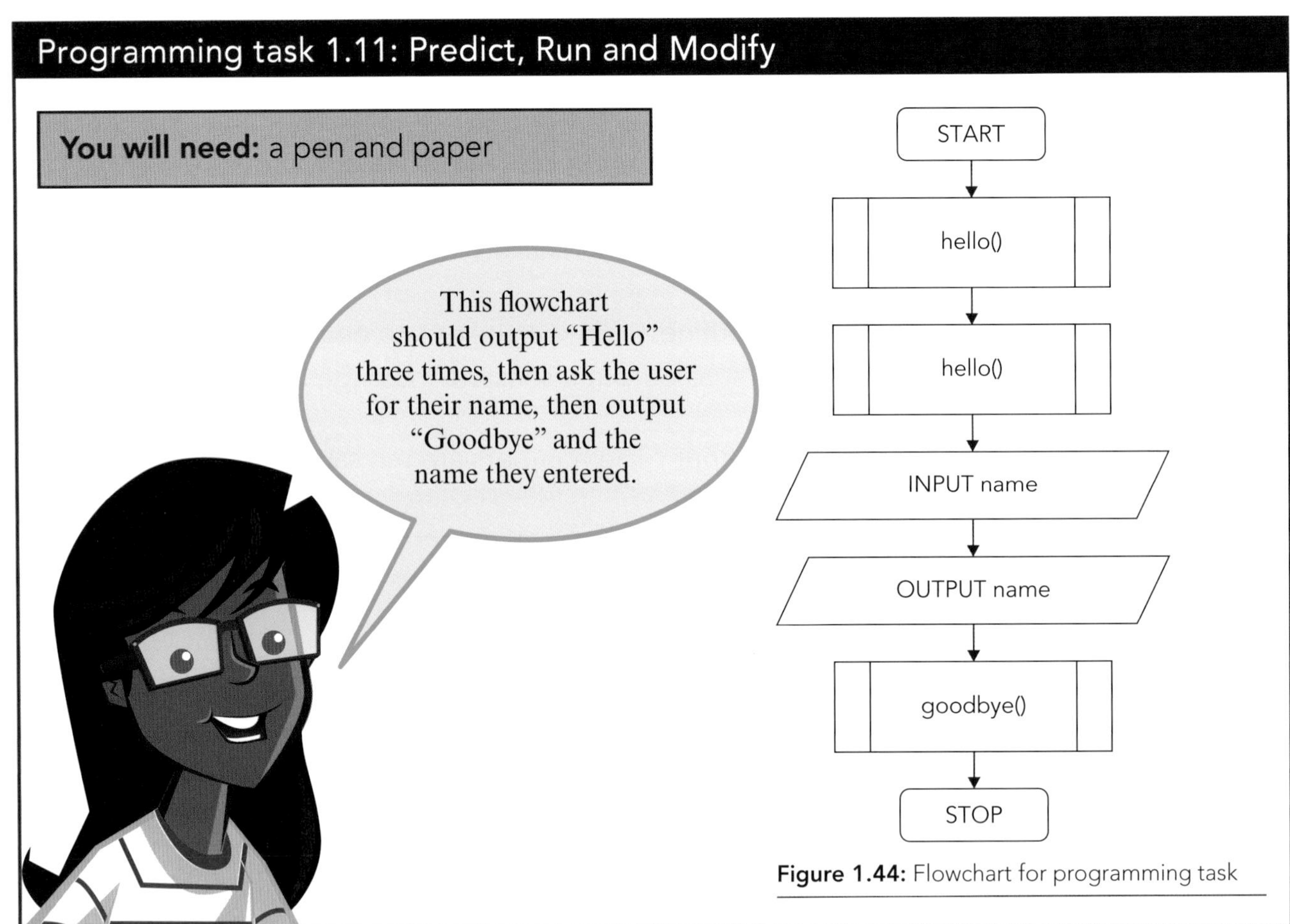

Figure 1.44: Flowchart for programming task

Continued

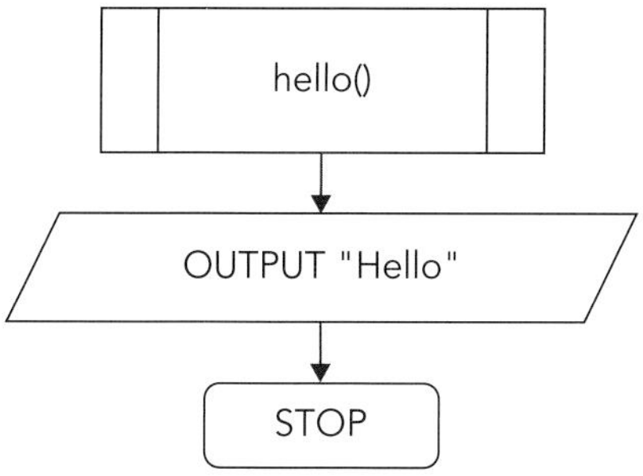

Figure 1.45: Sub-routine 1 for programming task

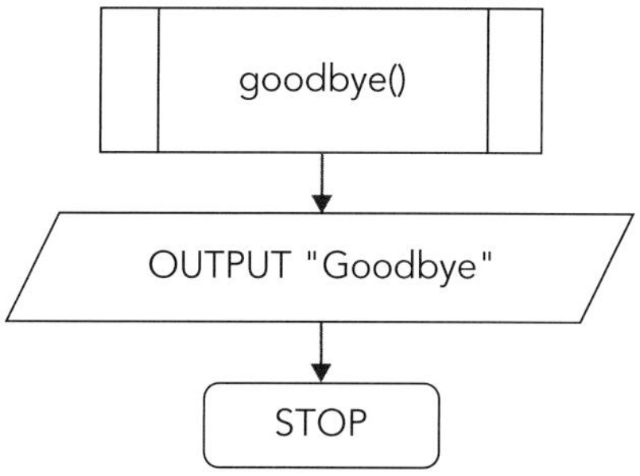

Figure 1.46: Sub-routine 2 for programming task

Predict: On your own, write down what the flowchart should output if Zara enters her name.

Compare your prediction with a partner. Discuss any differences and agree what should happen.

Run: Follow the flowchart with your partner. Compare the actions you perform with your prediction.

Write down the differences between what the flowchart should do, and what it actually does.

Modify: Join a group of up to four people.

As a group, select one of the differences between what the flowchart should do and what it does.

Discuss what needs to change in the flowchart.

Work with your partner to redraw the flowchart to correct the error.

Test whether the error has been corrected.

Repeat this process until all of the errors have been corrected.

Did you find it easier to find the error or to fix the error? Did you rely on other people to explain how to correct the error or did you contribute? How would you change your approach to the group discussion next time?

Did you know?

You are probably seeing and using sub-routines every day without realising! Have you ever read the lyrics to a song? When they get to the chorus they might say 'Repeat chorus' instead of writing the chorus again. What do you do when you get to this? You go back to the chorus, read this, then return to where you were before. This is a sub-routine.

Questions 1.7

1 What is a sub-routine?

2 What is the flowchart symbol for a sub-routine?

3 What features does a sub-routine have?

4 How do you call a sub-routine from another flowchart?

5 What happens when a sub-routine comes to the end?

6 Why are sub-routines useful when creating flowcharts?

Summary checklist

- [ ] I can describe what is meant by a pattern.
- [ ] I can identify a pattern in a description, a computer program or an algorithm.
- [ ] I can describe why pattern recognition is important when solving problems.
- [ ] I can state what a sub-routine is.
- [ ] I can describe the purpose of sub-routine.
- [ ] I can identify the flowchart symbol for a sub-routine.
- [ ] I can follow a flowchart that uses a sub-routine.
- [ ] I can change a flowchart that uses a sub-routine.
- [ ] I can find an error in a flowchart that uses a sub-routine.
- [ ] I can correct an error in a flowchart that uses a sub-routine.

> 1.4 Introduction to text-based programming

In this topic you will:

- know the difference between block-based and text-based programming languages
- understand how to create a program in Python
- understand how to use the print command to output a message to the screen in Python.

Key words

block-based language

editor

integrated development environment (IDE)

print

syntax

syntax errors

text-based language

Getting started

What do you already know?

- You may have used a block-based programming language before, such as Scratch, that allows you to create programs. You may have written programs to:
  - make a sprite move across the screen
  - make sprites speak
  - display text to the user
- When you had written your programs in Scratch, you would have run and tested them to see if they work.

Continued

Now try this!

Work in a group to create a mind map of all the different blocks you can remember from Scratch.

First do this from memory. Then open some Scratch programs that you created previously. Add any that you missed to your mind map.

Next to the name of each block, write its purpose.

Did you know?

No one knows exactly how many different programming languages there are, some current estimates are over 9000! Only a small number of these are used often though.

Text-based languages

There are a lot of different programming languages. Some are block-based like Scratch, and some are text-based like Python.

Block-based languages are really useful to help you learn about programming. It's a type of programming language that lets you drag and drop blocks of instruction to make a program. You don't have to remember the exact words to use, so you are less likely to make mistakes. However, block-based languages are limited, because there are fewer tasks you can do and you cannot always do exactly what you need. In a **text-based language**, you write statements instead of dragging blocks that already have the statements written on them.

In this book you will be learning how to use the text-based programming language Python.

All programming languages have their own **syntax**. Syntax is the grammar of the language, or the set of rules that have to be followed. When you are entering text-based code you need to make sure you are precise, or the programs may not run. For example:

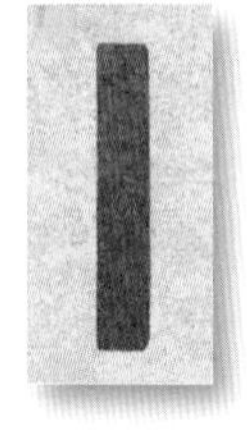

- Some words may be case sensitive. For example, 'PRINT' is not the same as 'print'.
- Some statements might need double quotation marks " " and some might need single quotation marks ' '.
- Some statements might need round brackets ( ) to open and close, and some might need square brackets [ ].

Even the most experienced programmers make **syntax errors** because nobody can remember everything all of the time. If you try and run a program that has a syntax error, the program will let you know that there is an error. It will often tell you where it is so you can fix it.

If you are ever unsure, look back at some of your previous programs, or use other resources such as this book, to check your syntax. Always remember that making mistakes is part of the programming process. It is nothing to worry about, and each time you correct an error, you are becoming a more confident programmer.

Did you know?

Python is not named after the snake. Guido von Rossum created the Python programming language while reading scripts from a 1970s comedy group named Monty Python.

Editors and integrated development environments (IDE)

Text-based programs are written using **editors**. A text editor is a special piece of software that lets you write the code. They often have extra features to help you, for example, colour code text so that you can check if you've written it correctly, or underline words that are incorrect.

Sometimes editors come in software called **integrated development environments (IDE)**. IDEs include more features than just an editor. They let you run the program and they tell you where any errors are.

There are many different editors and IDEs that you can use for Python. In this book, the two IDEs you will be introduced to are IDLE and PyCharm.

IDLE

IDLE is an IDE. When you write a program using IDLE, there will be two windows: one where you write the code, and one where the code runs.

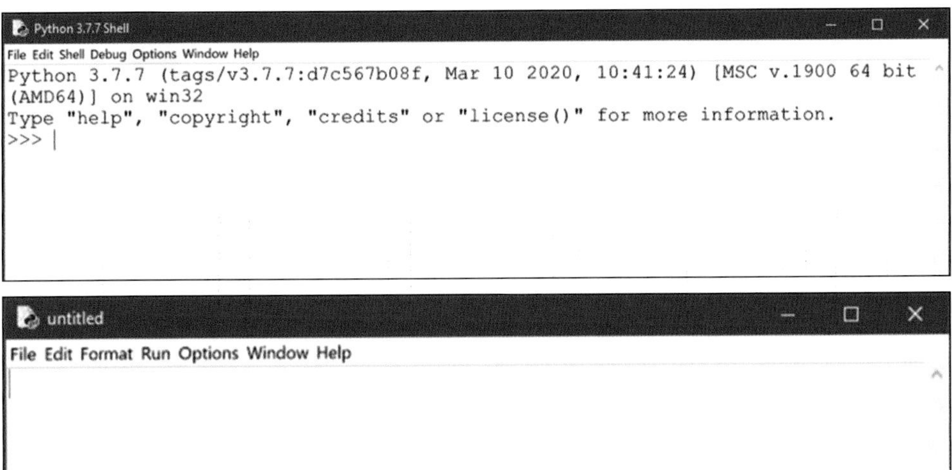

Figure 1.47: Example program shown in IDLE

Here's an example program. The code is shown on the right. To run the code, you click on Run and then Run Module (or press the F5 button). The results are shown on the left.

You will need to save your program with a sensible name before you can test your program.

If there is an error in your code so that it can't run, the error will appear in the Run window. There will be a message to explain the error. In this example, it says 'rint' is not defined. This is because it should say `print`.

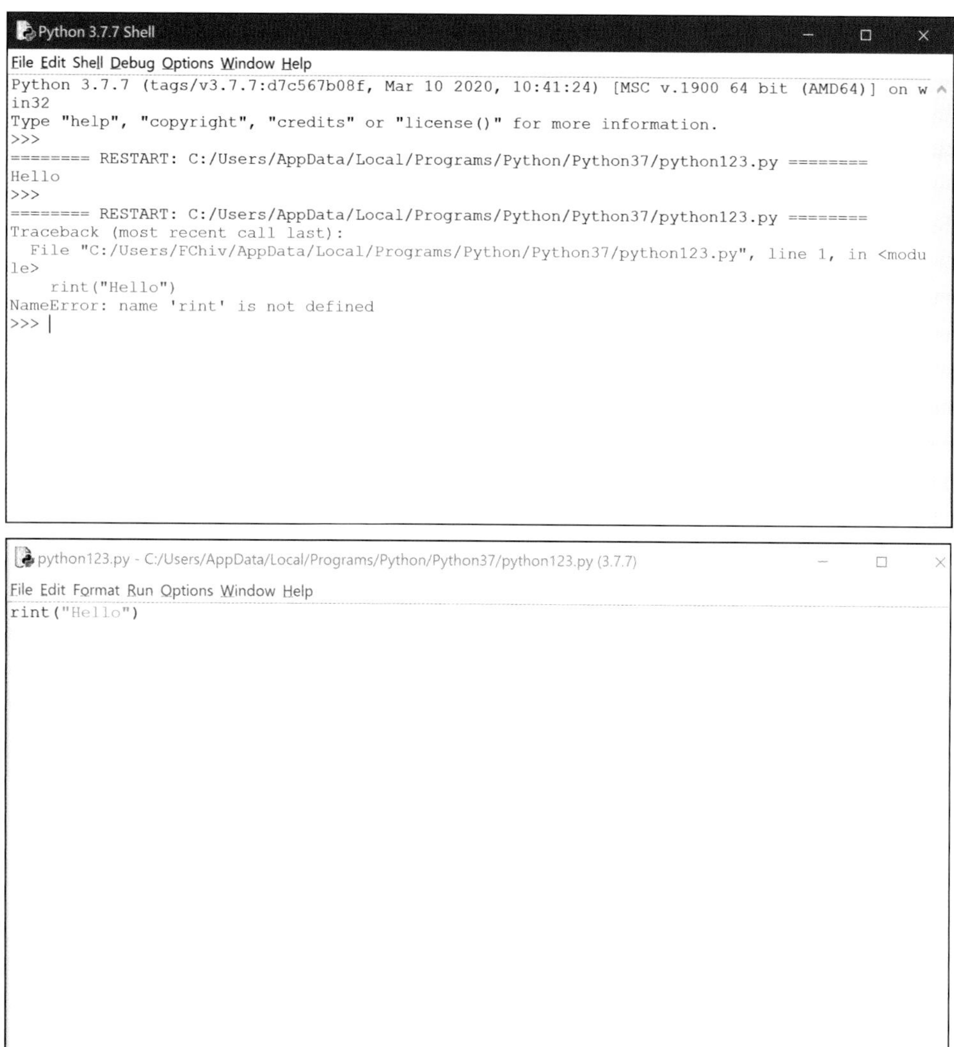

Figure 1.48: Error shown in IDLE

PyCharm

In PyCharm, you can write the code in the top window, and when the program is run, the results will appear underneath.

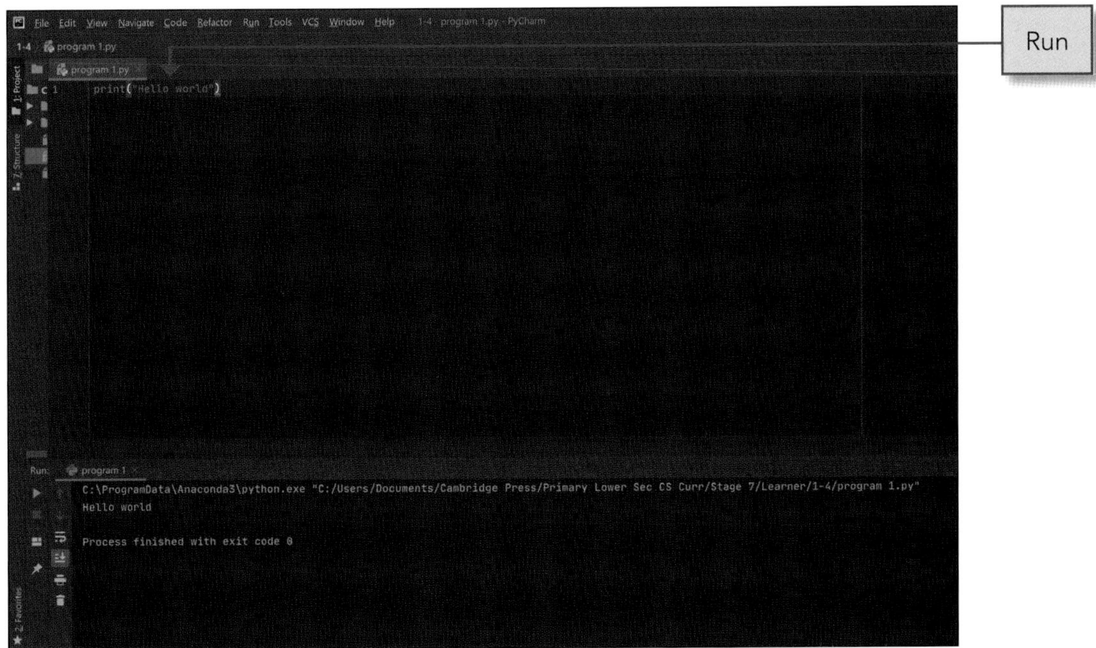

Figure 1.49: PyCharm

To run your program, you need to click on Run and then Run *filename*. If there is an error in your program, it might be underlined in red. When you try and run the code, PyCharm will tell you why it cannot run. In this image, it says 'rint' is not defined. This is because it should say `print`.

Figure 1.50: Error shown in PyCharm

Output in Python

The output command in Python is **print**. This is written: `print()`

This command word is always written in lowercase and has rounded brackets after it. You enter whatever you want to be output inside the brackets.

To output a message – for example, "This is my first message" – the text needs to have double quotation marks around it. This is to tell Python that you want these words output exactly as you have written them. If you put an uppercase letter, it will output an uppercase letter. If you put a lowercase letter, it will output a lowercase letter. You will learn more about this in the next chapter about strings and variables.

Here is an example line of code:

```
print("This is my first message")
```

What do you think will be output to the screen?

```
This is my first message
```

Notice how the double quotation marks were not output.

Unplugged activity 1.11

You will need: a pen and paper

Read this line of code with a partner.

```
print("My favourite colour is purple")
```

Write this line of code on the centre of a piece of paper, but change it so that it will output your favourite colour and your partner's favourite colour.

Annotate this to identify the main features, such as the command words and brackets.

Include a second example with an entirely different message to be output.

Programming task 1.12: Predict, Run, Modify and Make

You will need: a desktop computer, laptop or tablet with an IDE

Read this line of code:

```
print("Today is ?")
```

Predict: Tell a partner what you think will be output if this is run.

Run: Enter this code and run it. Was your output correct?

Modify: Change your code to output what day of the week today is.

Make: Create a new Python program to output a message about your favourite activity.

Output multiple statements

Here's an example of a Python program with two print statements:

```
print("I like sunny days")
print("I also like it when it rains")
```

Each `print` statement is written on its own line. Each statement will output text on a new line. Here's the result when the program is run:

```
I like sunny days
I also like it when it rains
```

Programming task 1.13: Predict, Run and Modify

You will need: a desktop computer, laptop or tablet with an IDE

Read this Python program with a partner:

```
print("Once upon a time there was a young girl.")
print("The girl lived in a village but liked to visit her grandmother.")
print("To visit her grandmother she would put on a red cloak and walk through the woods.")
```

Predict: Write down the output that the program will produce. Make sure you are careful to be exact.

Run: Enter this code and run it. Did the output you wrote match exactly or were there any differences?

Modify: Change this program to output the first three lines of a different story of your choice (you can make one up or use one you know).

Programming task 1.14: Make

You will need: a pen and paper, a desktop computer, laptop or tablet with an IDE

Make: Work with a partner to write a short poem. This can be on any topic you are interested in. It should be at least four lines long, but it doesn't have to rhyme.

Discuss where you will use capital letters, lowercase letters, and any other punctuation (full stops, commas, exclamation marks!).

Write a Python program by yourself to output your poem.

Run your program to make sure it works.

Compare your program with your partner's. Were they the same? Were there any differences? If there were, what was it in the code that made these differences?

Self-assessment

Give yourself a rating from 1 to 3 for your poem program.

1 means 'I completed this on my own without any help'.
2 means 'I needed some help to understand some parts, or to fix some errors'.
3 means 'I needed support to write my poem and to make sure it worked'.

Activity 1.2

You will need: a pen and paper, a desktop computer, laptop or tablet with internet access

Python is only one example of a text-based language. Different languages have different commands to output a message. Work with a partner to find out what the following languages use as a command to output:

- Visual Basic
- Java
- C.

Write down these commands. Can you find any other text-based programming languages that are not listed here? What do they use for output? Write these commands down with the name of the languages.

As a class, create a list of all the different commands that are used.

Common errors

You might have already had some errors when writing your output programs, or you might not have had any yet. It is OK for programs to have errors. Even the best programmers make errors all the time. How you find and correct the errors is how you learn to program.

Each line of code in this table should output the word "Hello", but each line has an error in it.

Code	Error
`rint("Hello")`	print is spelt incorrectly
`print "Hello"`	missing brackets
`print(Hello)`	missing double quotation marks
`print("Hello)`	missing one quotation mark
`PRINT("Hello")`	print should be lowercase
`output("Hello")`	output should be print
`print` `("Hello")`	the code should all be on the same line
`print("Hello").`	there is a full stop at the end of the line

Table 1.7: Common errors in code

Questions 1.8

1 What is the command word to output in Python?

2 What punctuation do you put around a message in Python to output the message?

3 What will be the difference between the output from these two print statements?

```
print("Good morning.")
print("good morning!")
```

4 What is the error in this statement?

```
print("The sky is blue)
```

5 What is the error in this statement?

```
PRINT("Grass is green")
```

6 Write a statement to output your name.

7 Write a Python program to output a list of facts about yourself.

Summary checklist

- [ ] I can write a program in Python.
- [ ] I can run a program in Python.
- [ ] I can write a print statement in Python.
- [ ] I can output a message to the screen in Python.
- [ ] I can output multiple messages to the screen in Python.

1.5 Python programming

In this topic you will:

- know that data comes in different data types
- understand the difference between Integer, Real and String data
- learn how to use the input command to read data from the user
- know how to store, or use, the value input from the user
- know how to store data of different types in variables in Python
- understand the importance of using the most appropriate data type in a program
- learn how to cast data from one data type to another
- understand the purpose of variables
- learn the rules of using variables in a text-based program
- know how to store, change and output data from a variable
- understand the function of the arithmetic operators +, −, *, /.

Getting started

What do you already know?

- Python is a programming language that is relatively easy to learn. You may have already used Python. For example, you may have:
  - changed programs to output different messages
  - written new programs to output messages
  - corrected programs that output messages.

Key words

arithmetic operator

assignment statement

casting

data type

initialising

input

reserved words

Continued

- A variable is something that can be changed.
  In programming, variables store data that changes.
  - In Scratch, you might have stored a score for a character, for example:

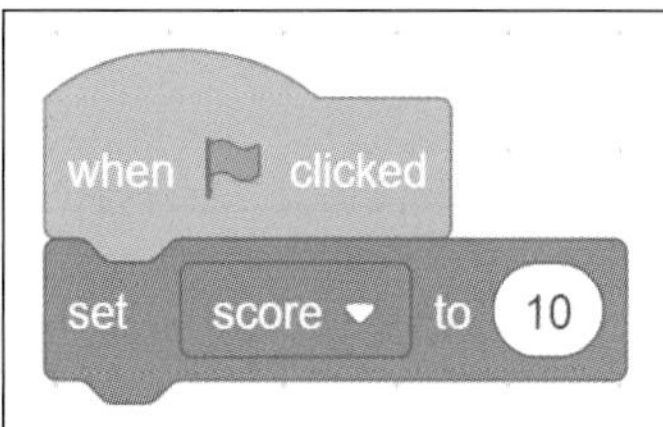

  - In a flowchart, you might have used a variable to store the result of a calculation. For example:

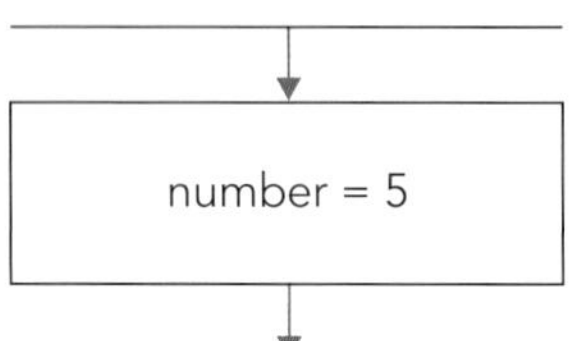

- Integer data is numeric. String data is a set of characters. Character data is one character.
- In maths, there is an order of priority of operations, for example BOMDAS or BIDMAS.

  The order is:

	Priority	
B for brackets	1	
I for indices	2	
D for division	3	Same priority
M for multiplication	3	
A for addition	4	Same priority
S for subtraction	4	

  So all you have to remember is the name – BIDMAS.

Now try this!

Work with a partner to discuss whether each item of data in this list is an example of an Integer (whole number), a String (one or more characters) or a Character (a single character).

Continued

Create a table with the headings: Integer, Character, String.

Write each item of data under one, or more, columns to identify its data type.

22	blue	H	horse	carrot	television	network
190	!	@	binary	11111001	7	fan
crocodile	mathematics	AND	byte	256	102	fan

Compare your answers with another pair and discuss any differences.

Variables and assignment

A variable is a space in memory that has an identifier. The variable stores data that can change while a program is running.

In Python, a variable is declared by giving it an identifier. This is a unique name that will be used to refer to that variable.

When selecting the identifier, you need to make sure you do not use any **reserved words**. A reserved word is one that Python already uses, for example `print`, `input`, `if`. You won't know what all of these are yet. But if you try and use a reserved word, Python will tell you when you try and run the program. Then you need to choose a different word.

The identifier cannot have any spaces in it, or symbols such as exclamation marks, commas and so on. But identifiers can have the underscore character _. They can include numbers, but cannot start with a number.

Questions 1.9

Identify whether each identifier is valid (allowed), or invalid (not allowed) for Python. If it is invalid, state why.

1 `myNumber`
2 `29Value`
3 `My Name.`
4 `print`
5 `the_Total`
6 `Number-entered`

Assignment

An **assignment statement** stores data in a variable. Here is the structure of an assignment statement in Python:

```
variable = data
```

If the data includes characters (for example, letters or symbols), the data needs to be in quotation marks. This is to tell the program that you want those characters saved, otherwise the program will try and find a variable with the same characters.

The variable on the left-hand side of the equals sign will store the data that is on the right-hand side. If you are reading it like a sentence, you can replace the = with the word 'stores'.

Let's have a look at an example:

```
myData = 20
```

`myData` is the variable, and 20 is stored in `myData`. `myData` stores 20.

```
myColour = "Purple"
```

This can be read as '`myColour` stores `Purple`'.

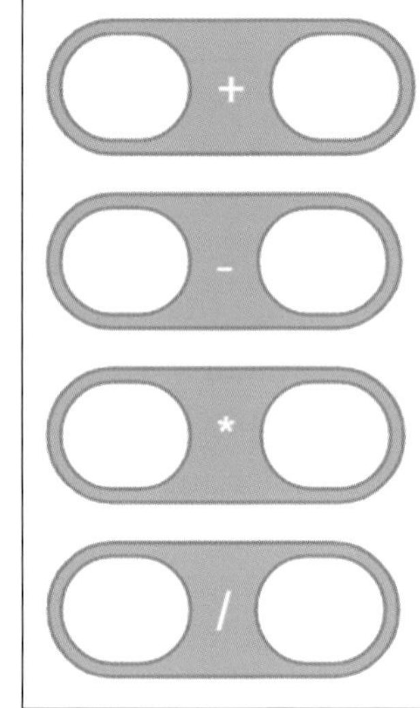

Figure 1.51: Arithmetic operators

Arithmetic operators

You will have come across **arithmetic operators** in mathematics. These are usually +, −, ×, ÷. In computing, arithmetic operators are +, −, *, /.

These operators are used between numbers, or variables, to perform calculations. They are the same as those you will have used in Scratch and are described in this table.

Arithmetic operator	Description	Example
+	Addition Adds together the numbers on either side of the +.	`number = 2 + 3` `number` will store 5
–	Subtraction Subtracts the second number from the first.	`number = 3 - 2` `number` will store 1
*	Multiplication Multiplies the numbers on either side of the *.	`number = 5 * 2` `number` will store 10
/	Division Divides the first number by the second.	`number = 10 / 2` `number` will store 5

Table 1.8: Arithmetic operators in computing

The operators are used on the right-hand side of the assignment statement (the right of the = sign).

Here are some examples:

```
numberStored = 100 + 20
```

`numberStored` will now store 120 (100 + 20).

```
numberStored = 20 * 3
```

`numberStored` will now store 60.

If you are using multiple operators, you might need to use brackets. The order of operations works in the same way as it does in mathematics.

The calculations inside the brackets are done first. Then those outside are done afterwards. For example:

```
value1 = 1 + 2 * 3 + 4
```

This will do the multiplication first.

1 + (2 * 3) + 4

1 + 6 + 4

7 + 4

11

```
value2 = (1+2)*(3+4)
```

This will do the brackets first.

(1 + 2) * (3 + 4)

3 * (3 + 4)

3 * 7

21

By using brackets, you can tell the program in which order you want the operations to be done.

Combining variables and operators

Because variables store data, you can use a variable instead of a number in a calculation. You refer to the variable by its identifier. When the program runs, it will access the data stored in that variable.

Here is an example:

```
first = 10
second = 20
total = first + second
```

Let's look at each line in turn:

`first = 10`	`first` stores the number 10
`second = 20`	`second` stores the number 20
`total = first + second`	`total` stores the value in `first` + the value in `second`. `total` = 10 + 20 `total` stores 30

Table 1.9: Combining variables and operators

Unplugged activity 1.12

You will need: a pen and A4 card

Cut the A4 card into six evenly sized rectangles. You and a partner should each take three cards. Write the name of a variable on the front of each of your three cards. Write a value on the back of each card. For example:

Front:

`first`	`colour`
`thing`	`answer`
`total`	`last`

Back:

`20`	`"Red"`
`100.4`	`"yes"`
`66`	`"Z"`

Ask your partner to perform actions for each variable that is written on the front of a card. This could be to output the content, change the content, or input new content. For example:

- Output the content of a variable. For example, `OUTPUT first`
- Your partner should turn over the card with `first` on it, and read the value on the back (20)
- Store a new value in the variable. For example store 10 in `first`.
  Your partner should turn over the card with `first` on it, cross out the value, and write 10 in its place
- Use an arithmetic operator with the value. For example, add 10 to `total`.
  Your partner should turn over the card with `total` on it, add 10 to the value (66 + 10 = 76), cross out the original value and write the answer (76).

Programming task 1.15: Predict, Run, Modify and Make

You will need: a pen and paper, a desktop computer, laptop or tablet with an IDE

Predict: Read this program and tell a partner what the output will be.

```
one = 1
two = 2
three = 3
four = 4
total = one + two + three + four
print(total)
```

Run: Enter the program and test whether your output was correct.

Predict: On paper, draw a box for each of the variables in this program. Write the identifier of each variable on a box (Hint: there are 5 variables). Write the values that are stored in each variable at the end of this program in the box for that variable.

Modify: Change the program so that it multiplies the numbers together instead of adding them.

Modify: Change the program so that there is a new variable, `five`, that stores the number 5 in it. Include this in the multiplication.

Make: Create a new program that stores the numbers 10, 100, 1000 in variables. The program should calculate and output (1000 + 100) / 10.

Changing the value in a variable

You might need to change a variable by performing an operation on the data inside it. For example, if you are creating a computer game with a score, you might need to add 1 to the variable that holds the score. Or you could be keeping track of the number of lives left, and need to subtract 1 from the variable that holds the number of lives.

You can use a variable on both sides of the assignment statement.

Example 1:

```
score = 10
score = score + 1
```

This line of code will take the value in `score` (10), add 1 to it (10 + 1 = 11), and store this new value in `score` (11). So `score` now stores 11.

Example 2:

```
livesLeft = 100
livesLeft = livesLeft - 10
```

This line of code will take the value in `livesLeft` (100). It will subtract 10 from it (90). This value is stored in `livesLeft` (90). So `livesLeft` now stores 90.

Programming task 1.16: Predict, Run, Modify and Make

You will need: a desktop computer, laptop or tablet with an IDE

Predict: Read this program with a partner and write down the output.

```
number = 1
print(number)
number = number + 1
print(number)
number = number + 1
print(number)
number = number + 1
print(number)
number = number + 1
print(number)
```

Run: Enter the program in Python and run it. Check the output against your prediction. Were you correct?

Modify: Change this program so it outputs the numbers 1 to 10 in order. Use the variable `number` in each output.

Make: Write a new program to output a countdown for a rocket launch, for example:

5

4

3

2

1

Blast off!

You need to use a variable to store, decrease and output each number.

Initialising

If you need to change the value in a variable, you need to make sure it already has a value in it. You cannot add 1 to a number that is 'empty' (there is nothing stored in it). Setting a variable to a starting value is called **initialising**. Here's an example:

```
score = score + 1
print(score)
```

In this program, 1 is added to the value in `score`. `score` does not have a value in it, so 1 cannot be added to it. To fix this, we set `score` to start at a value, for example, 0.

```
score = 0
score = score + 1
print(score)
```

Now `score` is initialised to store 0 at the start of the program so 1 can be added to it.

Not all variables need initialising every time, but it is a good habit to get into to make sure errors don't occur later in a program.

Variables and output

In Python, you can output the content of a variable by using its identifier. The identifier does not appear in double quotation marks – for example, `print(number)` will output the data stored in `number`, whereas `print("number")` will output the word "number".

If you want to output two variables, or variables and some other text, you put a comma (`,`) between each item. Python will automatically put a space between each item when it outputs them.

In this example, the content of the two variables are output together.

```
number = 5
day = "Saturday"
print(number, day)
```

Here is the output:

```
5 Saturday
```

The same symbol (`,`) is used to output text and a variable.

For example:

```
day = "Saturday"
print("Today is", day)
```

Here is the output:

```
Today is Saturday
```

The text within the quotation marks is output as written in the program, and then the contents of the variable `day`.

You can use as many variables and text as you need. Just make sure that text to be output has quotation marks, and that there is a comma between each item.

Programming task 1.17: Predict, Run, Modify and Make

You will need: a desktop computer, laptop or tablet with an IDE

Predict: Work with a partner to identify the output from this program.

```
film = "Peter Rabbit"
print("My favourite film is")
print(film)
```

Run: Write the program in Python and check whether your prediction was correct.

Modify: Change the program so the message and variable contents are output using one print statement.

Make: Write a new Python program to:

- store your favourite food and animal in separate variables
- output a message that states what your favourite food and animal are using the values in your variables. You should only have one output statement.

Data types

Data can come in lots of different formats. You can have numbers, letters, dates and so on. A computer often needs to know what type of data you want to use because some data can be in more than one category. The **data type** is the format that a data comes in.

The computer will treat different data in different ways, and each data type can have different operations applied to it.

What do you think the output will be from "a" + "b"? Can you add together two characters? In Python, this will join a and b together to become "ab".

If you store a number, for example 000123, as a 'number' data type, it will remove the 0s at the front and leave you with 123. You might need those 0s though, so you may need to store 000123 as a different data type if you need them to stay.

This table has some of the common data types:

Data type	Description	Example
Integer	A whole number without a decimal	12 24 -10 49584
Real or Float	A number with a decimal	12.0 24.5 -10.9 49584.3321
Character	One character from: • lowercase letters • uppercase letters • numbers • symbols	"a" "B" "3" "!"
String	One or more characters from: • lowercase letters • uppercase letters • numbers • symbols • a mixture of all character types	"house" "APPLE" "A" "12" ":-)" "Banana" "road123" "Hello!" "I am here today :)"

Table 1.10: Data types

Did you know?

The word 'float' is short for floating-point number. This is a special type of binary number where the binary point (same as a decimal point but for a binary number) can move, so it's a moving binary point.

Unplugged activity 1.13

You will need: some coloured pens and pencils, poster paper

Work with a partner. Work together to create a poster about data types. This needs to include the *four* different data types in this chapter, and examples of each type of data.

Make sure that the difference between the data types is clear, and that you include examples of data that could be more than one data type.

Questions 1.10

1 Identify the most appropriate data type for each of the items described.

- Number of books that you own, for example: 25
- Favourite colour, for example: Purple
- Amount of money given each week, for example: 2.50
- The first letter of your first name, for example: V
- Age, for example: 12

2 Give *one* example of an Integer number.

3 Give *two* examples of data that can be a Character and a String.

4 What is the difference between an Integer and a Real number?

5 What is the difference between a String and a Character?

Data types in Python

If an item of data is a String or a Character, then it needs quotation marks around it. This tells Python that it is a String and not another data type like an Integer. Python will treat whatever is inside the quotation marks as text.

You do not need to tell Python what type of data you are going to store. You can store a string in a variable and then replace it with an Integer. For example:

```
myValue = "house"
myValue = 10
```

In this program, the String "house" will be stored in the variable `myValue`. Then this will be replaced with the Integer value 10.

You need to make sure you are using numbers in mathematical operations. For example:

```
number1 = "12"
result = number1 * 2
print(result)
```

In this program "12" is a String, so instead of multiplying the number 12 by 2, it will make 12 appear twice. Try the program and see what happens.

Casting in Python

You can tell Python that you want to change the data type of a value by using a function called **casting**. You can cast one value to a different data type. For example, a String can be cast to an Integer.

There is a command word for each data type: `int()`, `str()`, and `float()`.

Inside the brackets you put the data or the variable whose data type you want to change.

To change a value to an Integer, use the code `int()`.

Write the data, or variable, that you want to change to an Integer inside the brackets. For example:

```
number1 = "12"
result = int(number1) * 2
print(result)
```

This program will now change "12" into the Integer 12, multiply it by 2 (24) and store this in result. Try the program and see what happens.

To change a value to a String, use the code `str()`.

Write the data, or variable, inside the brackets. For example:

```
favouriteNumber = 5
print("My favourite number is", str(favouriteNumber))
```

This program will change the Integer 5 into the String "5" to output it. Try the program and see what happens.

In Python, a Real number is called a float. To change a value to a Real number, use the code `float()`

Write the data, or variable, inside the brackets. For example:

```
number = 10
print(float(number))
```

This program will change the Integer 10 into the Real number 10.0. Try the program and see what happens.

Programming task 1.18: Investigate and Modify

You will need: a pen and paper, a desktop computer, laptop or tablet with an IDE

Investigate: If you try to run this program it will report an error.

```
first = "10"
second = 60
total = first + second
print(total)
```

Work with a partner to write down the three variables and the data type of each.

One of these variables needs the data type to be changed. Work together to identify the value that is the wrong data type.

Write the program in Python and see what error is produced.

Modify: Change the program to allow it to add together the two values by casting one of the values to the correct data type. Change the value to a different one than in the program above.

Input in Python

Input means data entered by the user on their keyboard in Python. You can store this input and use it in your program. The command `input()` waits for the user to enter some data and press enter.

The data entered will need to be stored somewhere. This can be stored in a variable, used in an output or used in a calculation.

Example 1, storing in a variable.

```
myName = input()
```

Example 2, using an output.

```
print("Your name is", input())
```

Example 3, used in a calculation.

```
result = 10 + input()
```

Inside the brackets, you can write a message to be output to the user. For example:

```
myName = input("Enter your name")
print("Hello", myName)
```

This program will output the message "Enter your name" and wait for the user to enter some text and press enter. It will then output "Hello" and the data that the user entered. Try the program and see what happens.

Any data that is input will be stored as a String data type. If you want to enter a number, then you will need to cast it. For example:

```
number = input("Enter a number")
result = int(number) * 2
print(result)
```

This program will take the data that the user enters and store it in the variable `number` as a String. It will change this to an Integer, multiply it by 2 and store the result in the variable `result`. The data in `result` will then be output. Try this program and see what happens.

Programming task 1.19: Predict, Run, Investigate, Modify and Make

You will need: a pen and paper, a desktop computer, laptop or tablet with an IDE

Predict: Write down what this program will output if you enter your current age.

```
age = int(input("Enter your age in years"))
age = age + 10
print("In 10 years you will be", age, "years old")
```

Run: Enter this program in Python and run it to see if you are correct.

Investigate: Write this program on paper, or print a copy of the program. Annotate the program by identifying:

- the variable(s)
- the data type(s)
- the casting
- the arithmetic operator.

Modify: Change this program to output the age in 20 years.

Modify: Change this program to output the age 5 years ago.

Make: Write a new Python program to:

- take a number as input from the user
- output the multiples for the number input.

Work with a partner to test both of your programs at the same time. Check whether the output for both is the same. If it is not, discuss why there is a difference, and which is correct (or whether both are correct but just different).

Programming task 1.20: Make

You will need: a desktop computer, laptop or tablet with an IDE

Make: Write a new Python program to:

- take the user's name as input
- take the user's age as input
- calculate the year the user was born
- output a message using the user's name and the year they were born.

Test that your program works, and identify whether it does each of the actions in the four bullet points above. When you are sure your program works, ask a partner to test it as well.

Self-assessment

Give yourself a rating on how independently you worked on this programming task.

- On my own: I created the program on my own and solved my own problems.
- With some help: I needed a prompt of help with the program or to solve a problem.
- With support: I had help to write some, or all, of the program, or to fix any errors that I encountered.

Next time you write a program, what will you do differently? Will you do more planning before you start? Or revisit some of your past programs to help you identify what to do?

Questions 1.11

1 What is the command word to read input from the user?

2 Identify the error in this line of Python code.

```
input("Enter a colour") = colour
```

3 Describe what happens in this program.

```
first = int(input("Enter a number"))
second = int(input("Enter a number"))
print(first / second)
```

Common errors

You might have already had some errors when writing your programs, or you might not have had any yet. It is OK for programs to have errors – even the best programmers make errors all the time. How you find and correct the errors is how you learn to program.

Each line of code in this table has an error.

Code	Error	Correction
`10 = number`	The assignment is the wrong way around. The data must be on the right-hand side	`number = 10`
`number == 20`	Assignment is a single = not double	`number = 20`
`input = 100`	Input is a command word and cannot be used as a variable identifier	`numberInput = 100`
`value = "red`	The quotation marks need to be closed	`value = "red"`
`20 + 13 = total`	The assignment is the wrong way around. The calculation must on the right-hand side	`total = 20 + 13`
`first = 10` `total = First + 5`	The variable identifier is case sensitive. `first` has lowercase once and uppercase once	`first = 10` `total = first + 5`
`result = 100 × 10`	Multiplication is * not ×	`result = 100 * 10`
`colour = "purple"` `print("colour")`	The characters inside the quotation marks will be printed, colour, instead of the contents of the variable `colour` (in this case, purple)	`colour = "purple"` `print(colour)`
`score = 10` `score = + 5`	To add to a variable, the variable name is needed again	`score = 10` `score = score + 5`
`name = "Khad"` `print("Hello" name)`	Missing the comma to output two different items	`name = "Khad"` `print("Hello", name)`

(Continued)

Code	Error	Correction
`value = input(Enter number)`	The text inside the `input()` needs to be in quotation marks	`value = input("Enter number")`
`number = input("Enter number")` `result = number * 10`	Values input are Strings. To multiply, it needs to be cast to a number	`number = int(input("Enter a number"))` `result = number * 10`

`value1 = "12"`
`value2 = 13`
`total = value1 + value2`
	`value1` is a String. To add to a number it needs to be cast to a number	`value1 = "12"`
		`value2 = 13`
		`total = int(value1) + value2`

`value1 = 10`
`value2 = 20`
`value1 = 30`
`total = value1 + value2 + value3`
	The data in `value1` was overwritten. It should be 10 and was accidentally changed to 30 instead of using `value3`	`value1 = 10`
		`value2 = 20`
		`value3 = 30`
		`total = value1 + value2 + value3`

Table 1.11: Errors in code

Summary checklist

- [ ] I can identify Integer, Real and String data.
- [ ] I can write a Python program that stores data in a variable.
- [ ] I can write a Python program that uses +, –, * and /.
- [ ] I can write a Python program that changes the data in a variable.
- [ ] I can write a Python program that changes data from one data type to another.
- [ ] I can write a Python program that takes data as input from the user.

1.6 Software development and testing

In this topic you will:

- identify the positive and negative elements of a software prototype
- explain why project plans are used in software development projects
- identify the key features of a test plan
- use a test plan to test an algorithm
- understand the different ways errors can happen in a program
- test programs to find errors.

Key words

bug

debug or debugging

evaluate

interface

logic error

project plan

prototype

software development

systematically

test plan

Getting started

What do you already know?

- You should have seen prototypes and created a prototype for an interface (for example, with buttons and messages).
- You should have tested block-based programs using different types of data, for example:
  - normal data (accepted)
  - invalid data (rejected).

Continued

- You should have evaluated programs by identifying the positive elements, and considered how they could be improved.
- You should have followed a project plan when developing a project on your own or with others.
- You should have corrected errors in programs. These could be block-based programs or text-based programs.

Now try this!

Work with a partner. Tell each other about three different errors that you have had in your programs. These could be that a word was incorrect, a calculation didn't work or the wrong output was produced. Write a list of the different errors, and explain to each other how you found and corrected each error.

If you cannot think of any errors you have had, write down some errors that could take place. What words could you write incorrectly?

How many different types of errors did you identify together?

Did you both do the same actions to find the errors? Or did you do something different?

Prototypes

A **prototype** is an early version of an end product or, in this case, a system. It might only be for part of the system and might not be fully working. For example, it could just be the design for the **interface**. An interface lets you interact with the computer. It is what you see on the screen: the words, images and buttons that you read or click. Clicking on a button on a game controller or opening a window on your computer are both examples of using an interface.

Prototypes are created as part of the **software development** process where you design, create and test a program.

The prototype is then **evaluated**. This is where you look at the prototype, compare it against its original purpose and see how good it is. You do this by identifying the positive points and where it could be improved.

This feedback is then used to improve the prototype.

The process can be done repeatedly until a final product is created. Each time the prototype is evaluated, it is changed and new features can be added to it. This new version is then evaluated again, and then changed repeatedly until a final working product is created that everyone is happy with.

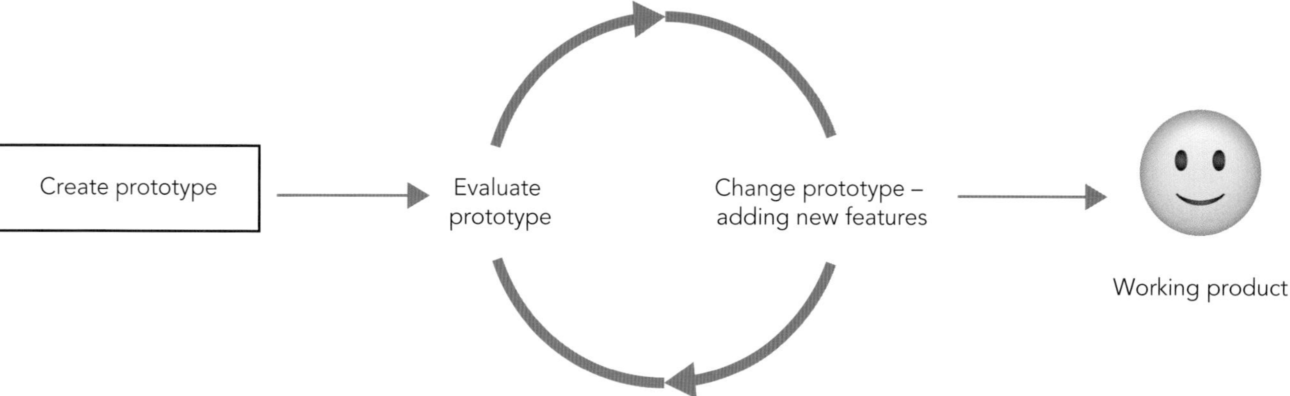

Figure 1.52: Software development from prototype to working product

Evaluating prototypes

When evaluating a system or product, you need to ask yourself a number of questions. Some examples are given here by Marcus, Sofia, Arun and Zara. Depending on the system, there might be others you want to consider.

Unplugged activity 1.14

You will need: a pen and paper

This prototype should display a menu for the user to select from. The user can either start a new game, load a saved game or leave the game.

```
Menu
Start new game
Load saved game
Quit
```

Work with a partner to answer each of these questions about the interface.

1 Does it meet the requirements?
Compare this prototype to the description at the start.
Does it display a menu for the user to select from?
Can the user either start a new game, load a saved game or leave the game?

2 Is the design appropriate?
Are the words, colours and layout easy to follow and read?

3 Is the method of input suitable?
How does the user know what to input?
How does the user know how to input (for example, type, select a button, joystick)?

4 Is the output suitable?
Is it text or images? Is this suitable? Can it be understood?

5 What are the positive features?
What do you like about the prototype? Do you like part of the design, or do you like that it meets some of the requirements?

6 How do you think this could be improved?
Now you need to think about what you don't like about it.
Make a list and then think about what needs to be done to improve it.
Be as detailed as possible, especially if there is a lot that you think should be improved!

Work with another pair. Compare your responses to each question.
Are there similarities? Are there differences?

Discuss whether or not there is always one right answer to an evaluation of a prototype.

Unplugged activity 1.15

You will need: a pen and paper

Arun is creating a computer game.
The game will have nine squares that are all blue. The aim of the game is to change all the squares to purple.

Clicking on a square will change the colour of at least two squares. These could be changed to blue, purple or an entirely different colour.

The player needs to keep on clicking on the squares until they are all purple.

This is a prototype for the start of the game.

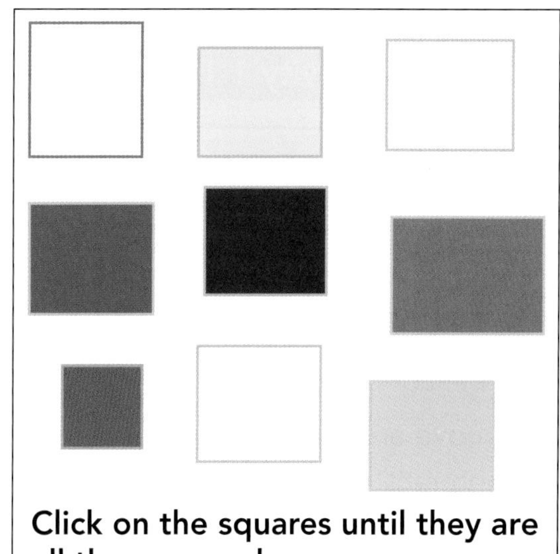

Evaluate this prototype on your own. Write a report that covers the six questions suggested above, as well as any of your own that you can think of.

Work in a group with up to three others. Compare your reports. Discuss the features you identified as positive and the ways you chose to improve the prototype. Combine your reports into one report that includes the points from each group member.

Present your group's evaluation to the class, explaining how you evaluated the prototype and the points you identified.

Self-assessment

Give yourself a colour for each of the statements based on your work in evaluating this prototype. Red = 'I needed help to do this'. Amber = 'I needed some help, but can do some on my own'. Green = 'I can do this confidently'.

1 I compared the prototype to its requirements.
2 I identified positive parts of the prototype.
3 I identified ways that the prototype can be improved.
4 I contributed to the group discussion.

Questions 1.12

1 What is a prototype?
2 When evaluating a prototype, what should you compare it to?
3 What should you think about when evaluating a prototype?

Project plans

Project plans are plans that are used to decide what you are going to do and when you are going to do it. You create a project plan before you start working on a project.

Unplugged activity 1.16

You will need: a pen and paper

Create a group with up to three other people.

A new computer game needs to be designed and created. The game will allow users to create a 3D character (avatar) that they will control. They will then need to:

- move around a virtual world
- interact with other characters and objects
- travel to different countries and solve puzzles.

The players will be able to play in the same virtual world over the internet by logging into an account.

The game development will be split between a large development team of artists, designers, programmers, testers and evaluators.

Discuss and create a list of what will need to be planned and decided before anyone can start working on this project.

Write a list of reasons why this planning is required.

Discuss your answers as a class. Together, create two lists: one that lists the items that need planning, and one that lists the reasons why planning is required.

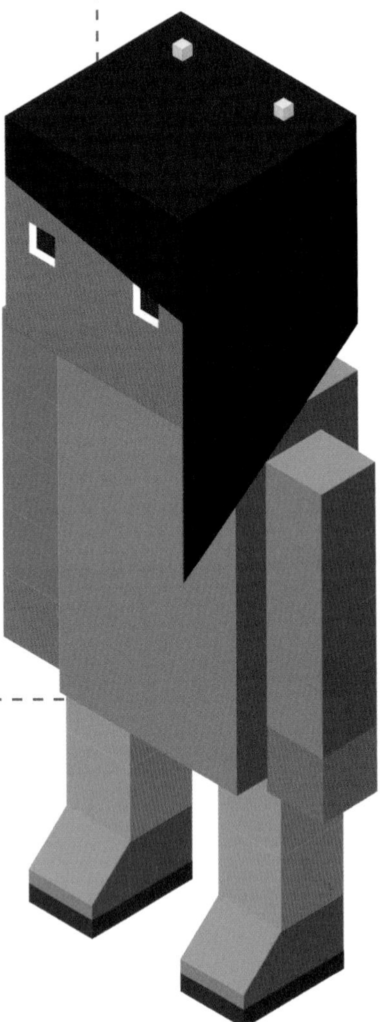

Projects need planning for a variety of reasons. Some of these reasons are shown in Table 1.12. You may have come up with some in your group discussion, but others may be new.

Reason	Explanation
To divide the project between team members.	Team members need to be always busy – and doing work that is suitable for them. Planning the project will make sure people are given suitable tasks and that they always have a task to be doing.
To identify deadlines.	Projects will have a final date when they need to be complete. Planning deadlines for each part of the project can help make sure this final deadline is met. Any problems along the way can be identified and other people can help out to make sure the project doesn't miss any deadlines.
To create an agreed set of requirements that everyone is working to.	Planning exactly what the project has to do, and how it will be done, will make sure everyone is working towards the same end product. If people think the system should do different tasks, then when they try and join all of the separate parts together, it will not work.
To make sure everyone knows what they are doing.	People need to know what they are doing and when to do it by. This will stop them from doing other people's work, or two people doing the same task, or even some tasks not being completed at all.
To reduce the risk of any problems during development.	If all elements are planned out, and this plan is referred to throughout the development, then people can keep referring to this if they are not sure what to do.
To identify which tasks need to be completed first.	Ordering the tasks will make sure that people are not working on tasks that cannot be completed until a previous task is finished. This stops people waiting for others to finish and makes it more likely that the final product will work when it is combined together.

Table 1.12: Reasons for creating a project plan

These reasons are not given in order of priority, because the priorities might change depending on the project.

Some small projects might not need detailed plans because there are not many tasks to do. For example, if only one or two people are working on a project, then they may not need to identify which tasks they are doing, or outline the deadlines in as much depth. However, they will still need to do these actions to make sure they can work together.

Larger projects might need several people to work together over several weeks or months. If there is no planning then people might not know what they are supposed to do. This can cause errors and make the project last longer than it should.

Unplugged activity 1.17

You will need: a pen and paper

You have been asked to lead a team of program developers to write a new computer game that will be available on a website. The company who has hired you would like you to get started immediately without spending any time planning.

Write a letter to the company that has hired you explaining why you think it would be more appropriate to plan the project before starting it.

Questions 1.13

1 How does planning help you to split work between team members?

2 Why is it important to identify deadlines in a plan?

3 How does putting the tasks in order help the project?

Test plans

Programs are tested to make sure that they work and to make sure that they cannot break.

You have probably already tested lots of programs without thinking about it! You will have run programs (in Scratch or Python) to see what happens.

You should have already tested some of these programs with a range of data. This means you test the program many times, not just once with data that you know will work. You will have tested it with lots of different data, some data that should work and some that shouldn't, to see what the program does.

For example, suppose a program needs to ask the user to input two numbers and then output the result of these two numbers added together.

input_A + input_B = result

To test it with a range of data, you could use the test data in Table 1.13.

Test data type	Description	Example inputs	Expected output
Normal	Test data that is typical (expected) and should be accepted by the system. Normal data should be allowed and give a correct output.	1 2	3
Invalid	Test data that the program cannot process and should not accept. Invalid data should not be allowed and should not give a result.	"house" 3	Error because "house" is not a number
Unsual	Test data that is not expected or usual but is OK to use. Unusual data should be allowed but might not be seen often.	-3 2.5	-0.5

Table 1.13: Different types of test data

It is really important to test programs to make sure they always work.

Did you know?

You can get a job as a software tester, for example, a tester for a new computer game. It's not all fun and games though. A test plan will be provided (it might look different to the one you are using) that you have to follow. Tests might include making a character walk into every part of a wall to make sure that they can't walk through it. They could include hundreds of tests that you then have to record the result of. Have you ever played a game where the character has gone through the wall? The angle at which you hit the wall might not have been tested.

The tests you are going to perform need planning. This is to make sure that you have tested all parts of the program. It also helps you keep a record of what you have tested and what the result is. This can stop you repeating the same test lots of times. By keeping a record, you can go back to check what happened the last time you ran the test.

A **test plan** is a formal way of recording your testing.

- Before you start testing, write down all the tests you will use, and what the result should be.
- Then you write the program.
- When you think you are finished, you return to the test plan, carry out each test and record the results.

If the results are all correct, then you have finished! If one does not work, then you can make changes, and then repeat the tests a second time. You will need to repeat all tests because if you have made a change, one of the other tests may no longer give the correct result.

Test plans can appear in different formats. Table 1.14 shows an example of a test plan in a table, with some example data for a program that takes two numbers as input, multiplies them, then outputs the result:

input_A * input_B = Result

This is the program:

```
Input_A = input("Enter a number")
Input_B = input("Enter another number")
Result = Input_A * Input_B
print(Result)
```

Test number	Description	Input	Expected output	Actual output
1	Are normal numbers multiplied together?	2 4	8	
2	Are decimal numbers multiplied together?	1.5 2.5	3.75	
3	Are negative numbers multiplied together?	-1 -2	2	
4	Are large numbers multiplied together?	1000 2000	2 000 000	
5	Do words stop the program?	"purple" 2	error program stops	

Table 1.14: Example test plan

Unplugged activity 1.18

You will need: a pen and paper

Work with a partner.

Read the example test plan shown in Table 1.14. Identify what the purpose is for each of the columns and write down your answers.

Then, discuss your answers with the rest of the class.

The first four columns are completed before the program is tested.

Column 1

Test number	Description	Input	Expected output	Actual output

Each column is given a number. This helps you look back at a test if you need to by stating which number it is.

Column 2

Test number	Description	Input	Expected output	Actual output

This says what is being tested. In a small program, it might be the whole program. In a larger program, it could just be one small part.

Column 3

Test number	Description	Input	Expected output	Actual output

This is what you, as the user, will use to do the test. It might be the data that you are going to type in, or the buttons that you are going to click. Make sure you list all the inputs needed.

Column 4

Test number	Description	Input	Expected output	Actual output

This is what should happen if everything works properly: what the program should do, what should appear on screen, or what number(s) or message(s) should appear.

The expected output might only give one part of the output. This is because it is only focused on one section of the program. However, all the inputs are needed.

Column 5

Test number	Description	Input	Expected output	Actual output

The final column is completed while you are testing the program.

When you test the program, using the inputs in this test plan, you fill in what happens. Write down what data, numbers(s) and/or message(s) are displayed.

If the test passes, then the expected output and actual output are the same.

If the test has failed, then the expected output and actual output are different.

If you are given a test plan to follow, then you need to:

- work through each test in the order given
- input the data given
- write down the output
- compare the actual and expected outputs.

A test plan can be used with a text-based program (for example, Python), a block-based program (for example, Scratch) or any other type of algorithm (for example, a flowchart).

In the next three activities, you will need to follow a test plan for a flowchart, Scratch and Python program.

Programming task 1.21: Investigate

You will need: a pen and paper, a desktop computer, laptop or tablet with Scratch

Work with a partner. Work together to replicate this Scratch program.

There are two sprites: Bear-walking and Lightning. These can be replaced with other sprites if needed.

There are two variables: Wait and Points.

The blocks for Bear-walking are:

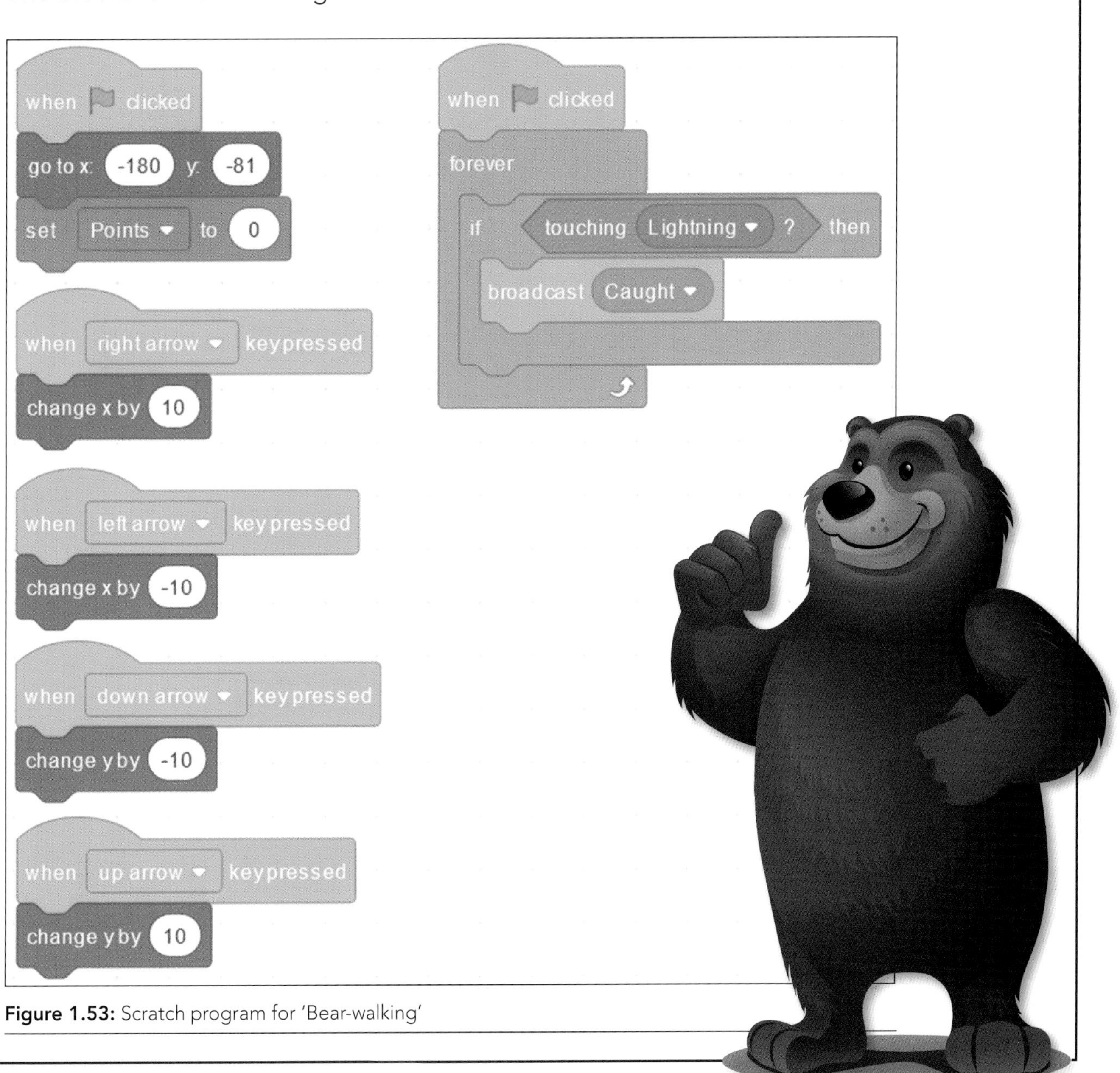

Figure 1.53: Scratch program for 'Bear-walking'

Continued

The blocks for Lightning are:

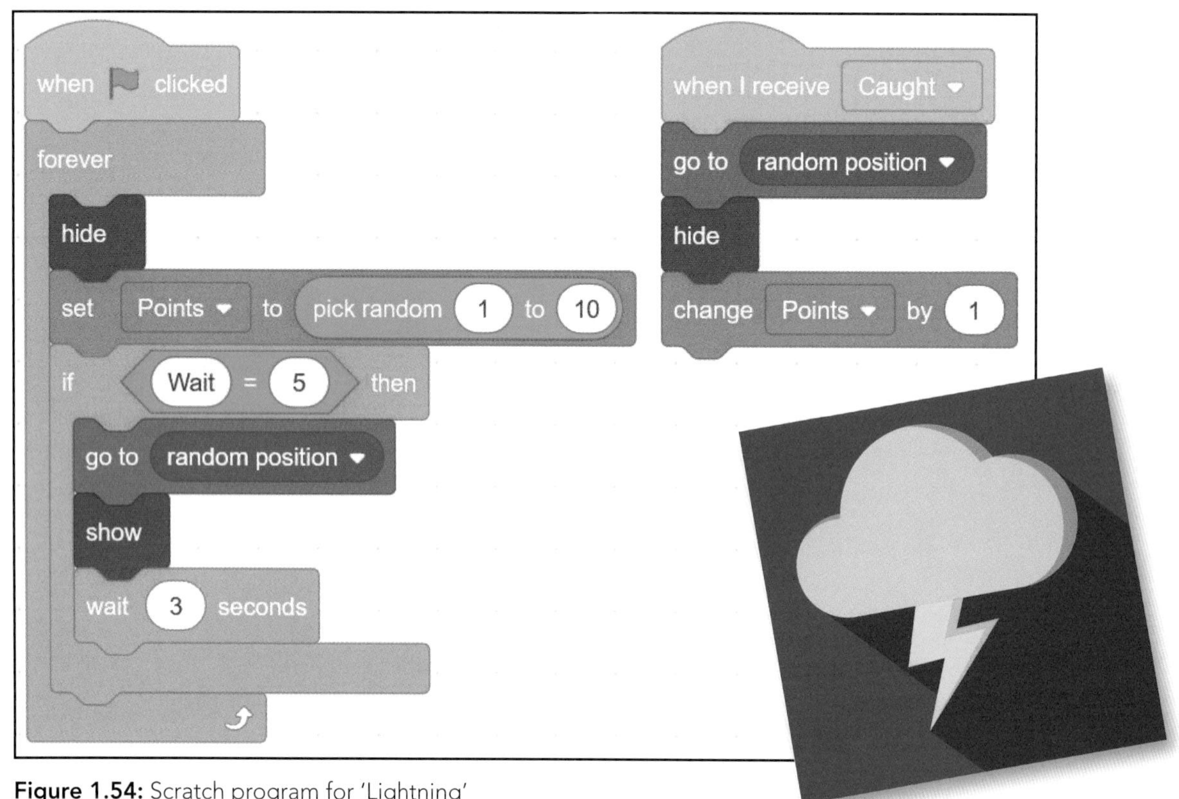

Figure 1.54: Scratch program for 'Lightning'

Create the test plan shown in Table 1.15. Fill in the final column by performing each test on this program.

Test number	Description	Input	Expected output	Actual output
1	The Bear returns to the starting position.	Click green flag. Move Bear. Click red stop. Click green flag.	Bear returns to starting position.	
2	The Bear moves up when the up arrow is clicked.	Click green flag. Click up arrow on keyboard.	Bear moves up.	

(Continued)

Continued

Test number	Description	Input	Expected output	Actual output
3	The Bear moves down when the down arrow is clicked.	Click green flag. Click down arrow on keyboard.	Bear moves down.	
4	The Bear moves right when the right arrow is clicked.	Click green flag. Click right arrow on keyboard.	Bear moves right.	
5	The Bear moves left when the left arrow is clicked.	Click green flag. Click left arrow on keyboard.	Bear moves left.	
6	Lightning changes places every 3 seconds.	Click green flag.	Lightning appears for 3 seconds, then appears somewhere else for 3 seconds.	
7	Points start at 0.	Click green flag. Use arrow keys to move Bear to touch Lightning and change points. Click red stop. Click green flag.	Points start at 0. Points increase when Lightning is touched. Points are 0 when flag clicked second time.	
8	Points increase by 1 when the Lightning is caught.	Click green flag. Use arrow keys to move Bear to touch Lightning once.	Points start at 0. Points change to 1 when Lightning is caught.	

(Continued)

Continued

Test number	Description	Input	Expected output	Actual output
9	Points increase each time the Lightning is caught.	Click green flag. Use arrow keys to move Bear to touch Lightning several times.	Points start at 0. Points increase by 1 each time Lightning is touched.	

Table 1.15: Test plan for Scratch program

Self-assessment

Did all of your actual outputs match the expected output?
What does this mean for the program? Does it work? Or is there an error?

Can you think of some other tests that would be appropriate to include?

Programming task 1.22: Make and Investigate

You will need: a pen and paper, a desktop computer, laptop or tablet with Python

Make: Work with a partner. Work together to replicate this Python program:

- takes two whole numbers as input
- adds them together
- multiplies the result by 2, then multiplies the result by 2 again
- takes the user's name as input
- outputs the user's name, and the answers from the 3 calculations.

```
name = input("Enter your name")
firstNumber = int(input("Enter a number"))
secondNumber = int(input("Enter another number"))
print(name, "your results are")
total = firstNumber + secondNumber
print(total)
total = total * 2
print(total)
total = total * 2
print(total)
```

Continued

Create the test plan shown in Table 1.16.

Investigate: Fill in the final column by performing each test on this program.

Test number	Description	Input	Expected output	Actual output
1	First output includes the name entered.	Sofia 1 2	First message is: Sofia your results are	
2	First output of numbers is correct.	Sofia 1 2	Second message is: 3	
3	Second output of numbers is correct.	Sofia 1 2	Third message is: 6	
4	Third output of numbers is correct.	Sofia 1 2	Fourth message is: 12	
5	Outputs are correct when a different set of numbers are input.	Sofia 20 9	Sofia your results are 29 58 116	
6	Outputs are correct when large numbers are used.	Sofia 100 200	Sofia your results are 300 600 1200	
7	Outputs are correct when negative numbers are used.	Sofia -1 -5	Sofia your results are -6 -12 -24	

Table 1.16: Test plan for Python program

Continued

Self-assessment

Did all of your actual outputs match the expected output? What does this mean for the program? Does it work? Or is there an error?

Can you think of some other tests that would be appropriate to include?

Programming task 1.23: Investigate

You will need: a pen and paper

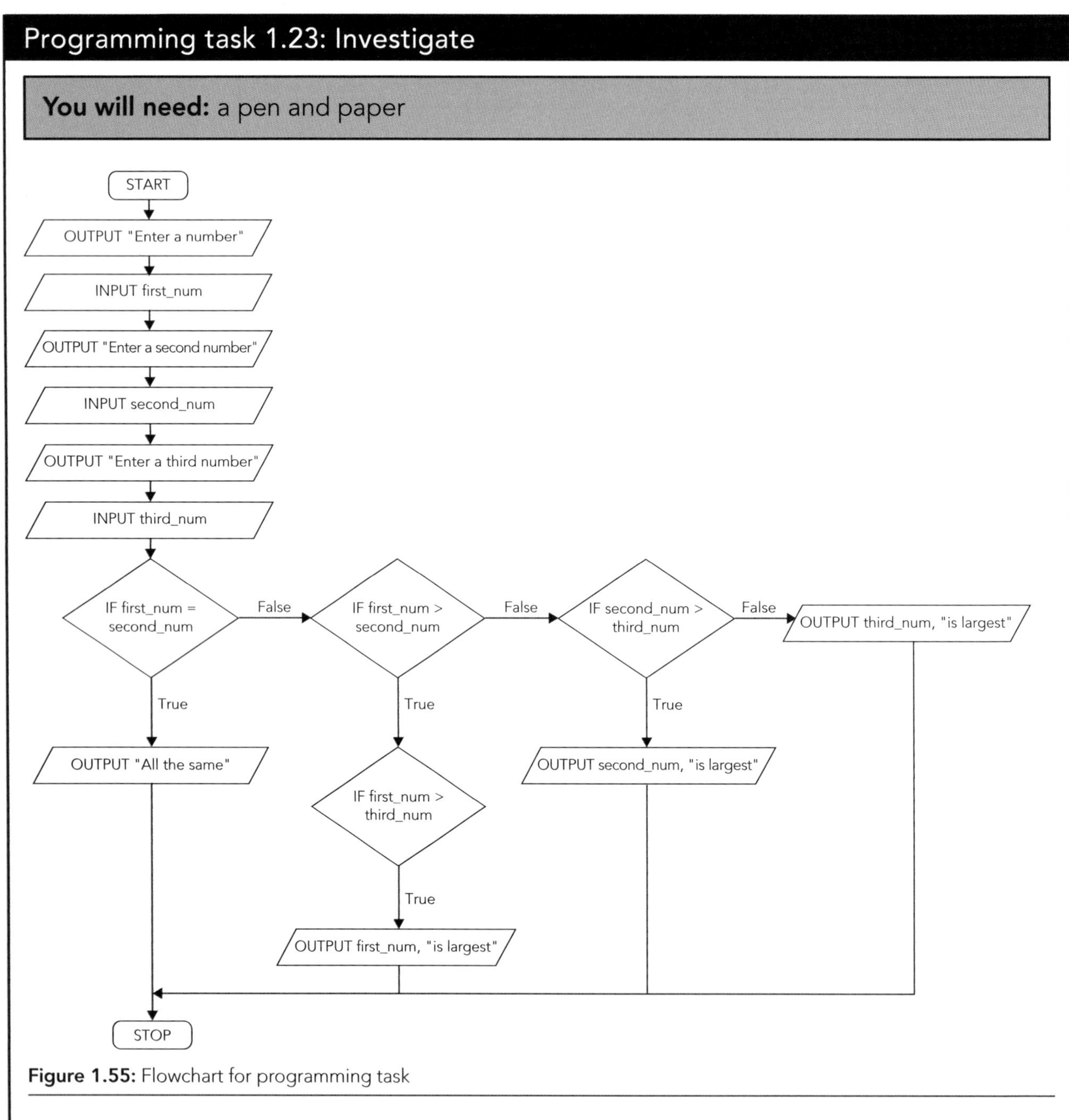

Figure 1.55: Flowchart for programming task

Continued

Work with a partner.

The flowchart shown in Figure 1.55:

- takes three numbers as input
- outputs a message if all three numbers are the same, or
- outputs the number that is the largest.

Create the test plan shown in Table 1.17.

Investigate: Fill in the final column by performing each test on this program.

Test number	Description	Input	Expected output	Actual output
1	The first number as largest is output.	10 2 1	10 is largest	
2	The second number as largest is output.	2 10 1	10 is largest	
3	The third number as largest is output.	2 1 10	10 is largest	
4	If all three are the same, a message is output.	10 10 10	All the same	
5	If the first two numbers are the same, and the third different, it outputs the largest.	10 10 20	20 is the largest	
6	If the second and third numbers are the same, and the first different, it outputs the largest.	20 10 10	20 is the largest	

(Continued)

Continued

Test number	Description	Input	Expected output	Actual output
7	If the first and third numbers are the same, and the second different, it outputs the largest.	10 20 10	20 is the largest	
8	Numbers that are very close together are output correctly.	99 100 98	100 is the largest	
9	Decimal numbers output correctly.	1.5 2.9 0.1	2.9 is the largest	
10	The first number, as a negative, is output as largest.	-1 -2 -3	-1 is the largest	
11	The second number, as a negative, is output as largest.	-4 -2 -8	-2 is the largest	
12	The third number, as a negative, is output as largest.	-100 -50 -22	-22 is the largest	
13	Negative and positive numbers work together.	-10 1 0	1 is the largest	

Table 1.17: Test plan for flowchart

Self-assessment

Did all of your actual outputs match the expected output?
What does this mean for the algorithm? Does it work? Or is there an error?

Can you think of some other tests that would be appropriate to include?

Questions 1.14

1 What is a test plan?

2 What are the contents of a typical test plan?

3 Why is it important to plan before testing starts?

How successful were you in following the test plans?

Could you predict which outputs were going to work and which weren't before running the tests?

Do you take any shortcuts, or did you follow the tests in sequence?

Errors in programs

You have probably found errors in programs that you have written – for example, a Scratch program that didn't work first time, or a Python program that you had to change so that it worked the way you wanted.

These errors can be put into different types of error: syntax errors and logic errors.

Syntax error

We saw in Topic 1.4 that syntax is the structure of a language. In a programming language, the syntax is the key words that you need to use and the order they need to appear in.

For example, the output syntax for Python is:

```
print()
```

The word print is written in lowercase, with opening and closing brackets.

A syntax error is when code is written that breaks these rules. For example:

```
print("Hello"
```

The closing bracket is missing, so this does not follow the rules of Python.

This code also has an example of a syntax error in it:

```
firstNumber = 10
secondNumber = 20
total := firstNumber + secondNumber
```

The third line has `:=` instead of `=`.

Unplugged activity 1.19

You will need: a pen and paper

Work with a partner.

Read this Python code. There are *three* syntax errors in it. Work together to identify each error. Rewrite the code with the correct syntax.

```
metres = int(input("Enter the number of metres")
centimetre = metres X 100
print(metres, "is", centimetre, "centimetres)
```

When there is a syntax error, your program will not run fully. It will either not start, with a message appearing telling you there is a problem, or it might run part way and then crash, with a message telling you there is a problem.

Logic error

A **logic error** is another type of error. This happens when the program has the correct syntax, but there is an error that means the program doesn't do what it was supposed to do and gives an incorrect output (or result). A logic error doesn't normally make the program crash.

In this example Python program, the syntax is all correct (the code makes sense and the program will run). The program is supposed to add two numbers together.

```
total = 1 - 5
print(total)
```

However, when the program is run, it subtracts the numbers instead of adding them. The logic error is that the minus sign (–) should be a plus sign (+).

When there is a logic error, your program will run completely from start to end. It will not tell you there is an error, and the only way you will know there is an error is when you test it and realise that it does not do what it was supposed to.

Some common logic errors are:

- an incorrect calculation; for example, adding instead of multiplying
- using the wrong variable; for example, `numberOne` instead of `numberTwo`
- changing the value in a variable when it should stay the same

- using the wrong comparison in a decision; for example, <= instead of <
- putting statements in the wrong order; for example, outputting before a calculation is performed.

Programming task 1.24: Run, Investigate and Modify

You will need: a desktop computer, laptop or tablet with Python

Join with a partner.

Copy this Python code.

```
number = 5
print(number)
number = number - 1
print(number)
number = number - 1
print(number)
number = number - 1
print(number)
number = number - 1
print(number)
number = number - 1
print(number)
print("Blast off!")
```

This program should output the numbers 5 to 1 and then output "Blast off!"

Run: Run the program and compare the output to what the program should do.

Investigate: There is a logic error. Discuss what the error is, and work out how it can be corrected.

Modify: Work together to change the program and then re-test it to make sure it works.

Were you able to find the logic error on your own or did you need the support of your partner? Did you use different approaches to find the error? Did you take the lead in finding the error or did you follow your partner's lead? How will you change your approach next time you need to find an error?

Debugging text-based programs

When you find a logic error in a program, you need to debug it. The error is known as a **bug** in the program. The process of finding this bug and correcting it is called **debugging**.

There are different ways to debug a program and, as your programs include more code, you might start using other methods. At this stage, you need to work through the code line by line. When you work through a process one step at a time from start to finish, it is called working **systematically**. There are different ways of doing this. You could:

1. read each line of code one by one from the start and check that it makes sense
2. write the variable names down and the values stored in them next to the names. Then check whether these values are correct
3. use a checklist to make sure the correct key words, operators and variables are used.

Programming task 1.25: Investigate, Run and Modify

You will need: a desktop computer, laptop or tablet with Python

1 **Read each line of code one by one from the start and make sure it is correct.**

This program should:

- take the number of bits as input from the user
- calculate and output the number of bytes and kilobytes.

Bytes is the number of bits divided by 8. For example, 256 bits is 32 bytes.

Kilobytes is the number of bytes divided by 1024. For example, 256 is 0.03125 kilobytes.

```
bitNumber = int(input("Enter the number of bits"))
byteNumber = bitNumber / 8
kilobyteNumber = bitNumber / 1024
print(byteNumber,"bytes")
print(kilobyteNumber,"kilobytes")
```

There is a logic error in this program.

Investigate: Read each line out loud and compare it to what the program should do. Check each line against the requirements until you find the error.

Work with a partner and discuss whether you have found the error.

Continued

If you have both found it, discuss if you have found the same thing and then how you can correct the error.

If only one of you has found it, that person should read the code out loud line by line and explain how they compared it to the requirements until the error was identified.

If neither of you has found it, repeat the process. This time read the code together and compare each line. If you still cannot find the error, join with another pair who have identified it and repeat this process.

Run: Once you have read through the code below, enter this program and run it.

Modify: When you have both found the error, change the program to correct this error.

Programming task 1.26: Run, Investigate and Modify

You will need: a desktop computer, laptop or tablet with Python

2 **Write the variable names down and the values stored in them next to the names. Then check whether these values are correct.**

This program should:

- take as input the number of items person 1 bought, person 2 bought and person 3 bought
- add together these values input
- output the total number of items bought.

For example, if person 1 bought one item, person 2 bought two items and person 3 bought three items, the total number of items output should be six.

Run: Enter this program and run it to see what the output is. There is a logic error.

```
total = 0
quantity = int(input("Enter quantity person 1 bought"))
quantity = int(input("Enter quantity person 2 bought"))
quantity = int(input("Enter quantity person 3 bought"))
total = total + quantity
print("The total number of items bought is", total)
```

Write down the names of the variables in the program, for example:

```
total
quantity
```

Continued

Investigate: Read each line of the program one at a time. If the code stores a value in a variable, write it next to the variable name. If the code uses the value in a variable, use the value next to the name.

Repeat this with different values being input until you can identify why the program does not work.

Work with a partner and discuss whether you have found the error.

If you have both found it, discuss if you have found the same thing and then how you can correct the error.

If only one of you has found it, that person should repeat the process and show their partner how they identified the error.

If neither of you has found it, repeat the process together. Look carefully at each value that changes in the variables and whether these changes are correct.

If you still cannot find the error, join with another pair who have identified it and repeat this process.

Modify: When you have found the error, change the program to correct this error.

Programming task 1.27: Run, Investigate and Modify

3 **Use a checklist to make sure the correct key words, operators and variables were used.**

This program should:

- take the amount of money a person will save each week as input
- take the number of weeks they are going to save money for as input
- calculate and output how much will be saved when that amount is saved for that number of weeks.

For example, if they save $10 for five weeks, the total output should be $50.

Run: Enter this program and run it to see what the output is. There is a logic error.

```
amountSaved = 0
numberWeeks = int(input("How many weeks are you saving money?"))
moneyEachWeek = real(input("How much will you save each
week in $"))
totalSaved = numberWeeks * moneyEachWeek
print("In",numberWeeks,"weeks you will save $",amountSaved)
```

Continued

Investigate: Use Table 1.18 as a checklist. Each row tells you what to look for in the program to help you find the error.

Feature to check	✓
Are all the values input that need to be input?	
Do the calculations use the correct operator(s)? + – / *	
Are the correct variable names used in each place?	
Are any variables changed when they should not be?	
Are the correct variables output?	
Are inputs changed to the Integer or Real numbers if numbers are being input?	
Are the lines of code in the correct order? For example, is a value output before it is used in a calculation?	

Table 1.18: Checklist to make sure the correct key words, operators and variables are used

Work with a partner and discuss whether you have found the error.

If you have both found it, discuss if you have found the same thing and then how you can correct the error.

If only one of you has found it, that person should identify which item on the checklist stated the error, and then support their partner in identifying where the error is.

If neither of you has found it, repeat the process together. Look carefully at each checklist item and make sure you both agree that it is correct.

If you still cannot find the error, join with another pair who have identified it and repeat this process.

Modify: When you have found the error, change the program to correct this error.

Questions 1.15

1 What is a syntax error?

2 What is a logic error?

3 How can you find an error in a program?

4 This program written in Python should take the number of marks out of 100 that a student got on three tests. It should then calculate and output the average mark.

Identify the *two* syntax errors in this Python program.

```
mark1 = int(input("Enter the first mark ")
mark2 = int(input("Enter the second mark "))
mark3 = int(input("Enter the third mark "))
average := (mark1 + mark2 + mark3)/3
print("The average is", average, "marks")
```

5 This program written in Python should ask the user for three numbers. It should then add the numbers and output the total. It should then multiply the numbers and output the result.

Identify the *two* logic errors in this Python program.

```
number1 = int(input("Enter the first number "))
number2 = int(input("Enter the second number "))
number3 = int(input("Enter the third number "))
total = number1 + number2 - number3
print(number1, "+", number2, "+", number3, "=", total)
multiplyTotal = number1 * number2 * number3
print(number1, "*", number2, "*", number3, "=", total)
```

Summary checklist

- [ ] I can describe the purpose of prototypes.
- [ ] I can evaluate a prototype by giving positive elements and ways to improve.
- [ ] I can explain why project plans are needed in software development projects.
- [ ] I know what a test plan contains and can identify the key features.
- [ ] I can follow a test plan to test a program.
- [ ] I can identify different errors that can occur in programs.
- [ ] I can test programs to find errors and correct errors in a text-based program.

› 1.7 Physical computing

In this topic you will:

- program a device to take multiple inputs and use these to produce multiple outputs.

Key words

accelerometer

gravitational force (g-force)

LED (light-emitting diode)

Getting started

What do you already know?

A micro:bit is a small hand-held computer that you can program to do all sorts of things. You may have used one before. It is a piece of hardware that has an LED display, buttons, sensors and many input/output features that you can physically interact with. Here are some other things a micro:bit can do:

- Output data, for example, to display a message.
- Read data from inputs, for example, when a button is pressed an image is output.
- You can use variables in a micro:bit, for example, to store a number or word.
- You can program a micro:bit to make decisions based on the inputs, for example, if the user pressed a button twice, an image is displayed.
- You can program a micro:bit to use loops to run code multiple times.

Continued

Now try this!

Work with a partner. Open the MakeCode website by micro:bit and create a new project. Make sure you give it a sensible name. You will see this page.

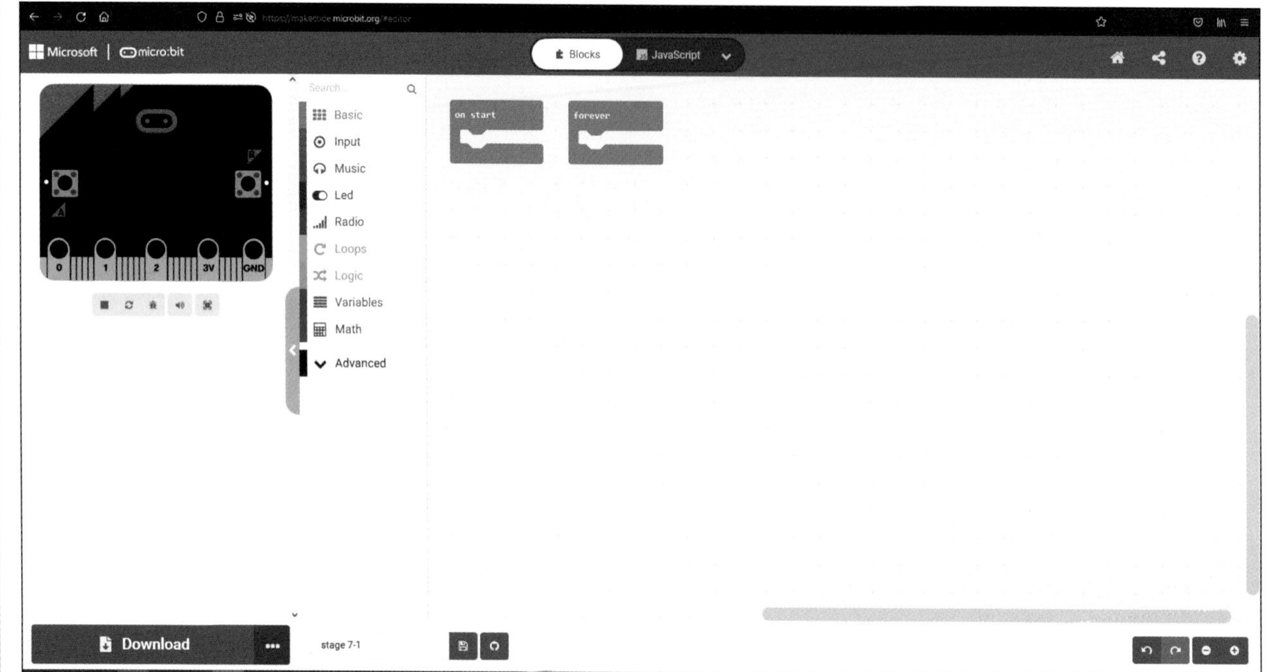

1 Write a program to display an image when button A is pressed.

2 Amend the program to display a different image when button B is pressed.

3 Amend the program to display a different image when the micro:bit is shaken.

Back to basics

In this section you can see the micro:bit blocks you should have already used, but some might be new. They are here in case you have forgotten how they work, or need a recap!

To create a program, you drag the blocks onto the screen. You can then run the code using the micro:bit on screen by clicking on it and selecting the buttons, or the movement options below it. If you have a physical one, you can download the file and then run it on your own micro:bit.

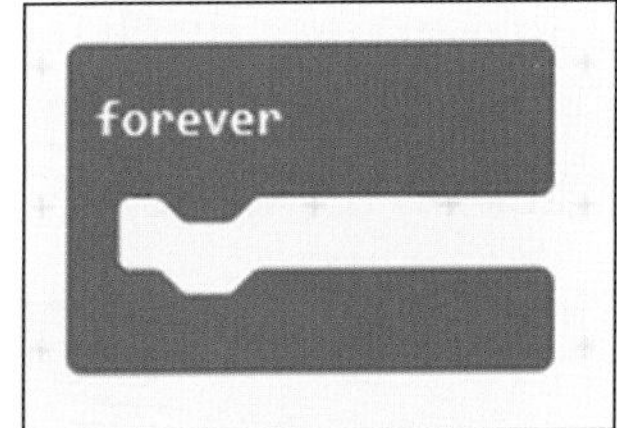

Figure 1.56: Forever block

The Basics menu has a 'forever' block. The blocks inside this will run as soon as the program starts, and will keep on running until the program stops.

As soon as this program starts, the large diamond will be displayed, then the small, then the large, then the small and so on. This will continue until you end the program.

The 'on start' block will run the code inside it as soon as the program starts. They will only run once through.

As soon as this program starts, the large diamond will be displayed, then the small. This will not repeat.

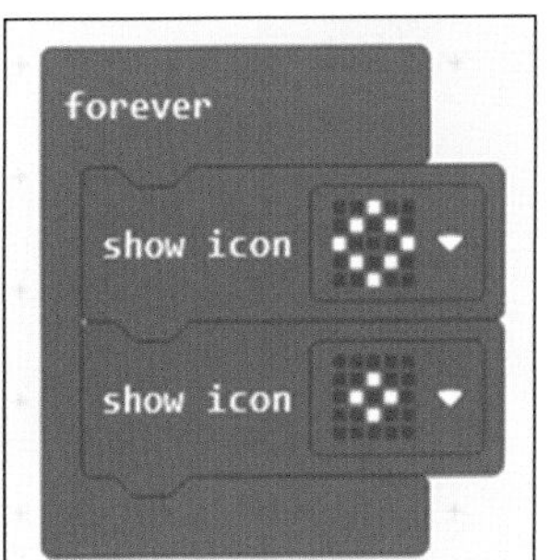

Figure 1.57: Forever block with two diamonds

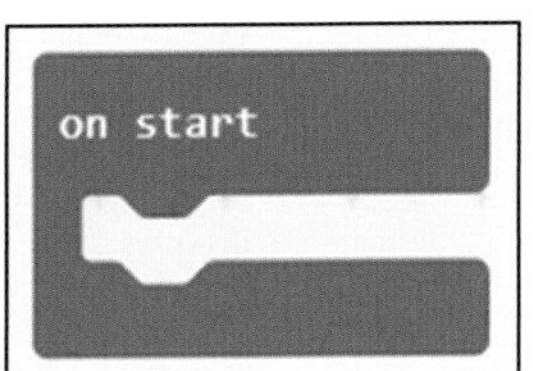

Figure 1.58: On start block

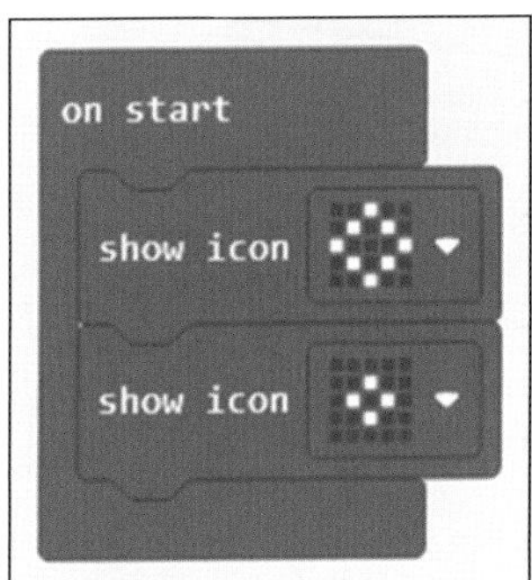

Figure 1.59: On start block with two diamonds

Outputs

The micro:bit has a set of **LEDs** arranged in a 5 × 5 grid. LED is short for light-emitting diode. This is a small light that can be controlled. LEDs can be combined to create a grid and can be lit individually.

On a micro:bit there is a grid of 5 × 5 LEDs (five vertically and five horizontally). By changing which LEDs are on and which are off, the grid can display words, numbers and images.

Click on the Basic menu to access the outputs options.

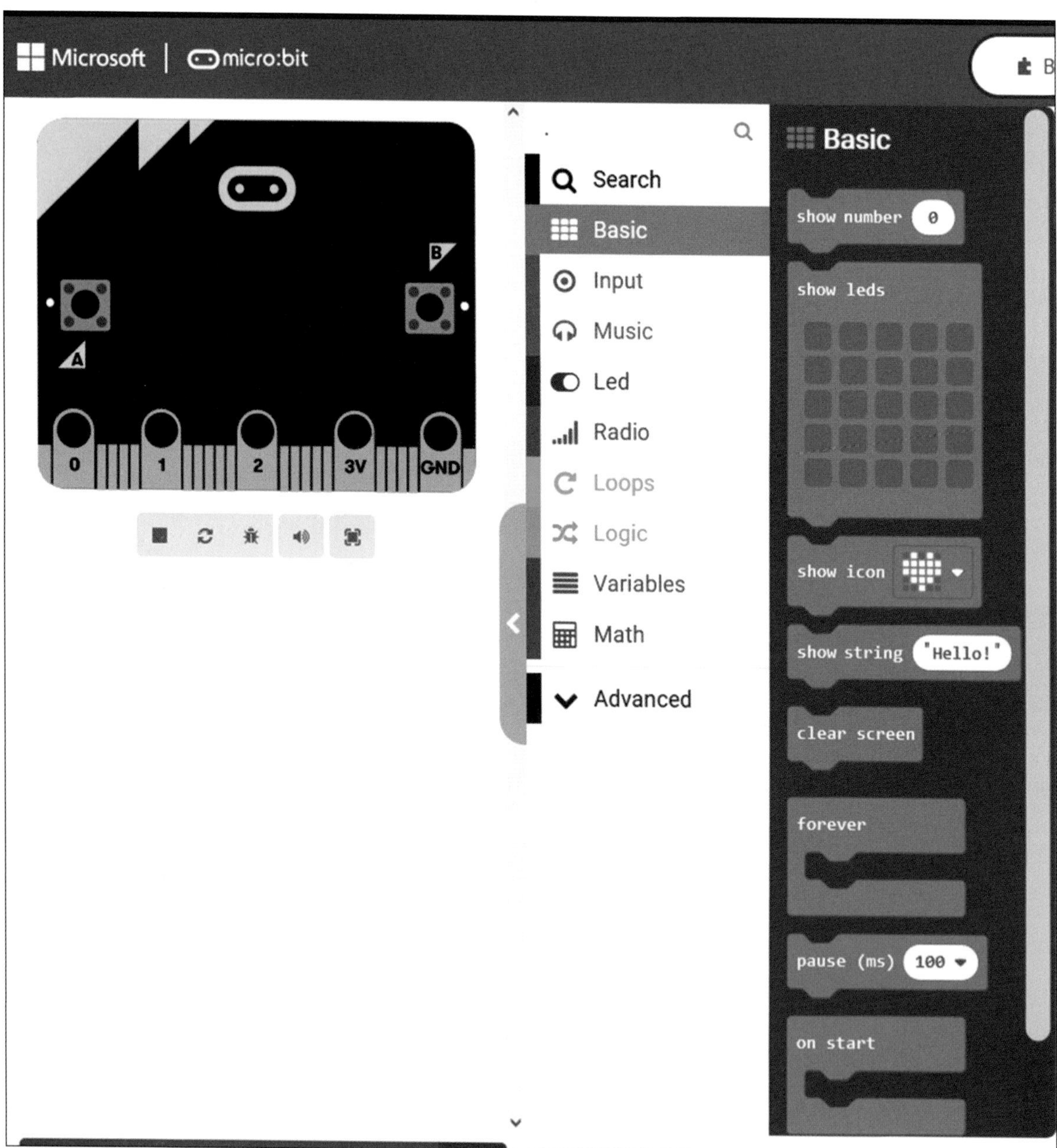

Figure 1.60: The Basic menu

Numbers

To use the 'show number' block, enter a number in the box (the white circle), and the program will display that number.

In this example, when the micro:bit starts, 1 then 2 then 3 will be displayed (see Figure 1.62).

Figure 1.61: Number block

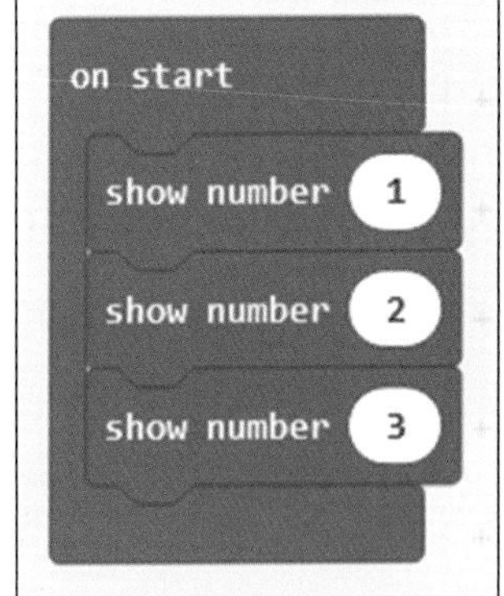

Figure 1.62: Number block with instructions on which number to show

String

The 'show string' block will display the characters you enter in the box.

In this example when the micro:bit starts, "I'm a micro:bit" will be displayed.

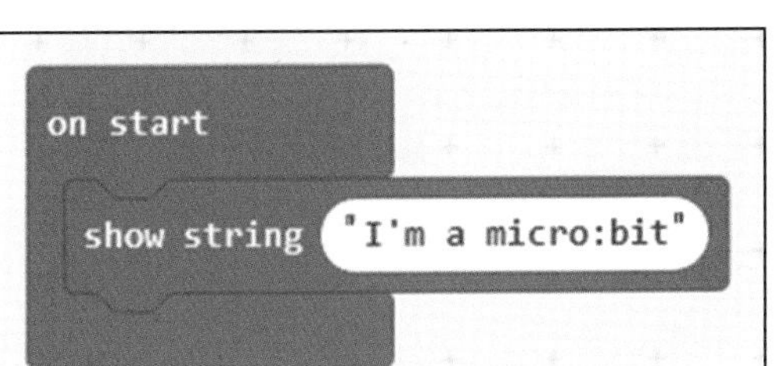

Figure 1.63: String block with instructions to show string "I'm a micro:bit"

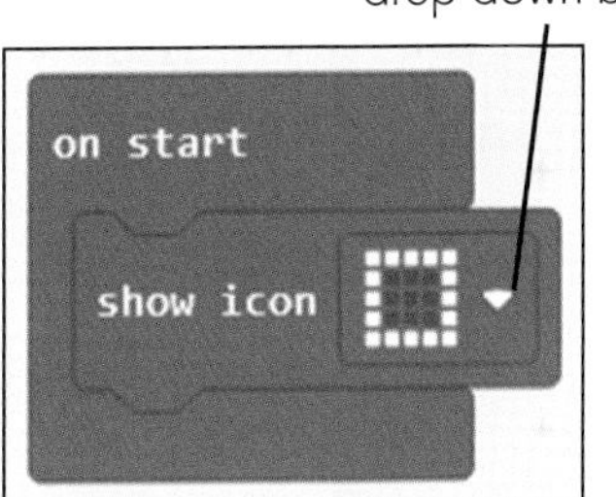

Figure 1.64: Icon block with instructions to show a square

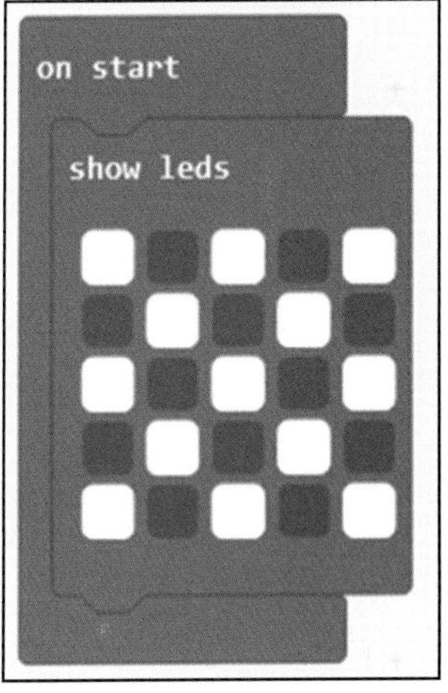

Figure 1.65: LED block with instructions to show a pattern

Icon

The 'show icon' block will display the image you select from the drop-down box.

In the example shown, when the micro:bit starts, a square will be displayed (see Figure 1.64).

Your own LED image

When you choose the 'show LEDs' box, you select the boxes that you want to be turned on.

In this example, when the micro:bit starts, the LEDs in white will be lit.

Programming task 1.28: Make

You will need: a desktop computer, laptop or tablet with access to the MakeCode website

Make: Create a micro:bit program that outputs your name and then an icon.

Sound

Another method of output is as sound. If you are using a physical micro:bit, you will need a speaker to attach to the pins.

Open the Music menu to view the sound blocks.

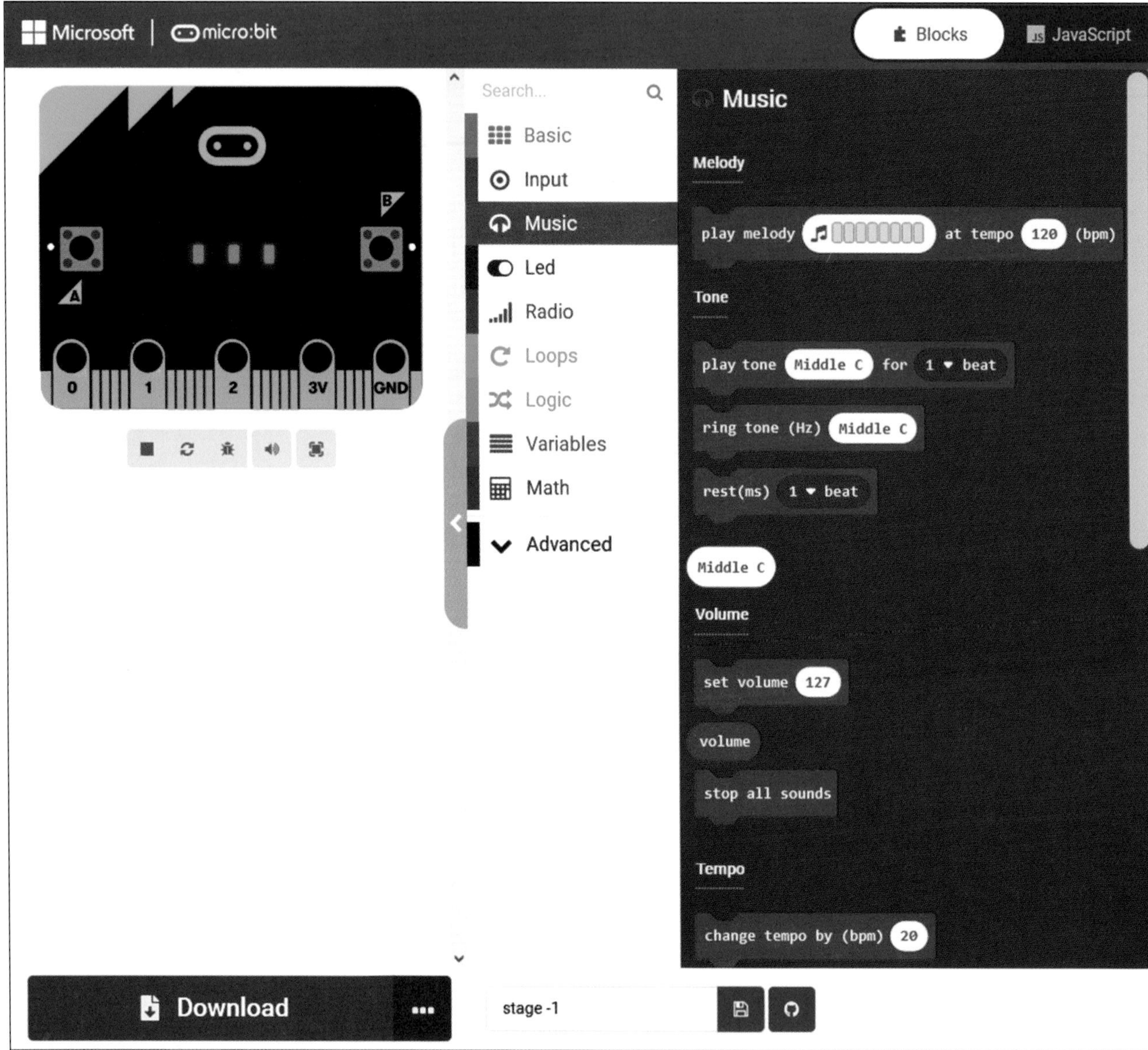

Figure 1.66: The Music menu

Scroll down to view more music options including melodies.

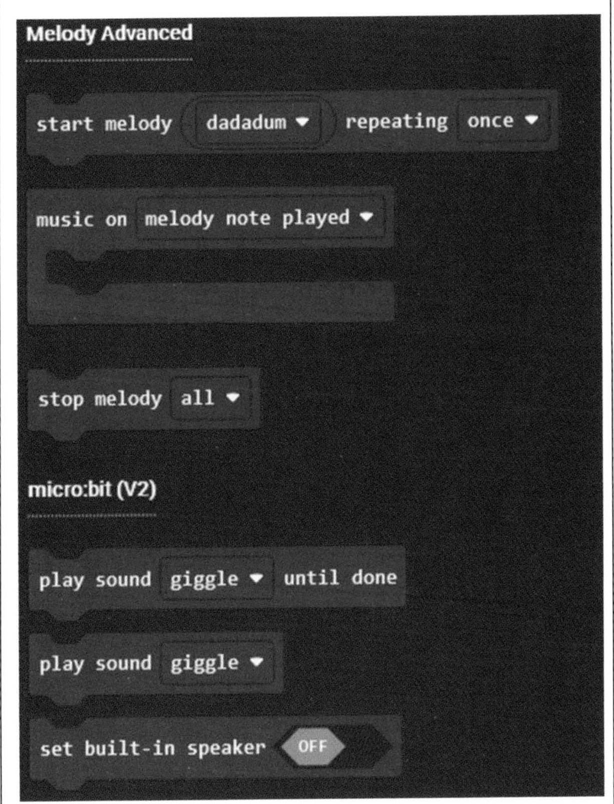

Figure 1.67: The Advanced melody menu

Figure 1.68: Melody block

The 'start melody' block lets you select and play one of the in-built tunes. You can select one from the drop-down menu, and then how many times you want it to repeat.

The program in Figure 1.69 will play the melody entertainer once as soon as the program starts. As 'once in background' is selected, it will play more quietly in the background.

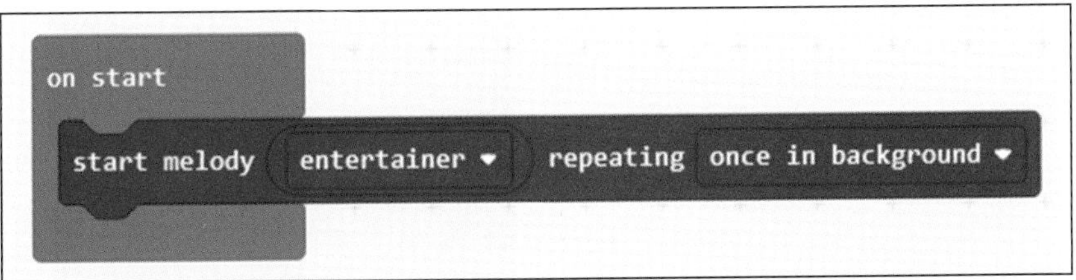

Figure 1.69: Melody block placed inside an 'on start' block

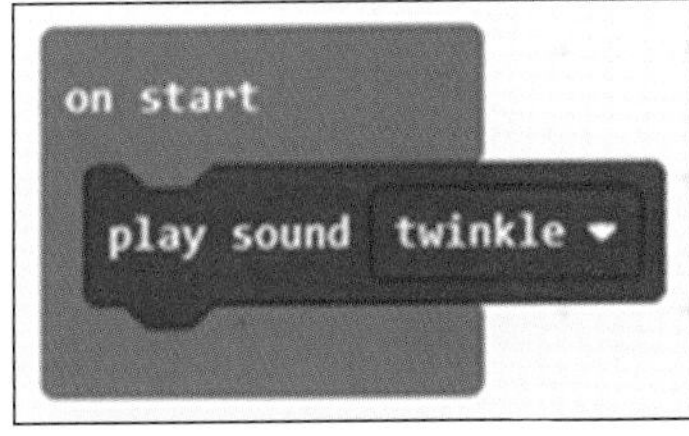

Figure 1.70: Sound block

The 'play sound' block lets you select and play one of the in-built sounds. You can select the sound from the drop-down box.

The program in Figure 1.70 will play the sound 'twinkle' when the program starts.

Inputs

A micro:bit has several different ways that data can be input.

Click on the Input menu and you will see a lot of different options.

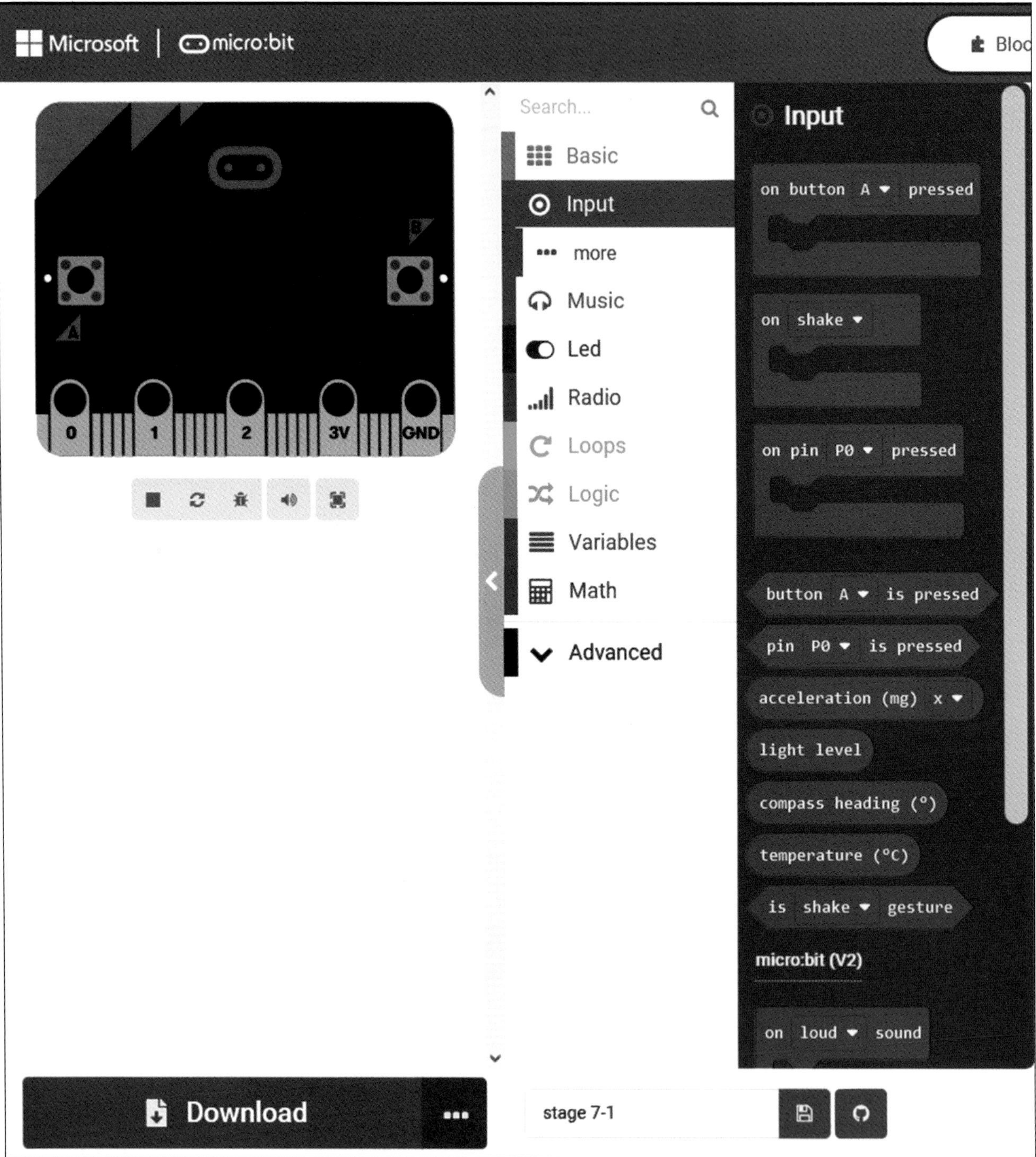

Figure 1.71: The Input menu

Motions

The second option is 'on shake'. Shake is a drop-down box. When this is selected, there are a lot of options to choose from. These use the in-built **accelerometer** to detect the movement. An accelerometer is a sensor that detects if it is moved up, down, tilted and so on. Each of these is an action.

3g, 6g and 8g are forces. The 'g' stands for **gravitational force** (g-force). Gravitational force is a measurement of acceleration. For example, how fast an object is moving. An increase in the g-force value will show that an object has accelerated (started moving faster). A decrease in the g-force will show that an object has decelerated (started moving slower or stopped).

For the micro:bit, it is the amount of force that it feels. For example, if it stops very suddenly, then it will detect a higher g-force.

Figure 1.72: The On shake menu

In this example, the micro:bit is tilted to the left, so a left arrow will be displayed.

Figure 1.73: On tilt left

Unplugged activity 1.20

You will need: a pen and paper

Write a set of instructions (called an algorithm) for a partner to follow. Your partner must lean one way, then depending on which way they are leaning, follow the appropriate instruction. For example, if they lean to the left, they could clap their hands. If they lean to the right, they could laugh.

Give your algorithm to your partner.

Instruct your partner to lean in different directions and follow your algorithm each time.

Programming task 1.29: Make

You will need: a desktop computer, laptop or tablet with access to the MakeCode website

Make: Create a micro:bit program that outputs your name when button A is pressed, and your favourite colour when button B is pressed.

Variables

Revisit Topic 1.1 to remind yourself about variables if you need to.

Click on the micro:bit Variables menu to load the options.
The button 'Make a Variable' lets you create a new variable, and give it an appropriate identifier (name).

Once you have made your variable, there will be new blocks to select from. You will be able to assign a number to the score using the 'set' block. You can change the score by a positive or negative value (increase or decrease the number assigned to score) by using the 'change' block.

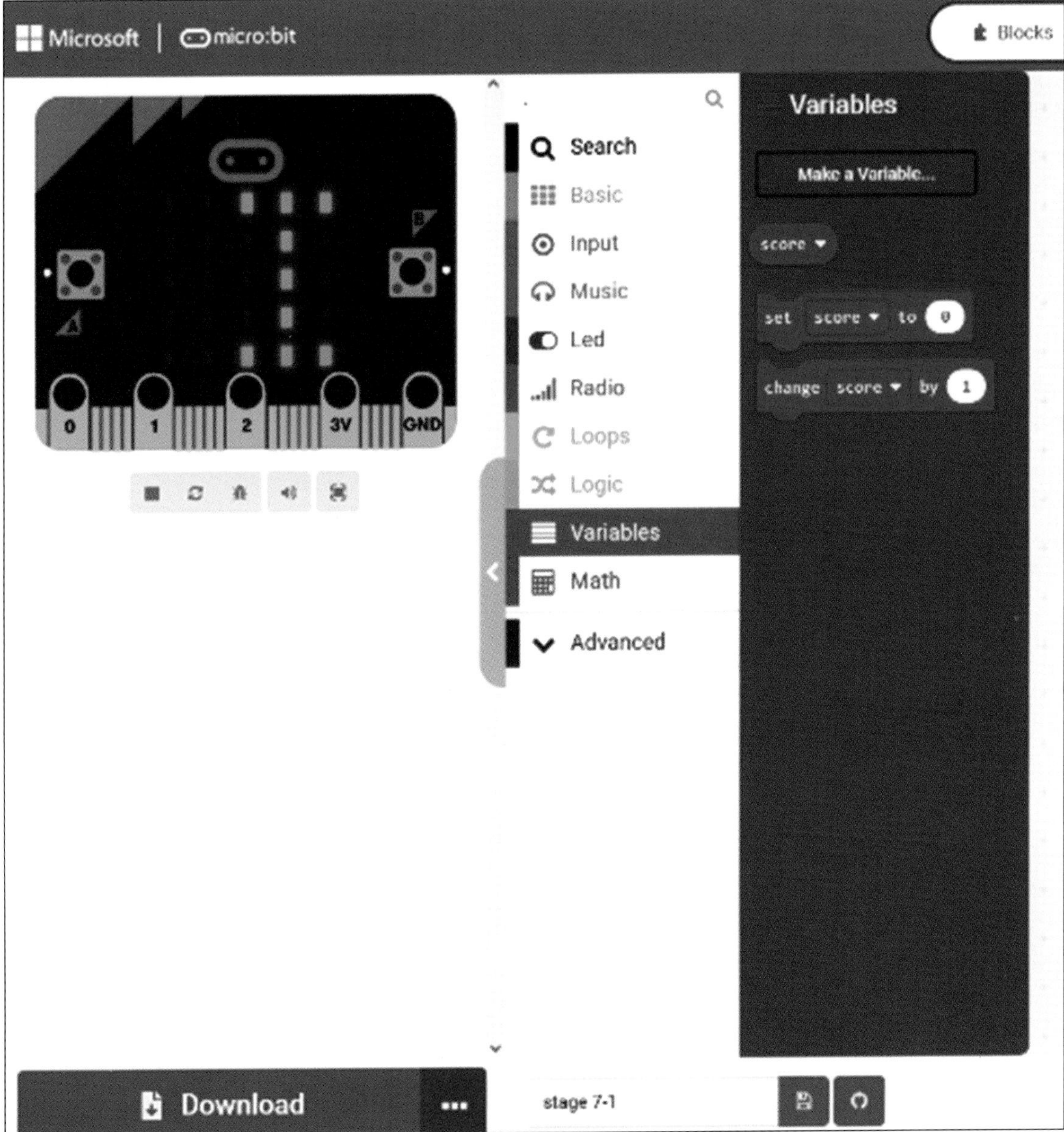

Figure 1.74: The Variables menu

In this example, the variable is named 'score'. When the program starts, the value in score is set to 0. Each time button A is pressed, the value in score will be increased by 1.

Figure 1.75: Using the variables block

Programming task 1.30: Make

You will need: a desktop computer, laptop or tablet with access to the MakeCode website

Make: Create a micro:bit program that outputs a maths question, for example: 'What is 1 + 1?'

The user should enter their answer by pressing button A that many times. For example, they press 'A' twice for the number 2.

The program should output the number of times they have pressed the button.

Maths

You can program the micro:bit to perform mathematical calculations, for example, addition and subtraction.

Click on Math from the menu to access these blocks.

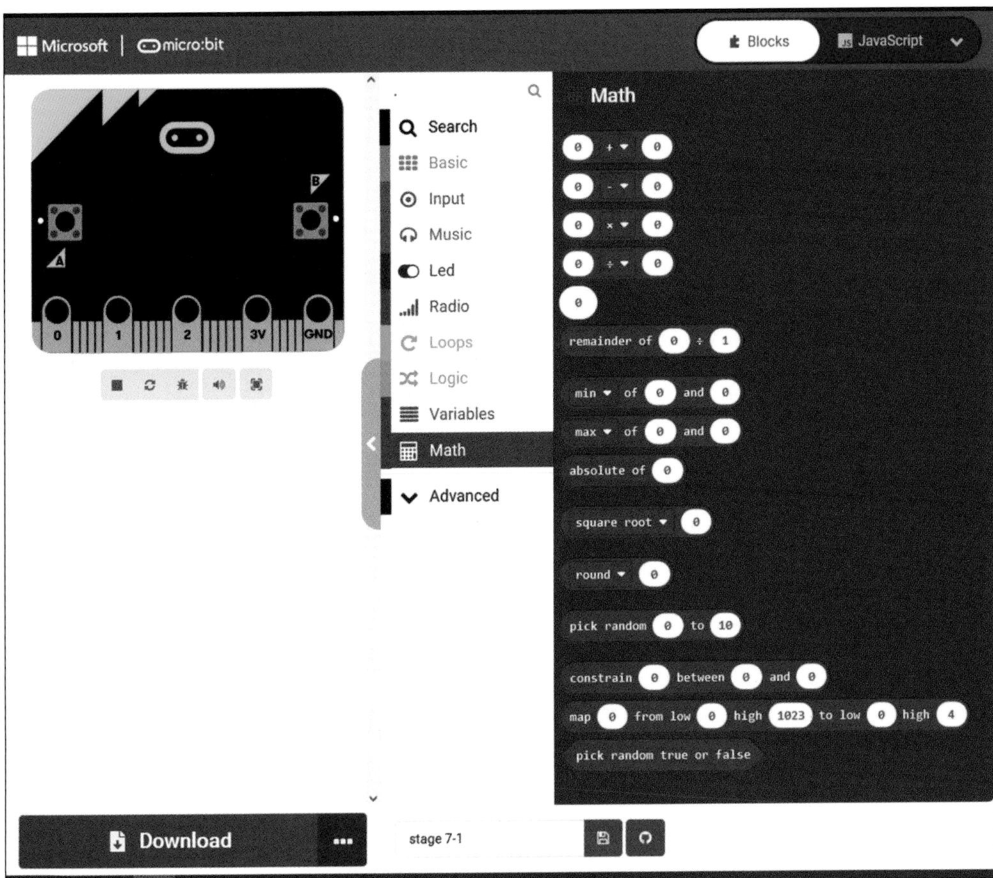

Figure 1.76: The Math menu

These blocks need to be joined with other blocks because they do not work on their own.

They could be put into an output. For example, this program will output 15 (10 + 5).

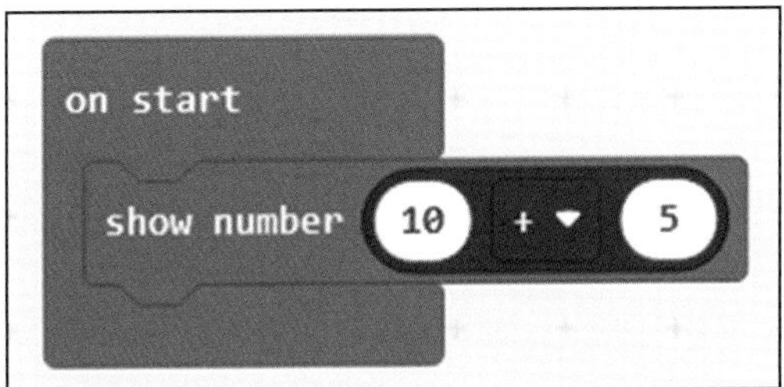

Figure 1.77: Using the math block to add two numbers

The result can also be stored in a variable. For example, this program will store 6 (3 * 2) in the variable score.

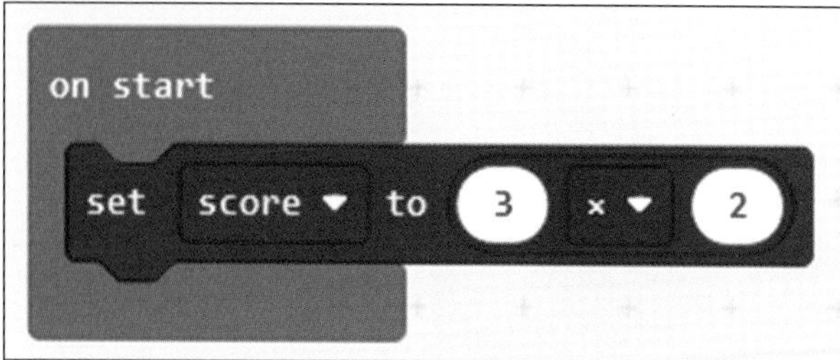

Figure 1.78: Storing a number in a variable

Variables can also be used instead of the number. This is done by inserting the block with the variable name from the Variables menu. In this example, the value in score is multiplied by 2 and then output.

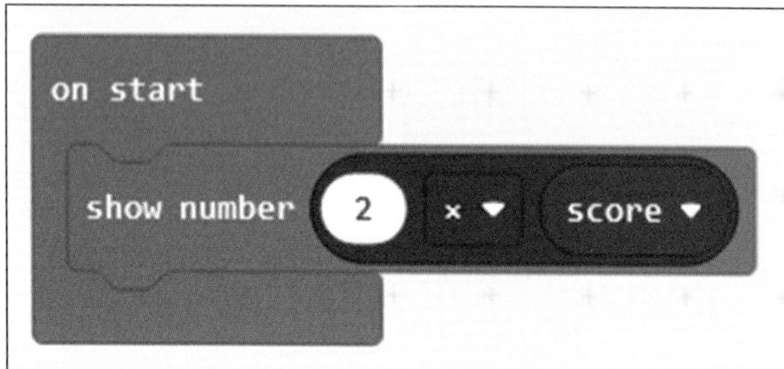

Figure 1.79: Using a variable instead of a number

Programming task 1.31: Make

You will need: a desktop computer, laptop or tablet with access to the MakeCode website

Make: Create a micro:bit program that stores the number 1 in a variable and outputs it.

Each time the user presses button A, 2 is added to this variable and the result is output.

Each time the user presses button B, 10 is added to this variable and the result is output.

Selection

Open the Logic menu to view the selection options. The micro:bit has selection statement blocks that you can use to test a condition. If the condition is true then one set of blocks will run. If the condition is false, another set of blocks can run.

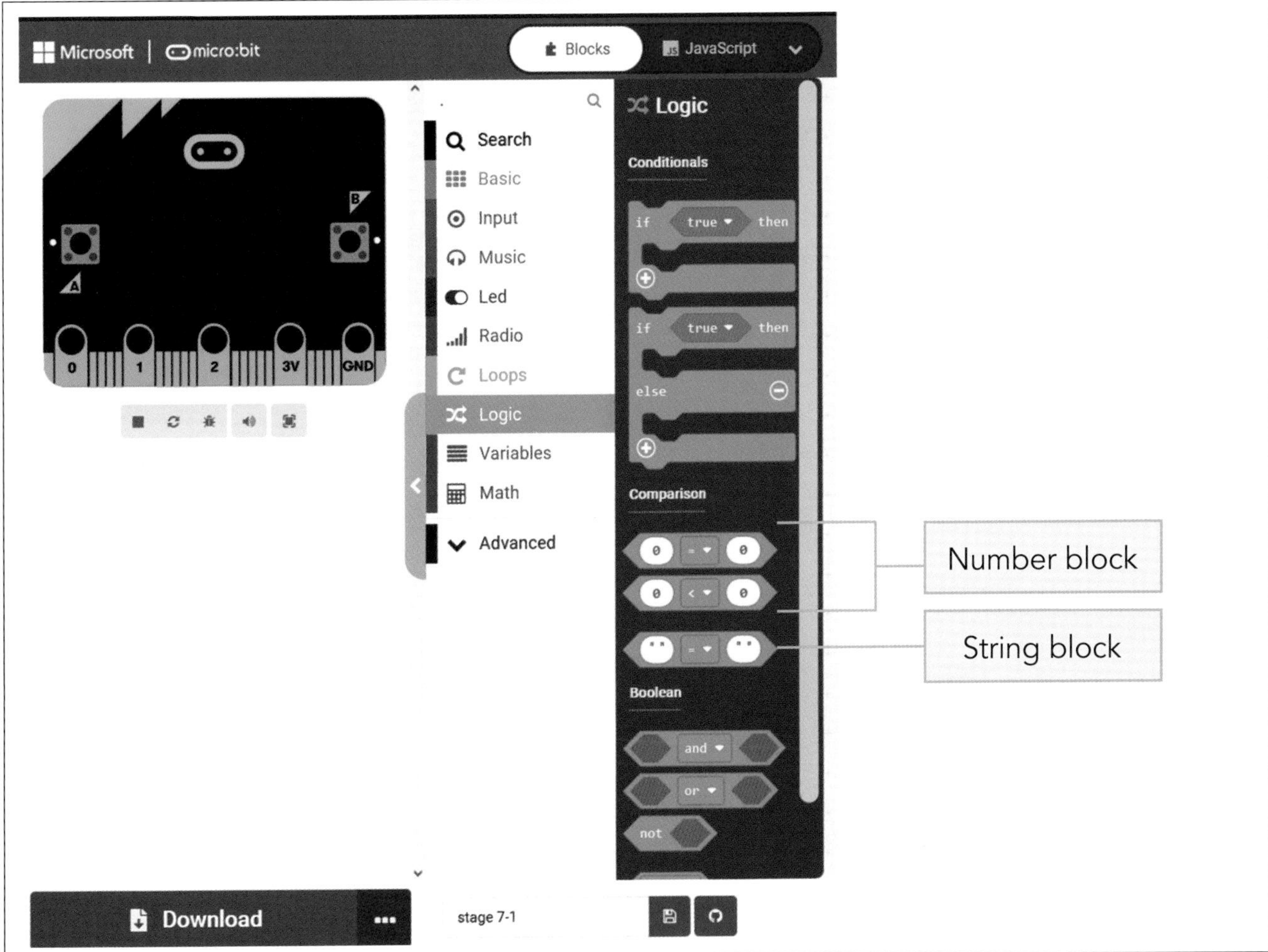

Figure 1.80: The Logic menu

Did you know?

Selection is used in almost every form of programming language. In almost all of these, it will have the same concept. There will be a condition, which can be true or false, and statements to run when the condition is true, and statements to run when the condition is false. All that changes is the format. Use the internet to find different languages and how they write selection statements!

Inside each conditional block there needs to be a comparison. These are the same mathematical comparisons used in Topic 1.3. For example:

```
IF 10 > 3
```

This statement is checking to see whether the number 10 is greater than the number 3.

There is one comparison block for strings and the other comparison blocks are for numbers. Make sure you select the number block if you are comparing numbers and the string block if you are comparing strings.

The drop down in the comparison lets you select the operator. On either side you can input numbers or words, depending on which block you chose.

In this program, if 0 is less than or equal to 10 then the words "Less or equal to" will be displayed. Otherwise, the word "More" will be displayed.

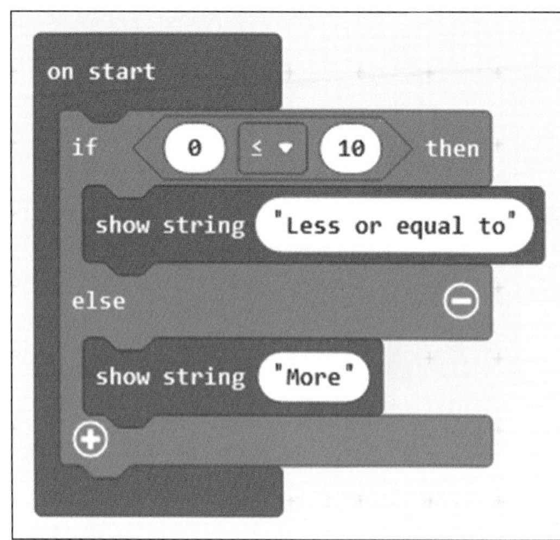

Figure 1.81: Using different blocks to create a program using the IF block

You can replace one or more of these values in the conditions with variables.

In this program, if the value in 'score' is less than 0 then "Game over" will be displayed.

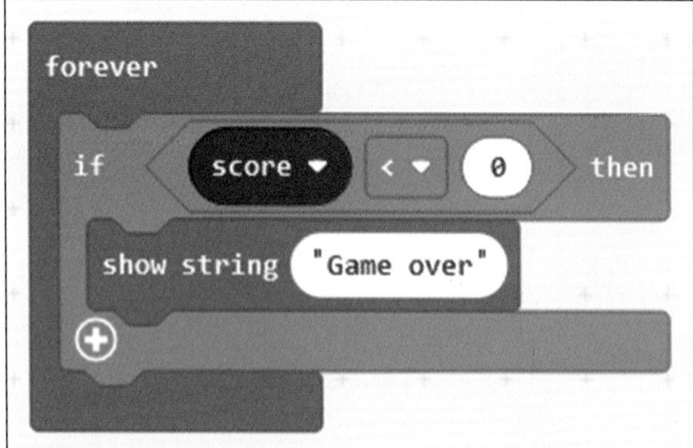

Figure 1.82: Using different blocks to create a program to display "Game over"

The Logic menu also uses the Boolean operators AND, OR and NOT. These blocks need to be combined with comparison operators.

- The AND operator needs the comparisons on both sides to be true.
- The OR operator needs one, or both, comparisons to be true.
- The NOT operator reverses the condition.
  If the condition gives true, the NOT turns this into false.
  The NOT operator only needs one condition to work (although it can have more).

See Topic 1.2 for more information on Boolean operators.

In this program, if both the score is more than 100 AND the number of lives is less than 1, then "Game over" is displayed.

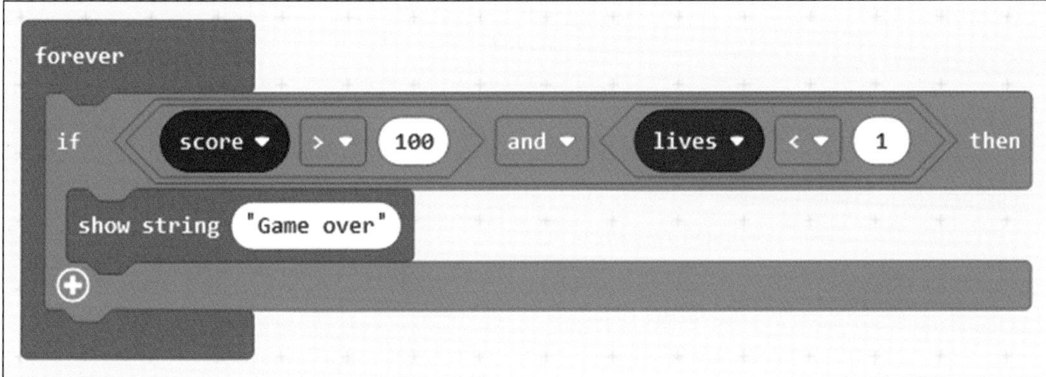

Figure 1.83: Using the AND logic operator

In this program, if 'player1score' is over 100, OR if 'player2score' is over 1, OR if both are true, then "Game over" will be displayed.

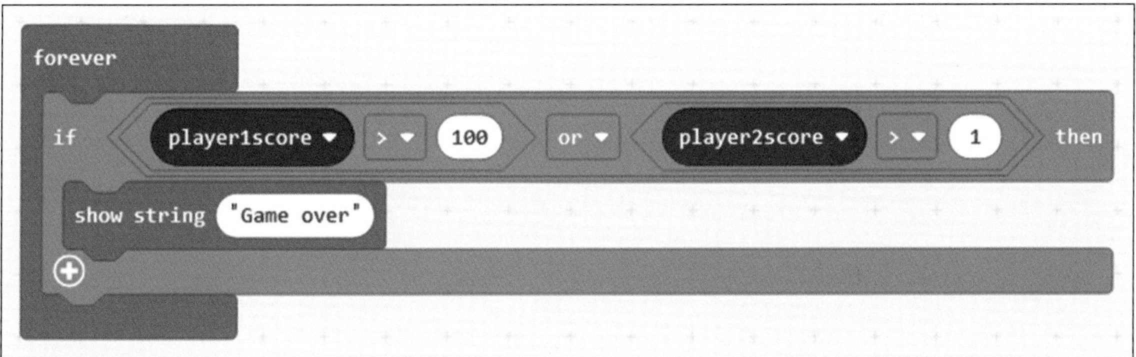

Figure 1.84: Using the OR logic operator

In this program, the NOT reverses the condition if the number stored in 'lives' is greater than 0, the condition is true.

The use of NOT will change this to false. So the text "Game over" will be displayed.

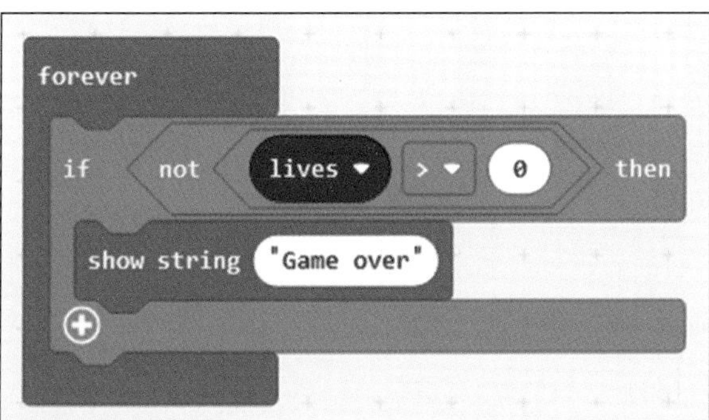

Figure 1.85: Using the NOT logic operator

Programming task 1.32: Modify

You will need: a desktop computer, laptop or tablet with access to the MakeCode website

Modify: Open your solution to Programming task 1.30.

The user enters their answer by pressing button A that many times. For example, the user presses A twice for the number 2.

The program outputs the number of times they have pressed the button.

Modify: Change this program so that:

- the user presses button B when they have finished inputting their answer using button A
- it outputs whether the answer the user input is correct or incorrect.

Loops

A loop is used when some blocks need to run more than once.
Loops can be found in the Loops option in the menu.

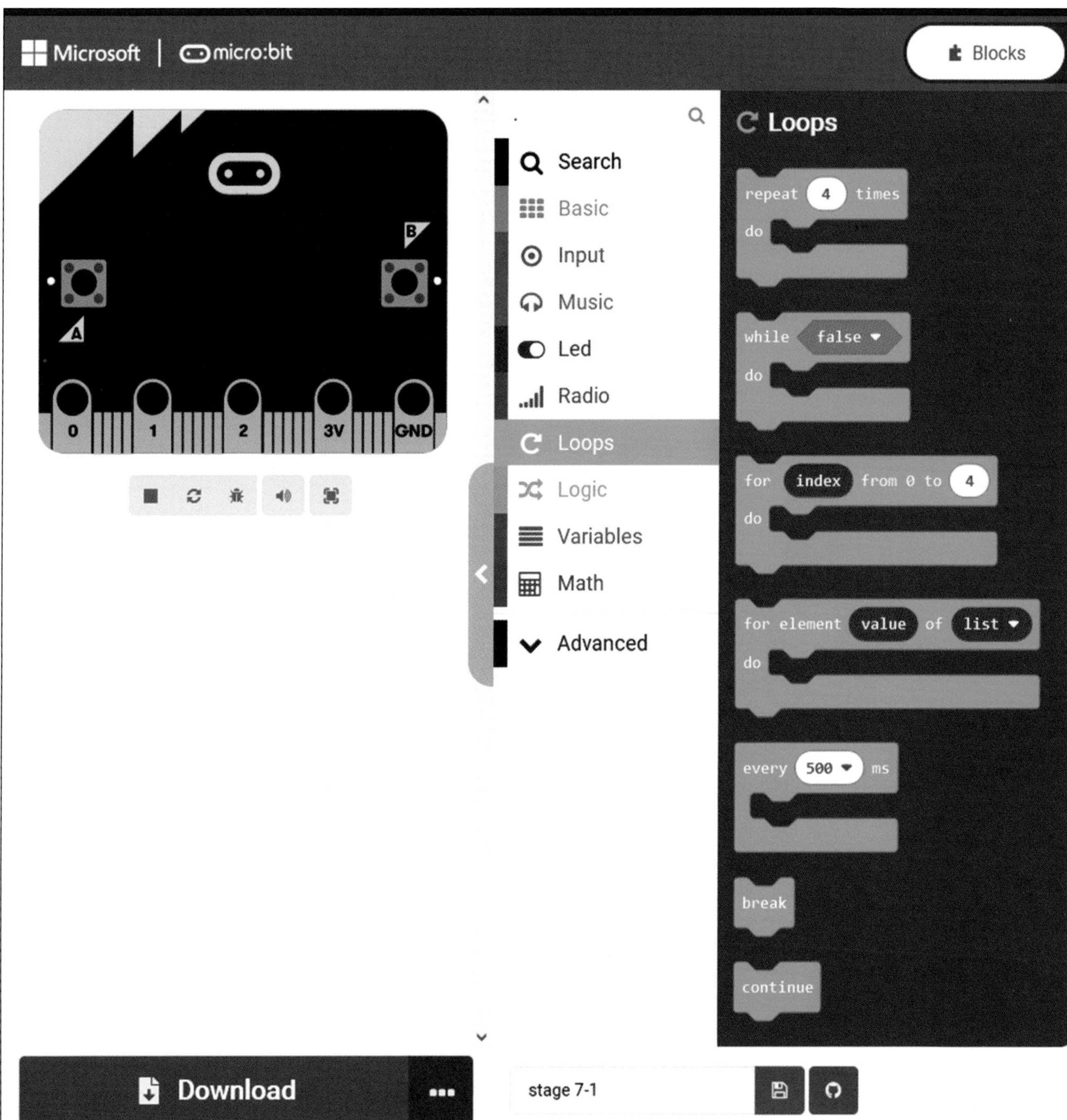

Figure 1.86: The Loops menu

The 'repeat' block will run the blocks inside it the number of times in the box.

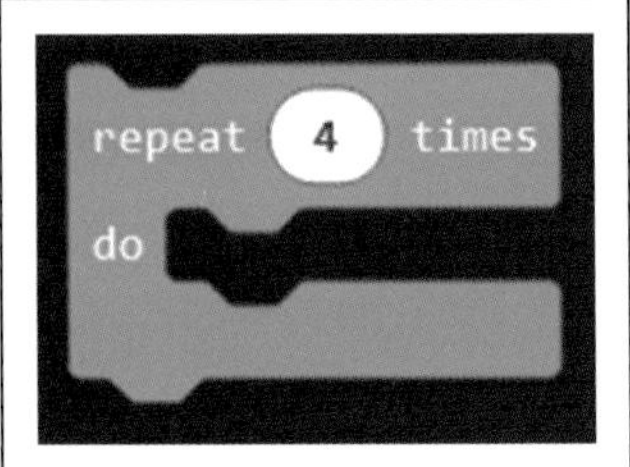

Figure 1.87: The repeat block

In this program, the large heart will be displayed, followed by the small heart, repeatedly for 10 times.

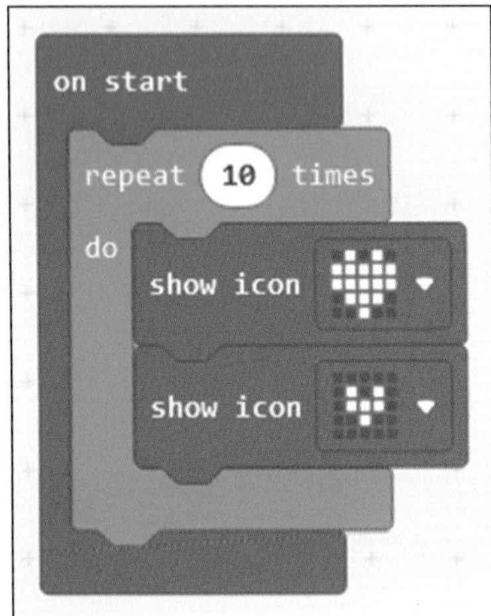

Figure 1.88: Using the repeat block with two hearts

The loop will run the blocks within it while the condition is false. It will stop only when the condition is true. The condition is checked and if it is false the block runs. The condition is checked again, and if is false the blocks run again and so on. This continues until the condition is checked and it is true.

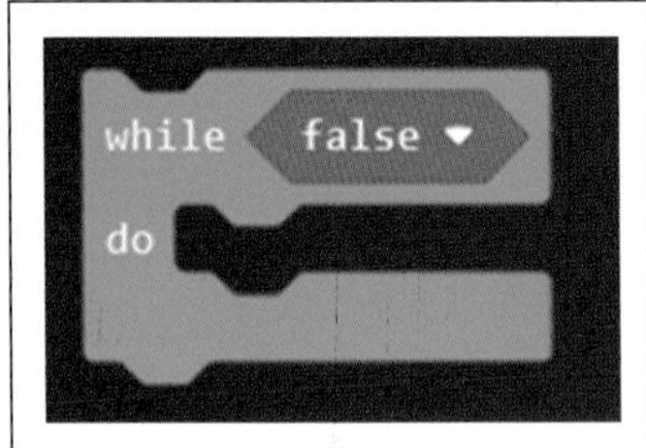

Figure 1.89: The while block

In this program, the heart will appear while the value in 'lives' is over 0. When the value in 'lives' becomes 0 or less, the 'while' loop will finish and the cross will display.

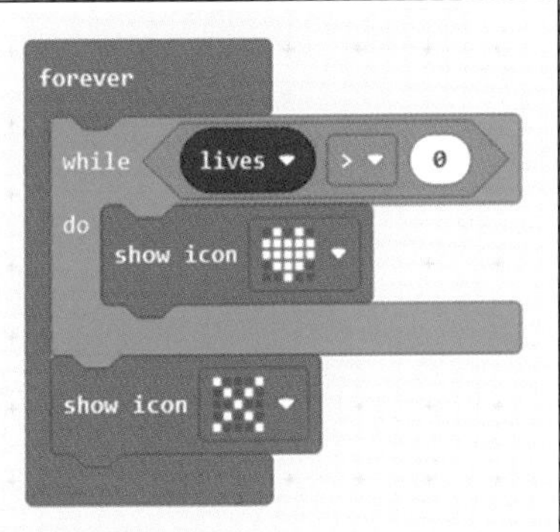

Figure 1.90: Using the while block to show lives over 0

Programming task 1.33: Make

You will need: a desktop computer, laptop or tablet with access to the MakeCode website

Make: Write a micro:bit program that uses a loop and a variable to output a countdown from 10 to 0. After 0 is output, a rocket should be displayed.

Programming task 1.34: Make

You will need: a desktop computer, laptop or tablet with access to the MakeCode website

Make: Write a micro:bit program that:

- adds 1 to a variable each time the micro:bit is tilted to the left
- subtracts 2 from a variable each time the micro:bit is tilted to the right

(while the value in the variable is less than 20).

When 20 is reached, the program changes to:

- add 2 to a variable each time the micro:bit is tilted to the left
- subtract 3 from a variable each time the micro:bit is tilted to the right

(while the value in the variable is less than 50).

When 50 is reached, the program ends and plays a tune.

Timer

You might need a program that times how long something takes. The micro:bit does not have a timer, but you can set it to keep track of time using a variable.

The micro:bit measures time in milliseconds. Each millisecond is one thousandth of a second. 1 second is 1000 ms. 2 seconds is 2000 ms.

The Basic menu has a 'pause' block.

When this block runs it will stop on this block for the number of ms in the box. When the time is up, the next block will run.

To create a timer, first create a variable and set it to start at 0.

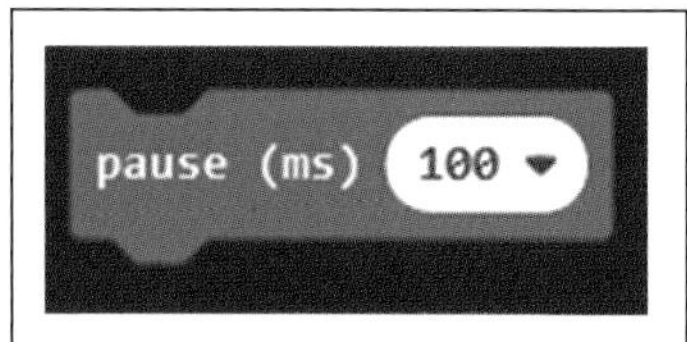

Figure 1.91: The pause block

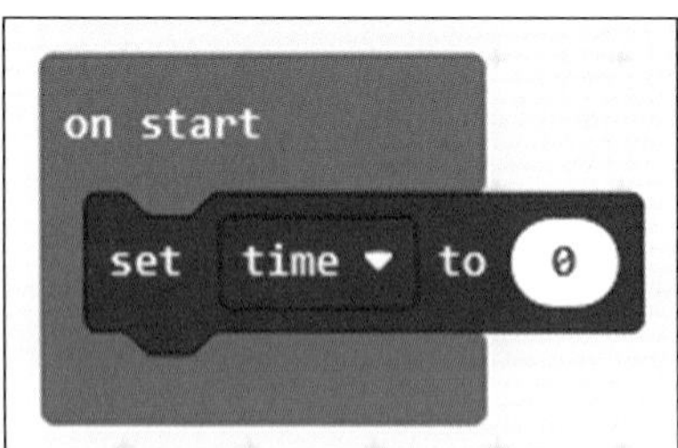

Figure 1.92: The time block

Inside a loop, change this variable by 1. Then pause. This will mean adding the pause block. If you want the timer to count in seconds, pause for 1000 ms. The first time, the variable will become 1, then it will pause for 1 second. Then the variable will become 2, and then it will pause for 1 second.

In this program the timer starts when button A is pressed, and the 'time' is output each time. Note that this program has the pause set to 100 ms.

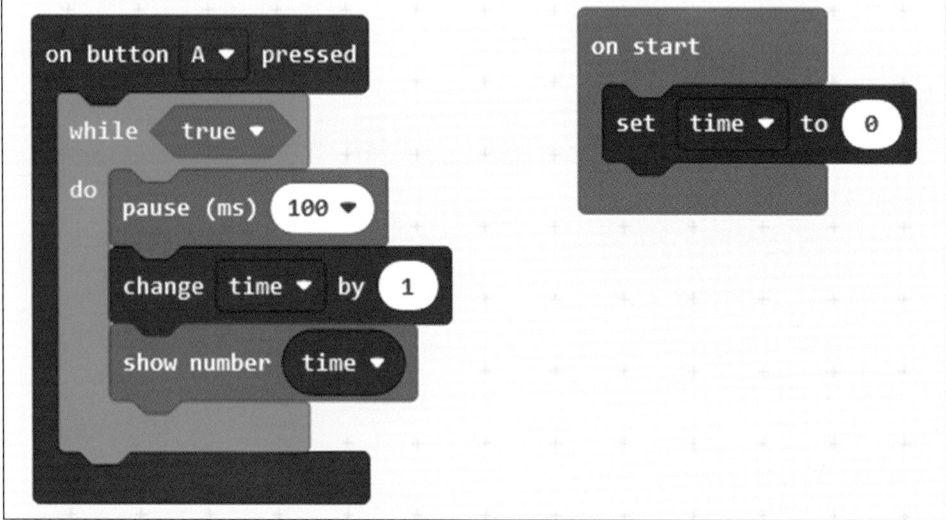

Figure 1.93: Pause and time in a loop block

Other blocks

There are a lot of other blocks that you might already know how to use, or ones that you might not be familiar with. This table has some more blocks that you might want to use.

Block	Description
`clear screen`	This will turn off all the LEDs on the micro:bit.
`pin P0 ▾ is pressed`	This input block will detect if one of the pins at the bottom of the micro:bit has been activated. This can be used with clips or additional micro:bit components.
`compass heading (°)`	This is an input that is stored like a variable. It will input the degree that the micro:bit is facing on a compass. 0 is north, 90 is east, 180 is south and 270 is east. Check the value to identify the way it is facing. North will be between 315 and 45. East will be between 45 and 135. South will be between 135 and 225. East will be between 225 and 315.
`temperature (°C)`	This is an input that is stored like a variable. It will input the current temperature around the micro:bit. The temperature is measured in Celsius.

(Continued)

<table>
<tr><th>Block</th><th>Description</th></tr>
<tr><td>plot x 0 y 0
unplot x 0 y 0</td><td>

'plot' allows you to turn on one LED, and 'unplot' allows you to turn off one LED.

The LEDs are in a 5x5 grid. The columns are x (0 to 4). The rows are y (0 to 4).

The LED in the top left is in position 0, 0. This grid shows the x and y values for each LED.

<table>
<tr><td>x 0, y 0</td><td>x 1, y 0</td><td>x 2, y 0</td><td>x 3, y 0</td><td>x 4, y 0</td></tr>
<tr><td>x 0, y 1</td><td>x 1, y 1</td><td>x 2, y 1</td><td>x 3, y 1</td><td>x 4, y 1</td></tr>
<tr><td>x 0, y 2</td><td>x 1, y 2</td><td>x 2, y 2</td><td>x 3, y 2</td><td>x 4, y 2</td></tr>
<tr><td>x 0, y 3</td><td>x 1, y 3</td><td>x 2, y 3</td><td>x 3, y 3</td><td>x 4, y 3</td></tr>
<tr><td>x 0, y 4</td><td>x 1, y 4</td><td>x 2, y 4</td><td>x 3, y 4</td><td>x 4, y 4</td></tr>
</table>

In this grid, the LED that is coloured in is position X3, Y1.

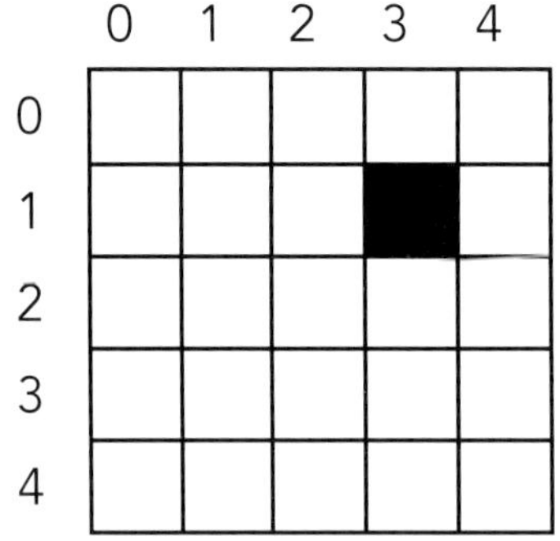

</td></tr>
<tr><td>

</td><td>

This block will give a number between two values, in this case 0 and 10. This number will be random, which means it does not follow a pattern. One time the number might be 2, and another it might be 4.

The 'random' numbers function is useful to help make decisions. For example, the computer can decide which image to display; if the random number is 3, then a smiley face is shown. If the random number is 5, then a sad face is shown.

</td></tr>
</table>

Table 1.19: Other kinds of micro:bit blocks

Activity 1.3

You will need: a pen and paper, a desktop computer, laptop or tablet with access to the MakeCode website

Open the MakeCode website and find *one* block that you do not already know how to use and is not included in this chapter.

Use the internet to find out how this block works and make a program that uses it.

On a piece of paper write the name of the block on one side and an explanation of what it does on the back.

Join with a group of up to 3 other people. Show the rest of your group the block that you have investigated and how it works.

Put each of your completed code descriptions on a table with the explanation face down. Take it in turns to point to a code block and explain what it does. Then turn it over and see if you were correct.

Peer-assessment

Rate your team members. Give them a mark from 1 to 5 for the difficulty of the block they chose and for how well they explained how it works.

1	2	3	4	5
easy		OK		difficult

Explain to your team members why you gave that mark for difficulty and discuss whether you all think the same concepts have the same difficulty.

Programming task 1.35: Predict, Run and Modify

You will need: a desktop computer, laptop or tablet with access to the MakeCode website

Work with a partner and read this micro:bit program.

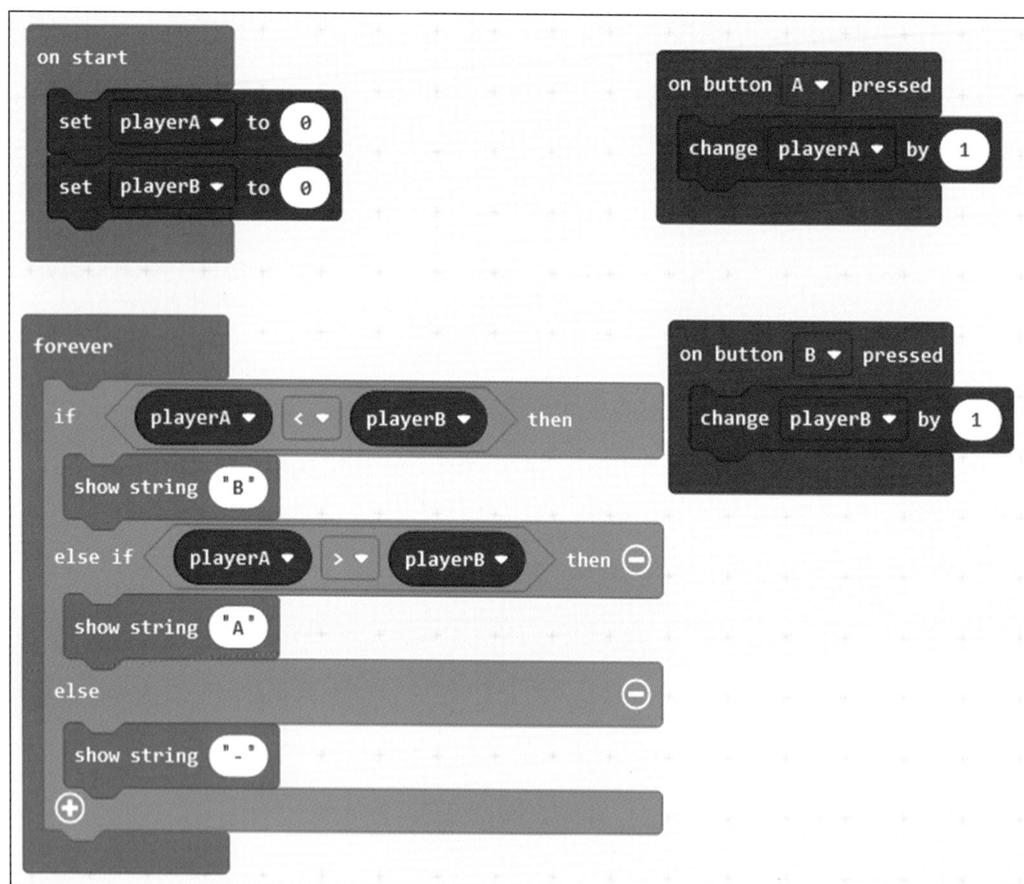

Figure 1.94: Micro:bit program for programming task

Predict: Discuss the purpose of this program, and what will happen when the buttons are pressed.

Run: Create the program on the MakeCode website and test it.
Was your prediction correct?

Modify: Change the program so that if both buttons are pressed at the same time, 1 point is taken away from both players.

Multiple inputs and outputs

You will need to be able to create a micro:bit program that has more than one method of input and more than one output. For example, the program might use both buttons for input, then output messages and images. Or the program might use the way the micro:bit is being tilted and the direction it is facing to output a message and a sound.

Programming task 1.36: Predict, Run, Investigate, Make and Modify

You will need: a desktop computer, laptop or tablet with access to the MakeCode website

Read through this micro:bit program by yourself.

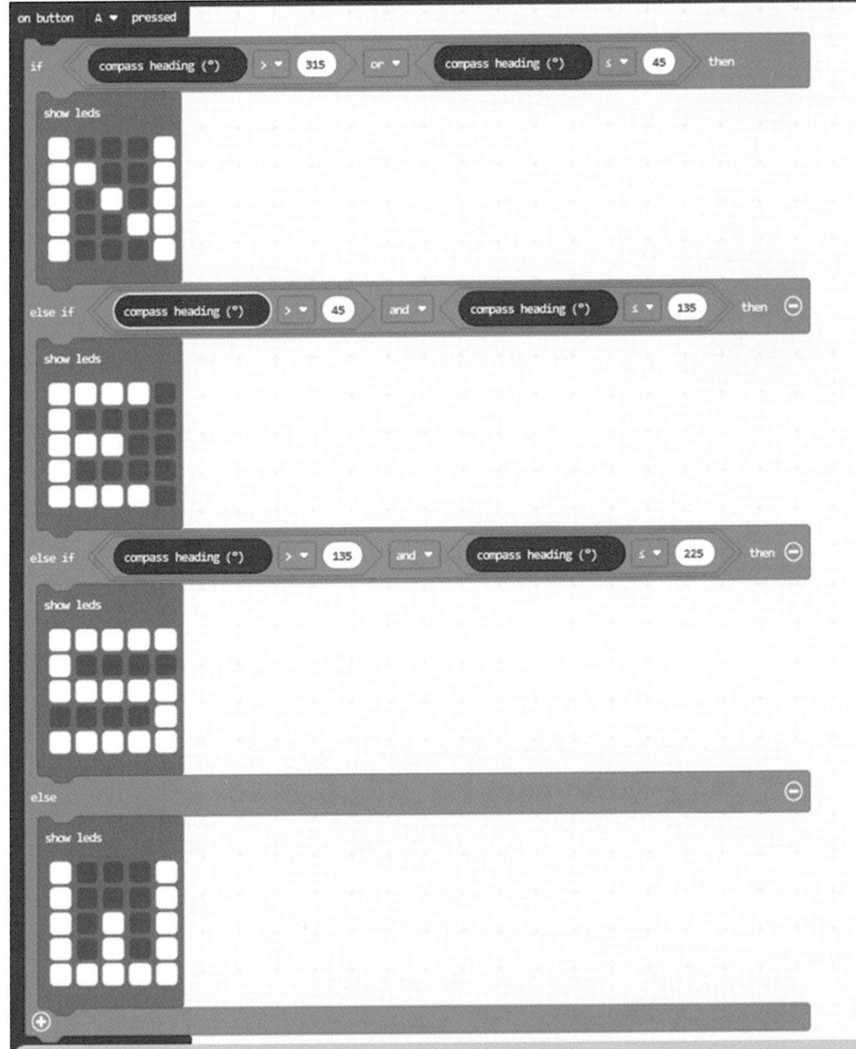

Continued

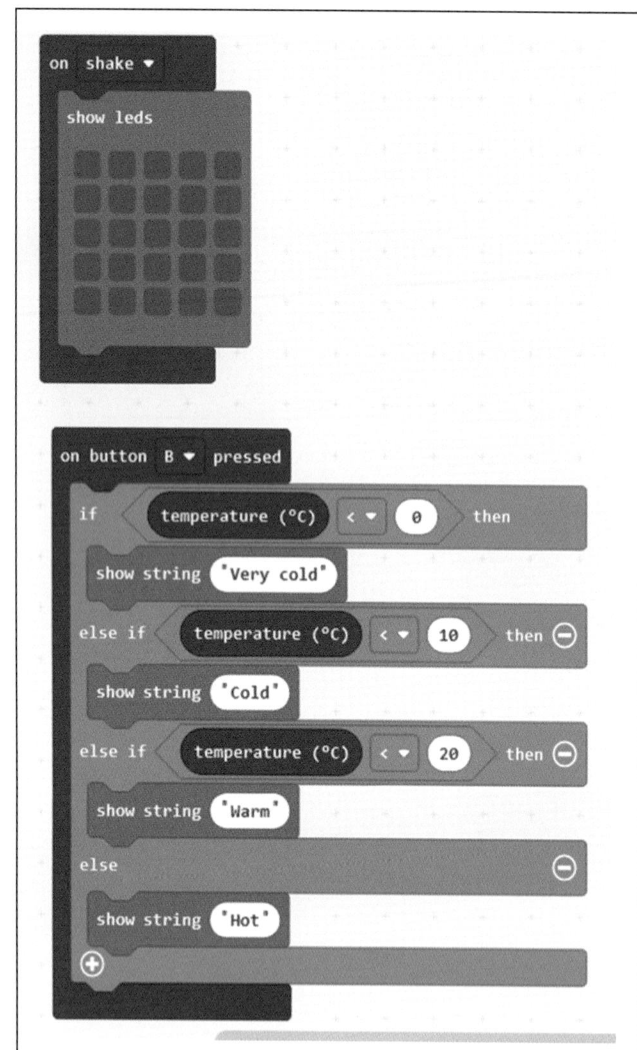

Figure 1.95: Micro:bit program for programming task

Predict: Join with a partner, and tell them what will happen when button A is pressed, button B is pressed and when the micro:bit is shaken.

Investigate: Work with your partner to identify the different inputs into the system and the different outputs from the system.

Run: Create the program with a partner and run it. Were your predictions correct?

Modify: Change the program so that the actions performed when button A is pressed run when the micro:bit is tilted to the left instead.

Modify: Change the program so that actions performed when button B is pressed run when the micro:bit is tilted to the right instead.

Continued

Make: Create a new micro:bit program that displays the current temperature and plays a different melody repeatedly depending on the direction the micro:bit is facing.

Self-assessment

How successful was your program? Give your final program a rating from 1 to 10, with 10 for a program that meets all the criteria, and 1 where it only meets some of the criteria.

Programming task 1.37: Make

You will need: a desktop computer, laptop or tablet with access to the MakeCode website

Make: Create a micro:bit program that:

- tells the user to press button A for images and button B for sound
- detects if the micro:bit is tilted to the left, right, has logo up or has logo down
- outputs a different sound or image for each tilt, depending on whether the user has selected images or sound.

How familiar were you with the micro:bit already? What new skills did you learn? Are there any similarities in your micro:bit knowledge and work in other topics?

Questions 1.16

1 What are the different inputs that can be used with a micro:bit?

2 What different forms of output can a micro:bit produce?

3 If you need to store a number in a micro:bit, what programming feature would you use?

4 What will be displayed on the micro:bit when the program in Figure 1.96 finishes?

5 What does the program in Figure 1.97 do?

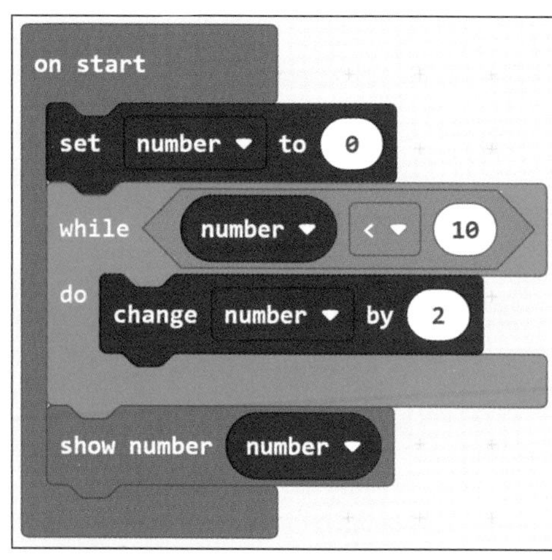

Figure 1.96: Micro:bit program

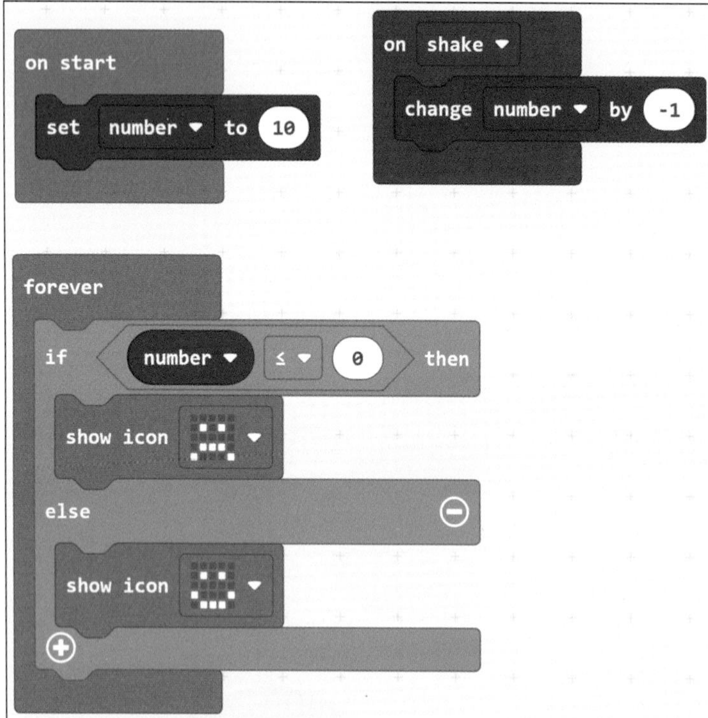

Figure 1.97: Micro:bit program

Summary checklist

- [ ] I can program a micro:bit to take multiple inputs from different input components.
- [ ] I can program a micro:bit to take different inputs from one input component.
- [ ] I can program a micro:bit to use selection.
- [ ] I can program a micro:bit to test multiple inputs and produce different outputs depending on the input.

Project 1: micro:bit bird

You need to develop an interactive bird using the micro:bit.

This bird needs to be visual; that is, an image.

Users need to be able to interact with the bird. For example, they might feed it, let it fly or put it in a tree.

You will need to work in pairs to do the following.

- Create a design for the bird and give it a suitable name.
- Decide how the user will interact with the bird. There must be at least two actions they can do.
- Decide what the input for each action will be, and the output. How will the user know what they have done?
- Produce evidence of testing your program.

You need to produce:

- a design for the bird
- a description of the inputs, processes and outputs
- a plan of how you will work together to produce the solution
- evidence of testing the program (for example, through a test plan)
- a final program that meets the requirements.

Challenge

Include at least one additional feature of your own design. This could be another method of interaction, a timer that makes the bird age or a game that the user can play with the bird. You need to use your imagination to identify something appropriate that you can program.

Project 2: Algorithm design

You need to work in groups to write a series of algorithm challenges.

These challenges are problems that need to be solved. Each challenge can state whether it should be solved using a flowchart, Python or a micro:bit.

Each challenge should be a description of a problem and should have a challenge rating. Bronze is the easiest level. Silver is a bit more difficult. Gold is the hardest level.

You need at least one bronze, one silver and one gold challenge. You need at least two challenges for all three methods (flowchart, Python, micro:bit).

In your group you need to decide:

- how many bronze, silver and gold challenges you are going to write
- whether you are going to divide the challenges between people based on difficulty, or programming language
- whether your team members will work individually, in pairs, or as a whole group.

For each challenge you need to create:

- a description of the problem
- a solution for the problem.

Your group should combine all of the challenges into one document and the solutions into a second document.

Groups should then swap their challenges and try to solve them.

You need to produce:

- a description of each problem
- a challenge rating and the method of solution required for each problem
- a solution for each problem
- at least one bronze, one silver and one gold challenge
- at least two flowchart problems, at least two Python problems and at least two micro:bit problems.

Challenge

For the gold challenges, include an extension task. This could be something extra to add to the solution, or it could be a task to research a new tool or feature that a user might not know how to use yet.

Check your progress 1

1 Draw the appropriate flowchart symbol around each of the flowchart statements.

Start

INPUT cost

totalCost = totalCost + cost **[3]**

2 Draw *one* line to match each description with its comparison operator.

Description	Operator
Less than or equal to	>=
Less than	<=
Greater than or equal to	>
	<

[3]

3 Read this flowchart and then answer the questions below.

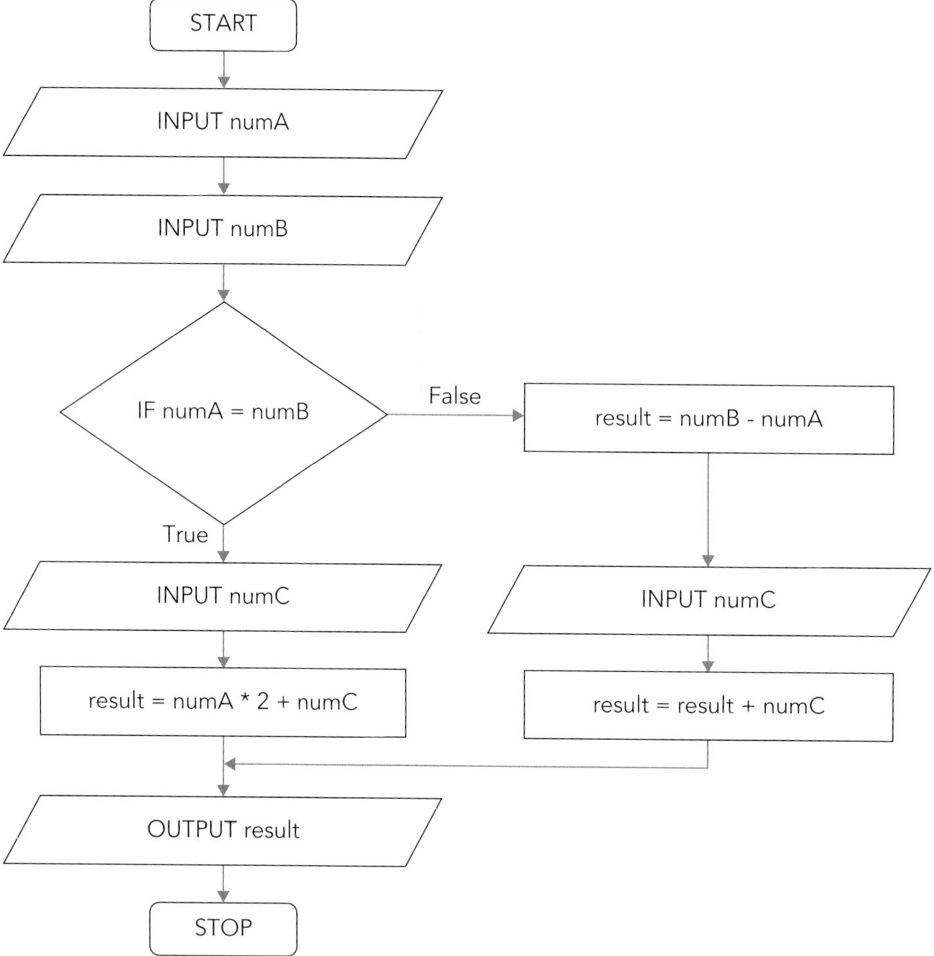

a Give the identifier of *two* variables in this flowchart. [2]

b Give the output when the numbers 1, 5 and 10 are input. [1]

c Give the output when the numbers 2, 2 and 5 are input. [1]

4 Complete the table by giving *one* example of each type of data.

Data type	Example
String	
Integer	
Real	

[3]

5 Complete this Python program to output the word "Programming".

`print(..............................................)` [2]

6 One mile is approximately 1.6 kilometres. The moon is 384400 kilometres away.
This Python program should convert and output the number of miles away the moon is.

```
conversion = 1.5
moonKm = 384400
moonMiles = moonKM / conversion
print("moonMiles")
```

The program contains *two* errors.
Identify each error and give the correction for each. [3]

7 Write a Python program to:

- ask the user to input their name
- read their name as input
- output the message "Hello" followed by their name. [5]

8 Give *two* ways an error can be made when writing a computer program. [2]

9 Read the following program for a micro:bit and then answer the questions.

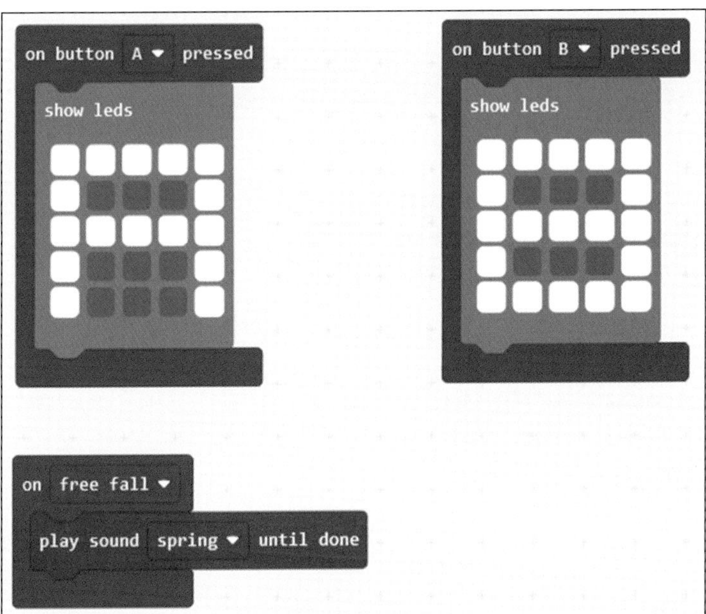

a Identify the different forms of inputs that the program takes. [2]

b Identify the different forms of output that the program creates. [2]

10 Marcus is designing a computer game and wants to make a project plan before starting.
Explain the reasons why it is a good idea for Marcus to make a project plan before starting. [4]

2 Managing data

2.1 Spreadsheets

In this topic you will:

- use conditional formatting to format a cell
- learn how to apply different styles of conditional formatting to a cell, depending on the data in the cell
- understand what a rule is
- learn how to write different types of rules.

Key words

analyse

cell

condition

conditional formatting

formatting

rule

spreadsheet

statement

Getting started

What do you already know?

- Spreadsheets are used for calculations, to create simple databases and to model solutions to a problem by using data to solve problems. They are made up of rows, columns and cells that you can type data into.
- We understand that different colours can mean different things. A red traffic light means you need to stop and a green traffic light means you can go. In some parts of the world, red means a warning and green means something positive.
- You may know that when you are using a spreadsheet, colours and text size can be used to help you easily see the most important information. For example, negative values that we are unhappy with (for example, −3) can be shown in red, and positive values that we are happy with can be shown in green (for example, 3).
- The mathematical symbol > means 'greater than' and the mathematical symbol < means 'less than'. These symbols (for example, +, −, ÷, ×, <, >) are called comparison operators.

Continued

Now try this!

Work with a partner. Ask your partner what they think when they see the things listed in this table.

Formatting	Examples
text that is bold	You **must always** look both ways when crossing the road.
text that is underlined	Never be mean to people.
text that is written in red	What does this red text make you feel about the words?
text that has a background colour that is green	Does this formatting feel positive or negative?
text that has a background colour that is yellow	Does this formatting feel positive or negative?

Then find out which text is bold in this book. Why is it bold?

You have just been thinking about what different formatting can mean when it is applied to text.

Spreadsheets

A spreadsheet is a computer file that lets you work with data to:

- make calculations
- create databases
- analyse the data (work out what the data means)
- model solutions to a problem. (Modelling is explained in Topic 2.2.)

Spreadsheets are made up of rows and columns. Data is typed into boxes called cells. A cell is an individual box where a column and a row meet.

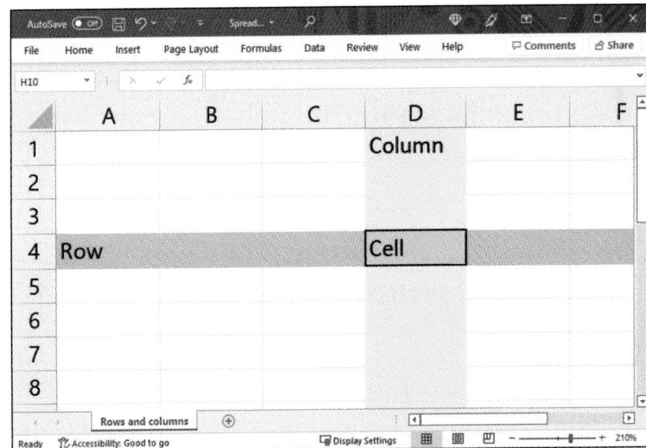

Figure 2.1: Rows, columns and cells in a spreadsheet

Some spreadsheets have thousands of cells with data stored in them. This can make it difficult to find the data that you need quickly. Conditional formatting can help the most important information stand out.

Conditional formatting

A **condition** is a test that gives a true or false result. For example, 'Is the value greater than 10?' **Formatting** is the style of certain aspects of a document. For example, the font, size or colour of text, or the fill colour of cells. Conditions and formatting can be used together to make it easier to see useful data in a spreadsheet.

Conditional formatting is a style that is applied to cells containing data that meets certain conditions. For example, we might want to make it so that:

- if the value in a cell is greater than 10, the text in the cell turns blue
- if the value in a cell is less than or equal to 10, the text in the cell turns green.

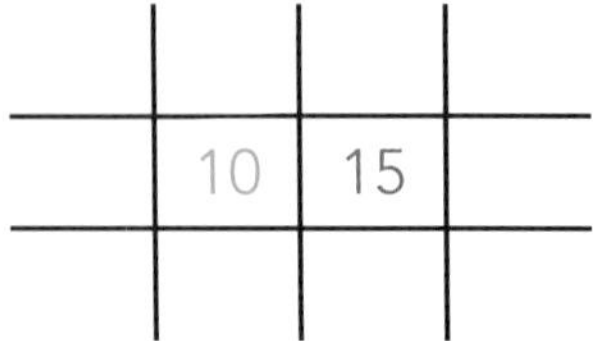

Table 2.1: Conditional formatting on values in a cell

You can use conditional formatting to draw attention to certain information. Conditional formatting makes the most important data look different from other data in the spreadsheet. This makes it much easier to see patterns in the data and analyse it. In our example above, the condition could be:

the value <= 10

If the condition is true, the text in the cell will turn green. If the condition is false, the text in the cell will turn blue.

Conditional formatting is applied to a cell by writing a **rule**. A rule is a sentence that includes:

1. a condition, and
2. the type of formatting that is applied to the cell based on the outcome of that condition.

For example:

(1) (2)

if the value in the cell = 0, format the background colour as orange.

This sentence is called a **statement**.

The owner of an ice cream van has used a spreadsheet to record:

- the amount of money the business has earnt from sales
- the amount of money the business has spent on its costs.

One of the cells in the spreadsheet shows how much money the business has in the bank.

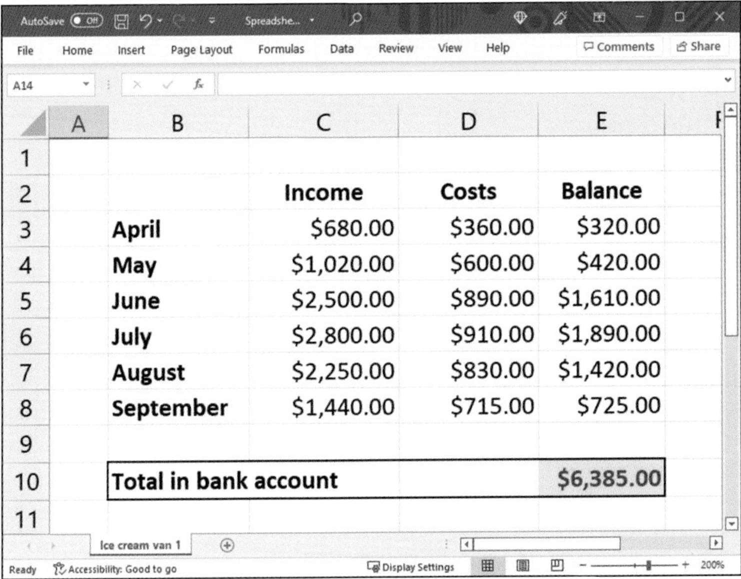

	A	B	C	D	E
1					
2			**Income**	**Costs**	**Balance**
3		**April**	$680.00	$360.00	$320.00
4		**May**	$1,020.00	$600.00	$420.00
5		**June**	$2,500.00	$890.00	$1,610.00
6		**July**	$2,800.00	$910.00	$1,890.00
7		**August**	$2,250.00	$830.00	$1,420.00
8		**September**	$1,440.00	$715.00	$725.00
9					
10		**Total in bank account**			**$6,385.00**
11					

Figure 2.2: Spreadsheet showing money in the bank

The cell will have a red background if the business is in debt. Being in debt means that the business has spent more money than it has received from sales. If the business is in debt, this cell will show a negative number on a red background.

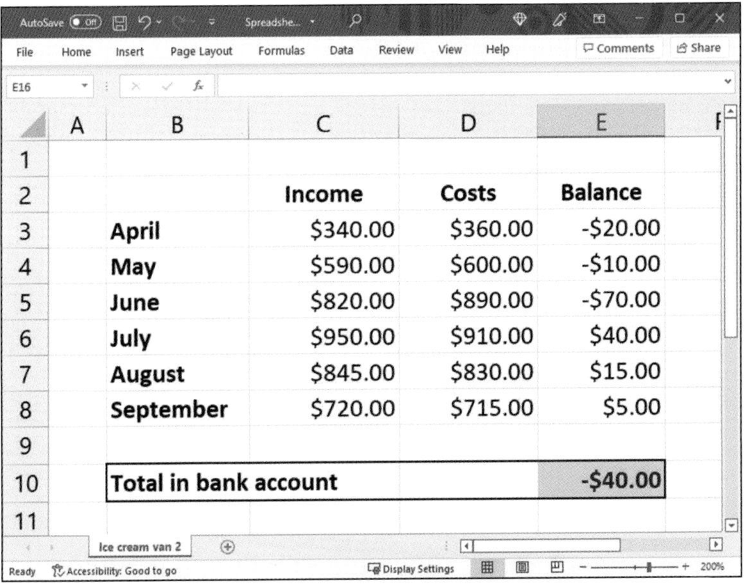

	A	B	C	D	E
1					
2			**Income**	**Costs**	**Balance**
3		**April**	$340.00	$360.00	-$20.00
4		**May**	$590.00	$600.00	-$10.00
5		**June**	$820.00	$890.00	-$70.00
6		**July**	$950.00	$910.00	$40.00
7		**August**	$845.00	$830.00	$15.00
8		**September**	$720.00	$715.00	$5.00
9					
10		**Total in bank account**			**-$40.00**
11					

Figure 2.3: Spreadsheet showing the business is in debt

Unplugged activity 2.1

You will need: a pen and a squared piece of paper

Write down ten important words from this topic. This could include some of the key words and any other words you have learnt more about in this chapter. Create a wordsearch that has your chosen words hidden in it.

Write a list of clues to help a partner find the hidden words, but do not write the words themselves. The clues should be hints about the meaning of the word, such as:

- a document made up of lots of cells
- how text or a cell looks, for example the font or colour.

Make sure you do not give any answers away by including parts of the hidden words in the clues!

Swap your wordsearch with a partner. Then try to complete their wordsearch using the clues to help you.

If this sounds too easy, you could give no clues and just tell your partner to find ten hidden words related to this chapter. When they find each one, ask them what it means. If they struggle to find ten, tell them the clues for the ones they can't find.

Did you know?

In many countries, red often means danger, a warning or something else negative. However, in East Asia, red means happiness and good luck. In China, gifts of money are given in red envelopes at special occasions and brides wear red on their wedding day. Therefore, when you see red formatting on a spreadsheet, do not assume that it always means the same thing!

Practical task 2.1

You will need: a desktop computer, laptop or tablet with source file **2.1_drama_society_accounts.xlsx**

You are going to apply conditional formatting to a youth drama society's accounts spreadsheet to see whether the society has earnt more than it has spent on its recent show.

Open the file 2.1_drama_society_accounts.xlsx. It shows the following data:

Income	
Ticket sales	$2,050.00
Merchandise sales	$350.00
Refreshment sales	$470.00
Total sales	**$2,870.00**

Costs	
Building hire	$800.00
Lighting hire	$200.00
Costume hire	$260.00
Merchandise costs	$150.00
Refreshment costs	$230.00
Total costs	**$1,640.00**

Balance	$1,230.00

Table 2.2: The youth drama society's accounts

Cell C16 shows the balance value for the society (how much of the income is left after costs have been paid). You are going to apply conditional formatting to this cell. The value in cell C16 shows how much money the society has in the bank. You are going to make the data in the cell change to:

- green if it is greater than 0
- red if it is less than 0.

Continued

Select cell C16. Select the conditional formatting option from the tool bar.

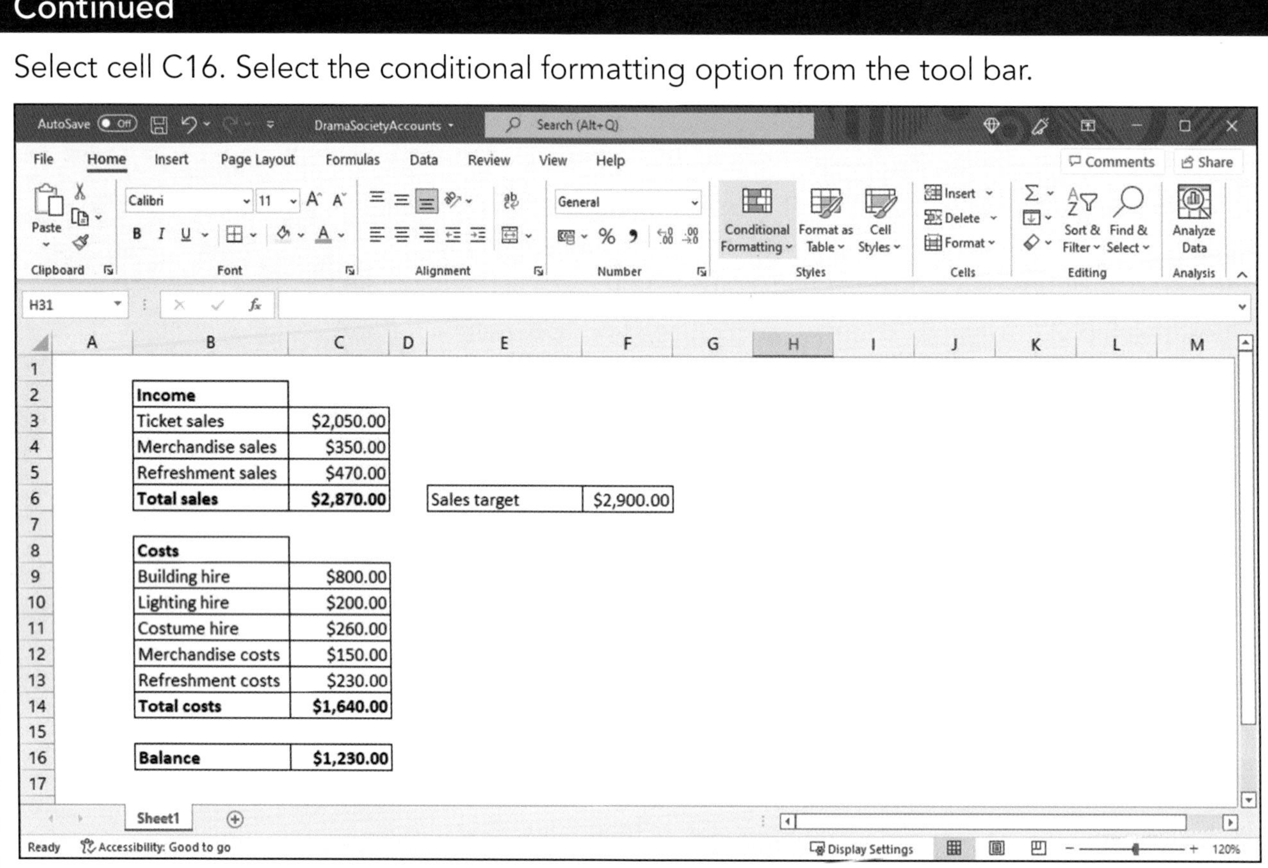

Figure 2.4: 'Conditional Formatting' button in Microsoft Excel (highlighted, top, right of centre)

In Microsoft spreadsheet software, you will see a menu of options:

1 Select the option 'Highlight Cells Rules'

2 Select the option 'Greater Than'.

This will open a box. You can input data for the condition on the left and choose formatting options on the right. If you are using different spreadsheet software, take a moment to find out how to use the conditional formatting tools in your software.

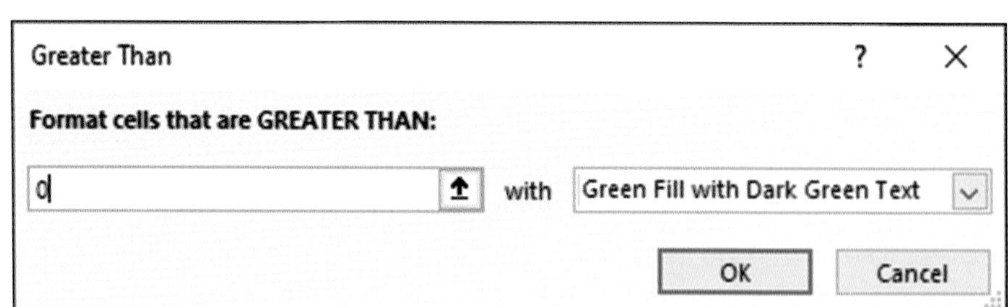

Figure 2.5: Setting conditional formatting using the 'Greater Than' rule

Continued

The 'Greater Than' option is a type of rule. This is a rule that will format the cell if it contains *a value greater than another value*.

Value greater than another value is the condition.

Tell the software to format cell C16 green if the value in the cell is greater than 0.

1 Type 0 in the text box on the left-hand side.
2 Select the option 'Green fill with dark green text' from the drop-down menu on the right.
3 Select OK.

You will now see that cell C16 has a green background and dark green text. This is because the value in it is greater than 0.

Income	
Ticket sales	$2,050.00
Merchandise sales	$350.00
Refreshment sales	$470.00
Total sales	**$2,870.00**

Costs	
Building hire	$800.00
Lighting hire	$200.00
Costume hire	$260.00
Merchandise costs	$150.00
Refreshment costs	$230.00
Total costs	**$1,640.00**

Balance	**$1,230.00**

Table 2.3: Cell C16 has a value greater than 0

You now need to tell the software to format cell C16 red if the value it contains is less than 0. See if you can use the instructions above to work out how to do this.

Now test whether your new rule works. Change the value in C3 to $800 to test your rule.

Continued

Self-assessment

Did you manage to find the right options to set the correct conditional formatting?

How did you know which ones to choose?

Did you change the value in cell C3 to test your rule? Did your rule work? If it did, why is the formatting for cell C16 now red? If it didn't, what do you think you need to do to make your rule work?

How confident did you feel doing this task? Show how confident you are using a smile or a frown (or something in between!).

Practical task 2.2

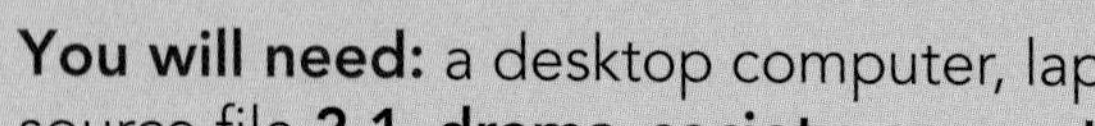

You will need: a desktop computer, laptop or tablet with source file **2.1_drama_society_accounts.xlsx**

You have added conditional formatting to make it easy to see if the value is positive or negative. But what will happen if the bank balance for the drama society is $0? For this, you could use the colour orange.

Now, you need to format cell C16 to be orange if the value it contains equals 0.

1 Select cell C16.
2 Select the 'Conditional Formatting' option from the tool bar.
3 Select the 'Highlight Cell Rules' option.
4 Select the 'Equal To' option.
5 Type 0 in the data box.
6 Select 'Custom Format ...' from the drop-down menu.

This will open a box that allows you to choose the formatting options for the cell. So far, you have been choosing formatting options from a limited list that was made when the software was created.

This time you are going to choose the formatting yourself.

1 Select the 'Font' tab (this may be showing already).
2 Find the 'Color' option and change it to a dark orange.
3 Select the 'Fill' tab and change the colour to a light orange.
4 Select 'OK'.

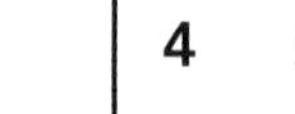

Continued

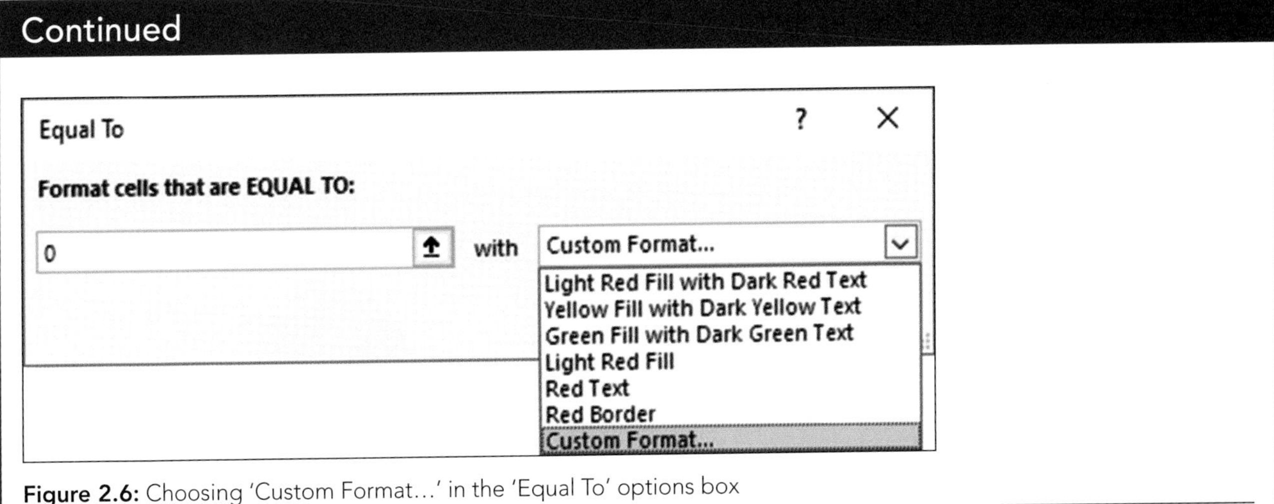

Figure 2.6: Choosing 'Custom Format...' in the 'Equal To' options box

You need to test that your rule works by changing the value in cell C3 again.

What do you need to change the value to so that you can test if the rule works?

Now see if you can change one of the conditional formatting rules you have created. You could set the format for cell C16 so that if the value = 0, the font is:

- Times New Roman
- italics
- size 14.

To change a rule, click 'Conditional Formatting' and choose 'Manage Rules...' from the bottom of the drop-down menu. Then select one of your rules and click 'Edit Rule...'. Then choose your formatting. Remember to test whether your rule change has worked!

Questions 2.1

1 Write down one condition that you have used so far.

2 Write down one rule that you have created so far.

3 Why is it useful to apply conditional formatting to cells in a spreadsheet?

Conditional formatting based on another cell

So far, the conditional formatting you have done has been based on the value in the cell you are formatting: you have told the formatting of cell C16 to change based on the value in cell C16.

Sometimes, you need to format the value in a cell based on the value in a different cell. The following practical task will tell you how to do this.

Practical task 2.3

You will need: a desktop computer, laptop or tablet with source file **2.1_drama_society_accounts.xlsx**

Cell C6 in **2.1_drama_society_accounts.xlsx** shows what the total sales value is.

Cell F6 also shows what the sales target for the society is.

You are going to format the total sales value in cell C6 based on the sales target value in cell F6. The total sales value needs to look different if it is greater than the target amount.

1 Select cell C6.
2 Select the conditional formatting option from the tool bar.
3 Select the 'Highlight Cells Rules' option.
4 Select the 'Greater Than' option.
5 Delete the value in the data box.
6 Click the cell F6 – The cell reference =F6 has appeared in the data box.
7 Select 'Custom Format ...' and choose your formatting.

You have now created a rule that formats the sales value based on the sales target value.

Now test your rule to see if it works. Can you think how you need to do this?

The society's treasurer is worried that they might not be able to cover all of their costs and will get into debt. She wants to make sure that the society doesn't spend too much.

1 In cell E14, type in 'Total cost allowed'.
2 In cell F14, type in '$1700'.
3 Now format C14 to show if the business has spent more than the total cost allowed. Use one style of formatting to show if the value is above (>) $1700. Use a different style of formatting to show if the value is equal to or below $1700.

Peer-assessment

Talk to a partner.

- Did you find it easy to choose which formatting to choose for the total sales value or did you find it difficult?
- Why did you choose the formatting you did?
- Did your partner choose the same formatting as you?
- Why did they choose the formatting they did?
- How effective do you think it was?

Activity 2.1

You will need: a desktop computer, laptop or tablet with spreadsheet software

A parent who runs a local computing club for 9- and 10-year-olds has asked for older children to come and run a session about how to use conditional formatting. Create a spreadsheet that:

- shows how helpful conditional formatting can be
- gives examples of what it can be used for
- explains how to set up conditional formatting.

To make your spreadsheet easier to understand, make sure you use a realistic life situation as an example. You could use:

- income and costs for a charity bake sale raising money for a particular goal
- a log of pocket money and savings goals
- scores in a game or competition
- high, medium and low priority changes to be made to a website.

Make sure your spreadsheet looks professional and works perfectly – the computing club members are hard to impress!

When you have finished making your spreadsheet, practise talking through it and using it to explain conditional formatting. Your talk should be no more than five minutes long. Then present your talk to a partner or small group.

Summary checklist

- [ ] I understand what a condition is.
- [ ] I can use conditional formatting to format a cell.
- [ ] I can apply different styles of conditional formatting depending on the data in the cell.
- [ ] I understand what a rule is.
- [ ] I can write different types of rules.

2.2 Modelling

In this topic you will:

- understand what a model system is and why they are used
- learn about different model systems, including simulators
- understand how model systems are used to model parts of real life
- understand how data is used in a model to test different conditions
- learn how a model system can be used in health, manufacturing and retail.

Key words

formula

function

mimic

model

modelling

outcome

scenario

simulator

spreadsheet model

Getting started

What do you already know?

- Data is very useful for all kinds of organisations. We can use data to help solve problems in industries such as health, manufacturing and retail. We can collect and analyse data (look at it in detail to see what it means) to see what has happened, why it has happened and what could be done to change a situation.
- Data can be entered into spreadsheets. Spreadsheet tools can then be used to help investigate and make sense of the data.

Continued

Now try this!

It is Gabriel's birthday. You need to plan a birthday celebration meal for Gabriel and his family. You are given this data about the family's food likes and dislikes:

Name	Favourite food	Food they do not like
Carlos	salad, pizza, noodles	pasta, carrots
Sue	pasta, carrots, ice cream	seafood, pizza
Gabriel	seafood, salad, chicken	chocolate, couscous
Sebastian	chicken, salad, pasta	peas, seafood
Anika	couscous, chicken, chocolate	pizza, chicken burger

Table 2.4: Data for Gabriel's birthday meal

What would you plan for the birthday meal?

Discuss the following with a partner.

- How did the data help you plan the meal?
- What did you think was important to be aware of in the data?
- How did you decide what meal to plan?

Modelling real-life systems and scenarios

In the Getting started task, you were presented with a problem and you used the data to make a decision and plan a solution. You were given a small amount of data to do this.

Organisations may need to solve problems daily. They often need to work with large amounts of data to solve these problems. Data can tell us a lot about why a problem has happened and what we can do to solve it. Working with data can also help people to plan solutions for problems that might happen in the future.

One way that an organisation can use data to learn why a problem has happened and plan a solution is by using a **model** system. A computer model is a representation of a real-life system or situation. People and organisations can use a model system to study what would happen in real-life situations if certain changes were made.

A **spreadsheet model** is a model created in a spreadsheet. The drama society accounts file that you used in Topic 2.1 is a spreadsheet model.

A basic model is made up of three types of information:

- **Data:** information we put into the model
- **Labels:** text that tells us what the information is
- **Calculations:** sums that are performed on the data to produce new information we want to find out.

Income				
Ticket sales	$2,050.00			
Merchandise sales	$350.00			
Refreshment sales	$470.00			
Total sales	$2,870.00		Sales target	$2,900.00
Costs				
Building hire	$800.00			
Lighting hire	$200.00			
Costume hire	$260.00			
Merchandise costs	$150.00			
Refreshment costs	$230.00			
Total costs	$1,640.00		Total costs allowed	$1,700.00
Balance	$1,230.00			

Table 2.5: Youth drama society accounts spreadsheet

Questions 2.2

In Table 2.5, the different types of information have been colour coded.

1 What colour are the data cells?

2 What colour are the labels?

3 What colour are the results of calculations?

Note: The **Total sales** amount in cell C6 is the result of a calculation. The Total sales cell adds up all the values under **Income**:

Total sales = Ticket sales + Merchandise sales + Refreshment sales

Unplugged activity 2.2

You will need: a pen and paper

To explain the calculation for **Total sales**, we have just used the labels on the spreadsheet rather than the values. The **Total costs** and **Balance** amounts in cells C14 and C16 are also calculation results. On a piece of paper, write down the correct calculations for these amounts using the labels.

Once a spreadsheet has labels, calculations and data, we can then change the data to see the different outcomes (results or effects) that could be produced. For example, the drama society could use this spreadsheet to see what would happen if building hire increased to $1,500.00 the next time the society needs to hire the theatre. What would the total costs change to?

Would the balance show that there would still be money in the bank account, or would the society get into debt?

Changing the values in a spreadsheet to see what outcomes the different values produce is called **modelling**. Modelling lets you create different **scenarios** (possible future situations) and see what the effects of these changes would be. For example, in our accounts model in Unplugged activity 2.2, we could see:

- what would happen if ticket sales for the next production were better or worse
- what would happen if merchandise costs increased or decreased
- what would happen if they used a different lighting hire company that charged a different amount.

Practical task 2.4

You will need: a desktop computer, laptop or tablet with source file **2.2_bike_model.xlsx**

Sofia's hobby is BMX biking. She wants a new bike, but the type she wants is very expensive. She gets $30 from her parents per month. She has saved up for a few months but still does not have enough for the bike.

Sofia's parents offer to lend her the rest of the money for the bike as long as she pays some back every month out of her pocket money. Her parents will also charge her a little bit of interest on the loan so that she learns how loans work. The longer she takes to pay back the loan, the more it will cost her!

Continued

Sofia needs to know how much the monthly repayments and final cost will be depending on the price of the bike, how much of the cost she can pay herself from what she's saved, how much interest her parents charge and how long she takes to pay back the loan.

Open the file 2.2_bike_model.xlsx and you should see Table 2.6:

Bike loan calculator		
Cost of bike:		• Purchase price of the bike
Deposit:		• Amount Sofia can pay by herself from her savings
Amount borrowed:	**$0.00**	• How much her parents will lend her (the loan)
Interest rate (%):		• Percentage of the loan that her parents will charge
Duration (years):		• Number of years Sofia would like to take to repay the loan
Duration (months):	0	• Number of months this is, and therefore how many payments
Monthly payment:	**#NUM!**	• How much Sofia needs to pay her parents back each month
Total amount to be repaid:	**#NUM!**	• How much Sofia will repay her parents in total
Total cost of bike:	**#NUM!**	• How much the bike will cost Sofia in total

Table 2.6: Bike loan calculator

- Sofia borrows money from her parents to buy the bike. This is the loan. She needs a loan for the cost of the bike minus the deposit that she pays.

  Cost of bike – Deposit = Loan

- Sofia needs to agree with her parents how long she will take to pay the loan back. She would like to pay it back over two years.

Continued

- Her parents will charge interest on the loan. This is a percentage of the loan amount added on as a fee for the service they are providing, to help Sofia learn how a loan works. Sofia's parents would like to set the interest rate at 3%.
- Sofia will then pay the same amount each month to her parents to pay back the loan and interest.

Enter these values into the white cells in the spreadsheet model:

Cost of bike:	500
Deposit:	80
Interest rate (%):	3
Duration (years):	2

Table 2.7: Data for Practical task

When you enter these values, the loan calculator will tell you:

- how many monthly payments are needed
- how much each monthly payment will be
- the total amount Sofia will repay
- how much in total the bike will have cost her at the end.

Questions

1 How much does Sofia need to borrow from her parents to buy the bike?

2 What is the monthly payment when you enter these values?

3 What is the total cost of the bike when you enter these values?

Sofia has seen a more expensive bike that she would really love, but it costs $540.00. She thinks she might be able to manage a deposit of $110, and she would prefer to pay back the loan in one year rather than two. Her parents are willing to lower the interest rate to 2.5%. If she gets a part-time job she will be able to make a monthly payment of $30 and still have enough left over for other things.

Change the values in the loan model to find the answers to these questions:

4 What are the monthly payments for the more expensive bike?

5 Will Sofia be able to pay the monthly payments and repay the whole loan in one year?

6 What is the lowest deposit Sofia would need in order to be able to repay the loan in one year?

7 What is the shortest loan duration that would result in monthly payments Sofia could afford? (Hint: the duration does not need to be whole years.)

You now know how to use a spreadsheet to model different scenarios, for example, taking out a loan to help you buy something expensive.

Spreadsheet calculations

To make a spreadsheet model, someone needs to write the calculations into the cells that need them. This is done using a simple type of code, which is a little bit like programming.

All calculations in a spreadsheet start with =. This tells the software that you want that cell to contain a calculation. You can use **formulas**, **functions**, or a mix of both to make calculations in a spreadsheet.

Formulas are simple calculations that use comparison operators like + and – with numbers and/or **cell references** (the column letter and row number of another cell, for example D4). Including a cell reference in a calculation means that whatever value is in that cell will be used in the calculation. Formulas look a lot like simple sums you might do on paper.

Functions are built-in chunks of code that tell the spreadsheet to do something a bit more complex. They avoid us needing to write a long formula using lots of operators and cell references. Each function has a name, which we write after the = when we want to use the function.

The basic formulas and functions you should know are shown in Table 2.8.

	Example	What does it do?
Formulas	=E4+6	adds numbers or cell values together
	=120–B4	subtracts one value from another
	=E4*0.8	multiplies one value by another
	=E4/12	divides one value by another
Functions	=SUM(E4:E8)	adds together all the values in cells in the range
	=COUNT(E4:E8)	counts all the cells in the range that contain numbers

Table 2.8: Simple spreadsheet formulas and functions and what they do

When you have written a correct calculation in a spreadsheet cell, pressing Enter or selecting a different cell will show the result of the calculation in the cell. You can double-click the cell to see or change the calculation.

With a partner, look at the bike loan calculator from Practical task 2.4 again and answer these questions.

Questions 2.3

1 What does the calculation in cell D6 do?

2 What does the calculation in cell D14 do?

3 Can you work out what the calculation in cell D10 does? Why is the ROUNDUP function needed?

How will you remember which formulas do a particular calculation? Can you think of any examples of how you might use the formulas in your daily life? Do you find the formulas easy to use? If not, what could you do to make it easier?

Activity 2.2

You will need: a desktop computer, laptop or tablet with spreadsheet software

Imagine you and your classmates are going to run a charity event. You want to model different outcomes for the money that will be raised by the event.

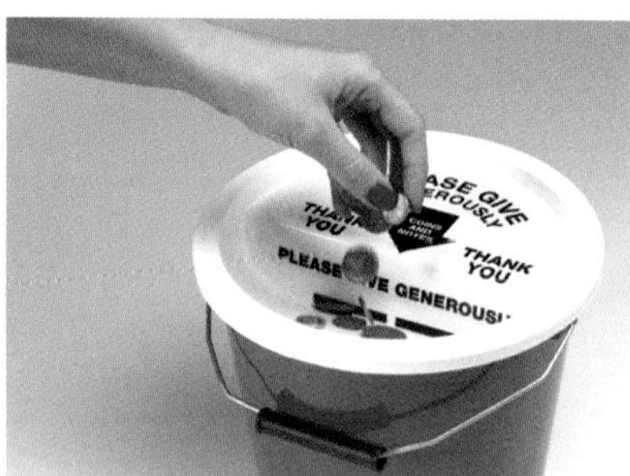

Figure 2.7: Charity donation box

1 In a small group, design a spreadsheet model for a charity event – it could be a party, a fair, a sporting event or a talent show. In one column, put the heading 'Costs'. Leave the next four columns blank, then in the next column put the heading 'Income'. Under these headings, make two lists:

- What kind of costs are involved in running the event – will there be food, entertainment, equipment you need to buy or hire?
- How will you raise money – will you sell tickets or goods, will people make donations?

Your spreadsheet might look something like this:

Costs					Income		
drinks					ticket sales		
cakes					donations		
bouncy castle hire					drink sales		
face paints					cake sales		

Table 2.9: The start of a charity fair costs and income spreadsheet

Continued

2 Once you have made the lists, discuss with your group which variables you will be able to change in your spreadsheet to model the costs and income for the event. Variables are the values that you can change to model different outcomes.

You might think of variables like:

- how many drinks to buy
- what price to charge for each drink
- how many tickets you could sell
- what price to charge for each ticket.

3 These variables fall into two categories. Can you work out what they are? See if you can add two new column headings next to the Costs heading and two next to the Income heading. Some values have been entered into the example below to help you.

Costs	?	?			Income	?	?
Drinks	500	$0.30			Ticket sales		
Cakes	450	$0.50			Donations		
Bouncy castle hire	1	$200.00			Drink sales		
Face paints					Cake sales		

Table 2.10: Charity fair costs and income spreadsheet being filled in

You will need to set the data type to 'Currency' for the cells that contain amounts of money (use the drop-down menu at the top of the screen that is usually set to 'General'), then enter all the data values into the columns.

4 Now think about what calculations your model will need. How will you find the amount that you will raise by selling tickets? How will you find how much you have left when you have paid all your costs? One example might be:

Income from tickets = price of tickets × number of tickets sold

Add a fourth column heading to each section of your spreadsheet for these calculations. Can you think of what to call it? Then add the calculations to the new columns, using the correct cell references (for example D5) for each value in the calculation.

5 Now add a row at the bottom with two more labels and calculations: one to add all your costs together and one to add all your income together. Then add another cell that subtracts the total costs from the total income to give the balance.

Continued

Once you have designed your spreadsheet model for the event, explain to the class in your group what you have done and how you can use your spreadsheet to model different scenarios.

Peer-assessment

You will need: three coloured cards (red, amber and green) and a piece of paper

Listen to the presentation from each group about their spreadsheet model. After each group has spoken, hold up a red, amber or green card.

- A green card means you have understood the design for the spreadsheet model and feel confident that you can answer questions about the design.
- An amber card means you understand most of the design but do not feel confident about answering questions about it.
- A red card means you do not understand the design for the spreadsheet model and need further explanation.

If you hold up an amber or a red card, think of one question that you would like to ask the group about their presentation.

Simulators

You have seen how a spreadsheet can be used to model the different possible outcomes of a scenario. Another type of computer program that can be used for modelling is a **simulator**. A simulator is a computer system that can be used to **mimic** real-life situations. To mimic means to imitate or behave the same way as something. Simulators can be used for research or for training people. Here are some examples of simulators.

Simulators in pilot training

Before a pilot is allowed to fly an aeroplane, they are trained in a flight simulator. This is much safer than training in a real plane. The simulator looks like a real cockpit (pilot's compartment) with all the same displays and controls, but it has computer screens instead of windows. These screens then show the pilot what they would see if they were really flying the plane. The pilot can see what happens when they use the controls and learn how to fly effectively, without needing to actually fly.

Figure 2.8: Pilot sitting in a flight simulator

Training in a simulator allows the pilot to:

- learn the basics without risk of damaging the plane or injuring anyone
- practise flying in dangerous weather conditions, such as a storm or heavy wind
- practise what to do in an emergency, for example, if a bird flew into the engine.

Using a simulator is also cheaper than buying and maintaining a real plane for training purposes, and no fuel or crew are needed.

Simulators can be used in many different areas of our lives. They are created by writing lots of rules and adding lots of data so that the simulator can mimic all the different scenarios that might be needed. This data is often collected and stored in large databases for the simulator to use. The amount and quality of data available to the simulator, and the quality of the programming used to create the rules, affect how good the simulator is.

Did you know?

Simulators are very important in preparing astronauts for their time in space. Simulators are used to mimic many aspects of space travel, and they can show how new equipment may behave in space.

Unplugged activity 2.3

You will need: a pen and paper

Imagine you are building a simulator to help people learn how to drive a car. What data would you need to give the simulator to help it know how to behave?

1 Write a list of as many things you can think of that the simulator would need to know, then share your list with the class. Did you miss out anything important?
2 Why is it important to give the simulator the right kind of data?
3 Can you think of any disadvantages of using a simulator to learn to drive?

Figure 2.9: Learning to drive in a simulator

How did you decide what data would be important for the simulator? What did you base this on? How did you decide what would be a disadvantage of using the simulator?

Simulators in health

Simulators are also used in healthcare settings. There are lots of ways that they can be used.

Simulators are used to train surgeons how to perform operations. Using a simulator, a surgeon can practise and learn the right skills without having to operate on real people. Simulators also help to develop new surgery techniques because it is safe to try out new ways of doing things in a simulated operation.

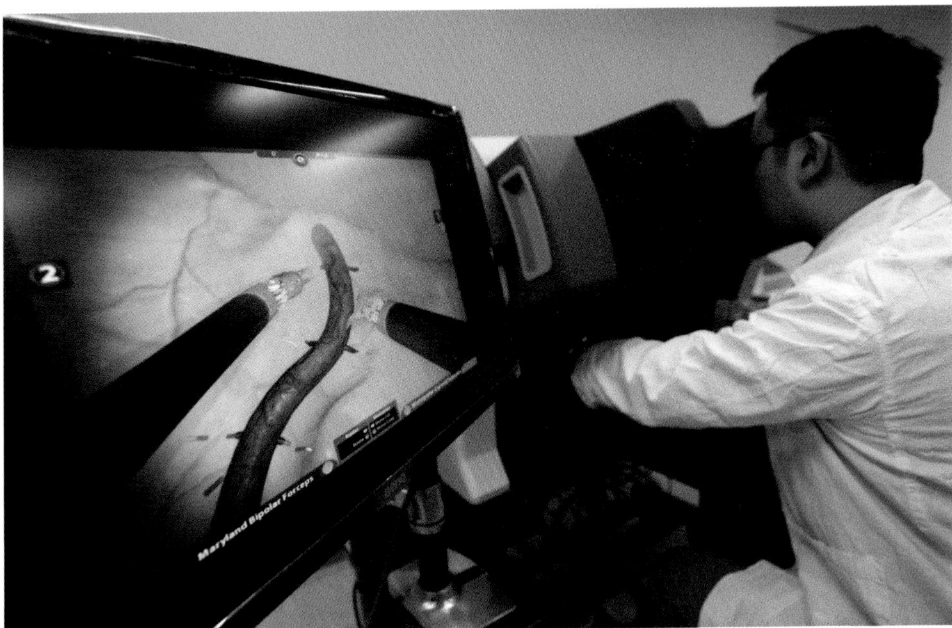

Figure 2.10: Surgeon practising heart surgery

Simulators can be used to plan for other healthcare issues. One example is when people need medical care after a natural disaster, such as an earthquake. A simulator can be used to mimic a natural disaster so that experts can plan how and where to send doctors, ambulances and other services to help people.

Simulators can also be used to design the layout of new hospitals. A simulator can be used to try placing different medical rooms in different places. A simulation can then be run to mimic different kinds of medical events. This allows the planners to see if the layout allows treatment to be provided in the quickest and most helpful way.

Simulators in manufacturing

Simulators are used in manufacturing (making goods in a factory). They are used to test how products behave in certain situations and to test whether a product meets certain criteria.

For example, a car manufacturer may want the model of their car to look a certain way. However, the car manufacturer may also want the car to reach a certain speed in a set amount of time (for example 80 km/h in 5 seconds). The car would need to have the right body shape to be able to do this, so a simulator could be used to test different designs. This is much cheaper and takes a lot less time than building the car first and then testing it in real life.

Figure 2.11: Simulated car tests

Simulators in retail

Simulators are used when a new shopping centre is being planned or an existing one is going to be renovated. Simulators help retail managers create a space that will be more efficient and enjoyable for shoppers. With a simulator, the retail managers model different layouts to see how customers will walk around the centre. This could help the managers to identify areas that could cause a problem.

Figure 2.12: Simulated shopping centre layout and customer traffic

Activity 2.3

You will need: a pen and paper, a desktop computer, laptop or tablet with internet access

Imagine you are an interior designer. A customer comes to you with the following information.

- Their living room needs rearranging as the current arrangement does not work for them.
- The room is 5 metres long and 4.5 metres wide.
- They would like to fit two large sofas, an ottoman (foot rest), an armchair, a fireplace, a TV stand, a large bookcase and a three small tables into the room.
- If you look at the room from above, there is a large window on the right-hand wall and a door in the middle of the left-hand wall. The door opens into the room.

The customer would like your help designing the room's new layout. It is not possible to move the door or the window, but the fireplace and furniture can go anywhere as long as the room can be used normally.

You are going to use a room layout simulator to find out if the customer's wishes are realistic. Your teacher will provide you with a room simulator website for this activity.

Figure 2.13: Interior design simulation of an apartment

Continued

1. Talk with a partner about what kind of things you need to model using the simulator. For example, think about where the different items of furniture need to be in relation to each other so that they are usable, and think about how people will move around the room.
2. Use the simulator to try out different layouts. Can all the customer's wishes be fulfilled? If not, explain why. Then use the simulator to help you come up with recommendations about what they could do instead.
3. On paper, write a summary of your findings and suggestions, then present them to a partner as if they were the customer. Show them how the model works to help them understand why you have made the recommendations you have.

Peer-assessment

Talk with your partner.

- How did you find using the room layout simulator? How useful was it?
- What were you able to do that would have been difficult or impossible without the simulator?
- How did you show the customer that putting different data into the model will change the outcome?
- Do you think the customer will be pleased with the model? Why or why not?

You have learnt about several different types of models and have seen that data can be given to computer models in many ways. Data input could be through the click of a button, typing the data in, or moving a mouse or a joystick. Can you think of any other ways the data could be given to the model?

Summary checklist

- [ ] I understand what model systems are and why they are used.
- [ ] I can explain different model systems, including simulators.
- [ ] I know how data is used in a model to test different conditions.
- [ ] I can explain how a simulator is used in health, manufacturing and retail.

> 2.3 Databases

In this topic you will:

- understand what a primary key is
- understand why a primary key is used
- learn how to select an appropriate field to be used as the primary key in a database
- learn how to create a query to search a database
- learn how to create a query using greater than (>), less than (<) and equal to (=) criteria.

Key words

database

field

primary key

query

record

table

unique

Getting started

What do you already know?

- You may have heard of databases or even used them. A database is a collection of data about the same topic. A database has tables that are separated into fields (columns) and records (rows).
- You already know that cells in a spreadsheet can have different data types. You changed the data type in the spreadsheet model you made in the previous topic. Each field in a database needs to have an appropriate data type too (for example a number or text).
- You can search for words or phrases in a database. A word or phrase must have double quotation marks around it when searching, for example, "2D platform". Searching for a phrase is called 'phrase searching'.

Continued

Now try this!

Look at this database of computer games:

Database 1

Game name	Age rating (Age+)	Genre
Bill & Betty	12	2D platform
Build Blocks	3	arcade
Ping Pong	3	arcade
Puzzle Place	8	puzzle
Super Adventurer	12	2D platform
Blocks Super Build	3	puzzle
The Great Race	3	racing
Work It Out	8	puzzle

Table 2.11: Database of computer games

Write down:

1 a field from the database
2 a record from the database
3 an appropriate data type for the Name
4 an appropriate data type for the Age rating
5 what you would enter into database software to search for all games that are puzzle games
6 the record(s) that would be output when the phrase search "Work It Out" is done
7 the record(s) that would be output when the phrase search "Build Blocks" is done
8 the record(s) that would be output when the phrase search "Super" is done.

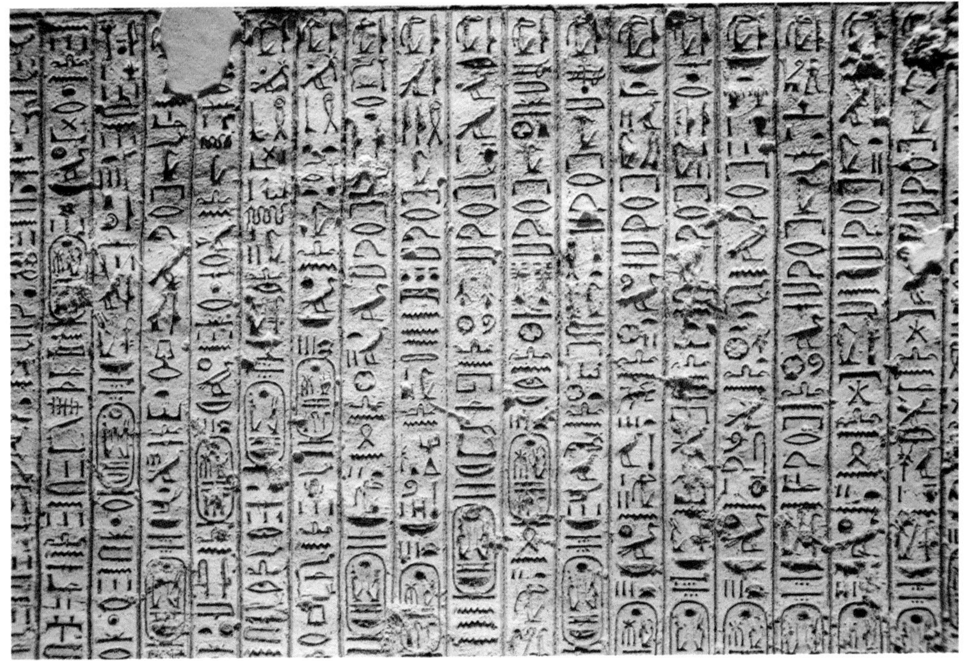

Figure 2.14: An Ancient Egyptian database

Did you know?

The Ancient Egyptians used databases to track and store information. These early databases were carved in stone and stored information, such as how many animals and crops were available, and information about buying and selling.

What is a primary key?

You may have looked at or even built a **database** before. A database is a collection of data about the same topic or type of thing.

Database 1

Game Name	Age rating (Age+)	Genre
Bill & Betty	12	2D platform
Build Blocks	3	arcade
Ping Pong	3	arcade
Puzzle Place	8	puzzle
Super Adventurer	12	2D platform
Blocks Super Build	3	puzzle
The Great Race	3	racing
Work It Out	8	puzzle

← **Record**

↑ **Field**

Table 2.12: Database of computer games

The kind of database you have seen or built probably had a single **table**: an organised set of data arranged into rows and columns.

- The columns in the table are called **fields**. A field is a collection of a single *type* of data in a table. For example, the names of all the computer games.
- The rows in the table are called **records**. A record is a set of data in all the fields about a single item in the database. For example, all the data about a single computer game.

It is important that every record has something that makes it **unique**. Unique means that it is the only one of its kind and there is no other record that is exactly the same. In the computer games database, data in some of the fields was the same in different records. For example, some games had the same age rating as each other, such as '12', and there was the same data in the Genre field, such as 'Arcade'.

However, a record is made up of different fields:

Name AND Age rating AND Genre

If you look at each record (the whole row), you will see that each one is unique.

The following database also shows the names of some players who like playing these games. Is every record in this database unique?

Database 2

Player	Game Name	Age rating	Genre
Mohammed Khan	Bill & Betty	12+	2D platform
Charlie Jones	Build Blocks	3+	arcade
Anisa Nababan	Ping Pong	3+	arcade
Mohammed Khan	Bill & Betty	12+	2D platform
Carla Estevez	Ping Pong	3+	arcade

Table 2.13: Database of computer games and players

In Database 2, there are two different people called Mohammed Khan who both like playing Bill & Betty. So every record in this database is not unique.

To make sure every record is unique, a database needs a **primary key** field. This column gives each record a unique number or code. In Database 1, the primary key is the Game Name because every entry in that field is different.

In Database 2, we need to create a new field for a primary key. Every entry in this new field needs to be different.

Database 3

Player number	Player Name	Game Name	Age rating	Genre
1	Mohammed Khan	Bill & Betty	12+	2D platform
2	Charlie Jones	Build Blocks	3+	arcade
3	Anisa Nababan	Ping Pong	3+	arcade
4	Mohammed Khan	Bill & Betty	12+	2D platform
5	Carla Estevez	Ping Pong	3+	arcade

Table 2.14: Database of computer games and players with the primary key (the column called 'Play number')

Unplugged activity 2.4

You will need: a pen and lined or squared paper, a ruler

Imagine you are a zookeeper and you want to create a database of all your animals. Draw a table on your paper with the fields shown in this example.

Animal	Name	Age	Gender	Food
giraffe	Aaliyah	17	F	leaves
monkey	Abu	12	F	fruit
giant panda	Bai Yun	8	F	bamboo

Table 2.15: Example rows in a database of zoo animals

Now fill your database with at least ten animal records.

Your table needs a primary key. Look at each field to see if one of them is suitable as a primary key. Which field do you think would be best to use? Draw a little key symbol in the field heading cell.

Setting a primary key

Practical task 2.5

You will need: a desktop computer, laptop or tablet with source file **2.3_computer_games.accdb**

Open the file 2.3_computer_games.accdb. You should see the computer games database.

You are going to choose the best field for the primary key and set it.

1. Open Microsoft Access and change the view to 'Design View'. The button for this looks like a triangle and ruler. (The software might ask you to save your table. Give the file a name and click OK.)
2. Select the field that you want to set as the primary key.
3. Select the 'Primary Key' button in the top left of the screen.

Another way of setting the primary key is to right click on the field and then choose 'Primary Key' from the drop-down menu that appears.

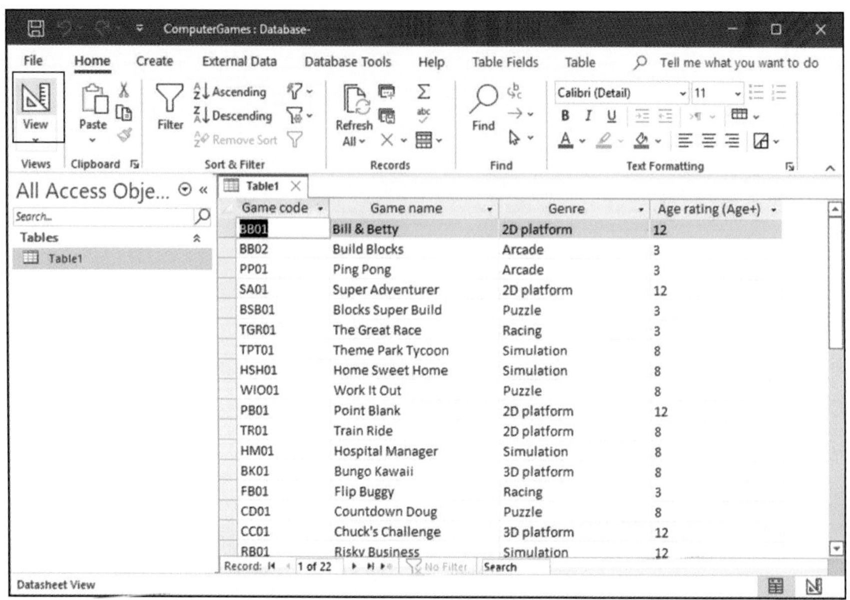

Figure 2.15: Selecting 'Design View' in Microsoft Access (highlighted, top left)

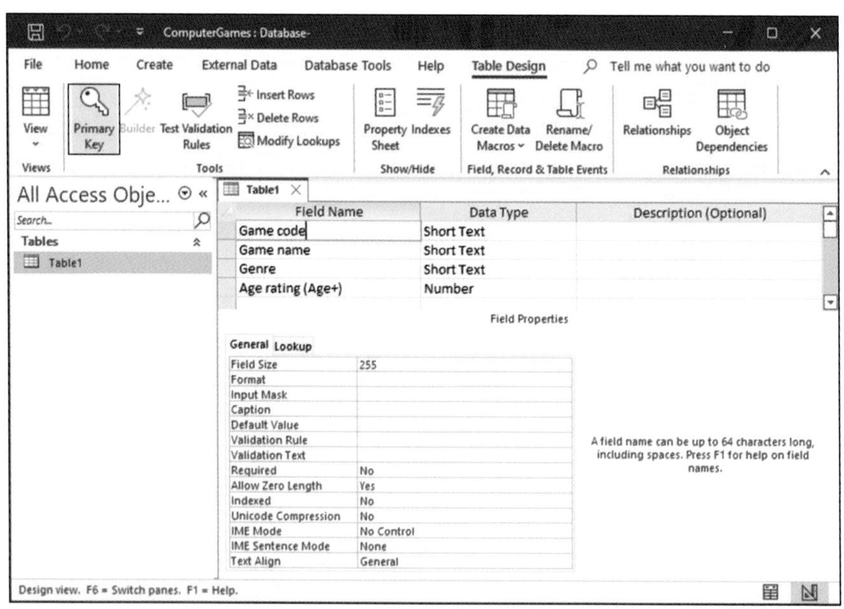

Figure 2.16: Selecting 'Primary Key' (highlighted, top left)

Continued

The field is now the primary key. If you have done this correctly, there will be a small key symbol in the grey box next to the field name.

Self-assessment

Check that you have set the Game code field to be the primary key. Check to see if there is a key symbol in the grey box to the left of the Game code field name. If there is a key in the box, you have set the primary key correctly. Well done!

If there is not a key symbol in the grey box, try following the instructions to set the primary key again.

If this still doesn't work, ask a partner to show you how they did it correctly.

Activity 2.4

You will need: a desktop computer, laptop or tablet with word-processing software

With a partner, create a questionnaire to find out what your classmates eat for breakfast. Think of five questions you want to ask. Use Microsoft Word or other word-processing software to create this questionnaire. Ask ten people to answer your questionnaire.

If you used the answers to your questionnaire to create a database, you would find that each question turned into a field. (You do not need to create the database.)

How would you create the primary key for this database? Is there a field that you could set to be a primary key or do you need to create a new field?

Creating a query

The computer games database only contains a small amount of data. Some databases can be very large. Looking for a piece of data or record in the computer games database would be easy. Looking for a certain piece of data in a database that has hundreds or thousands of records would take a long time if you had to do it with just your eyes.

Database software lets you create a type of search called a **query**. A query is a request for data that meets certain criteria. For example, a query could show you all the computer games that use a puzzle format. Or a business might want to query all the products that have been sold in the last month. You may have done something like this when you looked at phrase searches during previous learning.

To create a query in the database software:

- Select the 'Create' tab from the toolbar at the top of the screen.
- Select the option 'Query Design' from the toolbar.

This will open a new tab that is used to design a query. This is what the Query tab will look like in Microsoft Access:

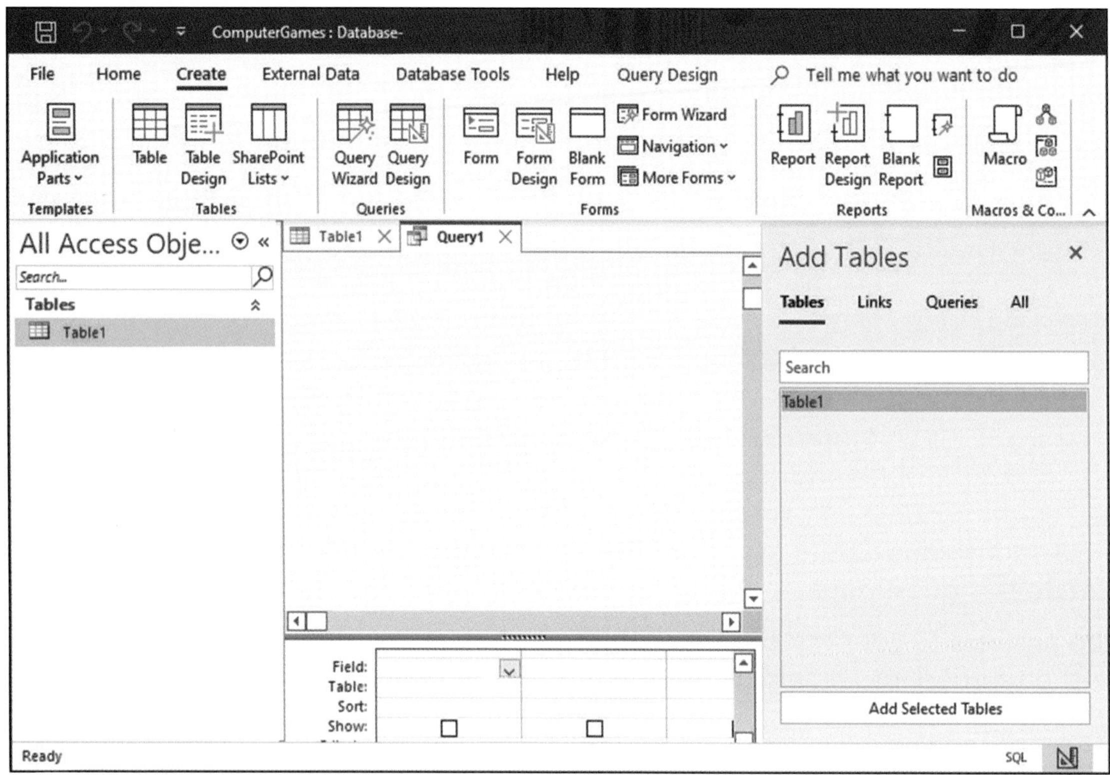

Figure 2.17: Query tab in 'Design View'

We are going to create a query that shows us all the simulation games in the database.

- Double click the table that you want to search from the 'Add Tables' panel on the right. This should display a list of the fields from the table in the middle of the screen.
- Select the fields that you need to use in the query. You will need to choose:
  - the fields that you want to use in the query
  - the fields that you want displayed in the result of the query.

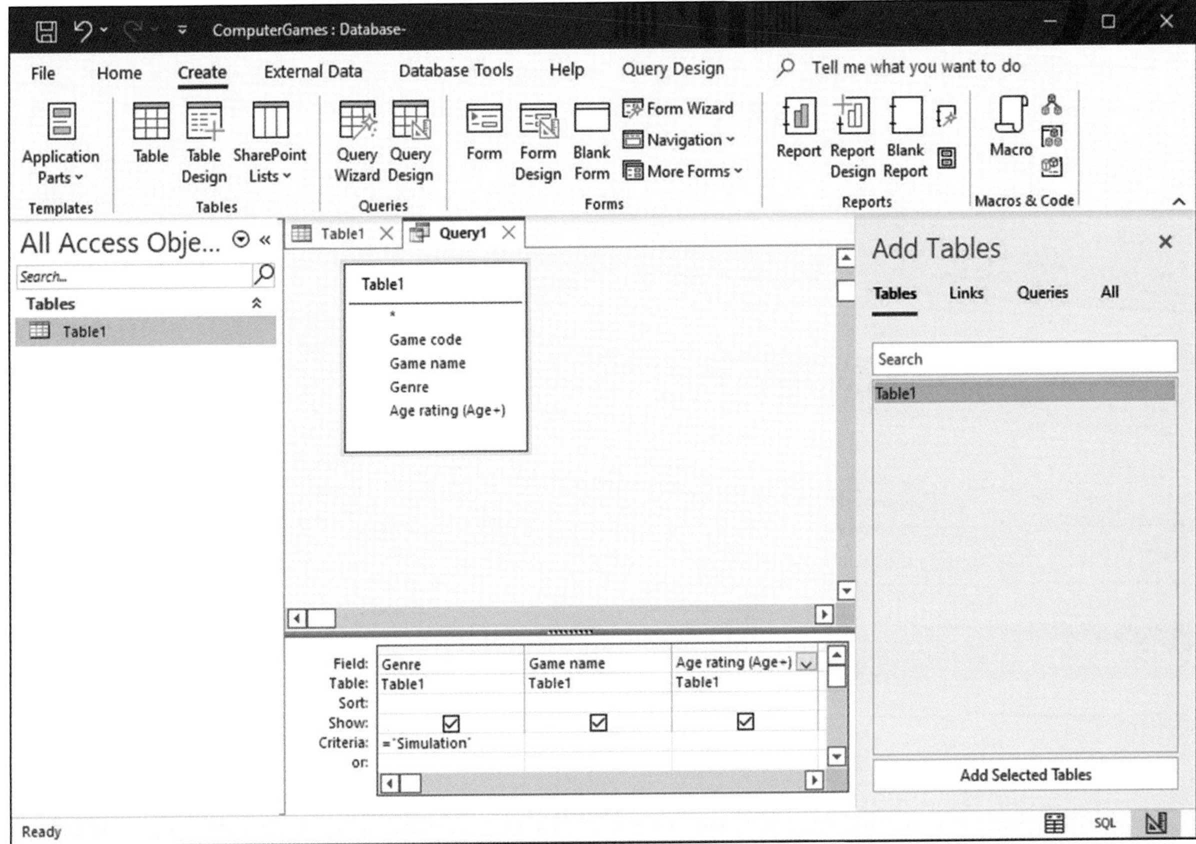

Figure 2.18: Query tab in 'Design View' with criteria entered

In the database in Figure 2.18, we have chosen to use the Genre field in the query, and the Game name and Age rating to be displayed as the result. You can either select these by double clicking on the field name in the list, or you can use the drop-down box in the table structure at the bottom of the screen.

- Add the criteria for the query in the criteria row at the bottom of the screen. Because we are searching for a word rather than a number, we need to put the criteria in double quotation marks, like this: "Simulation".
- Make sure to have the 'Show' box ticked for all the fields where you want the data to appear.

There are two ways to see the result of your query. You can change from 'Design View' to 'Datasheet View' by clicking the 'View' button in the top-left corner of the 'Home' tab. Or you can select 'Run' next to the 'View' button. You will now see all the data in the table that meets your search criteria.

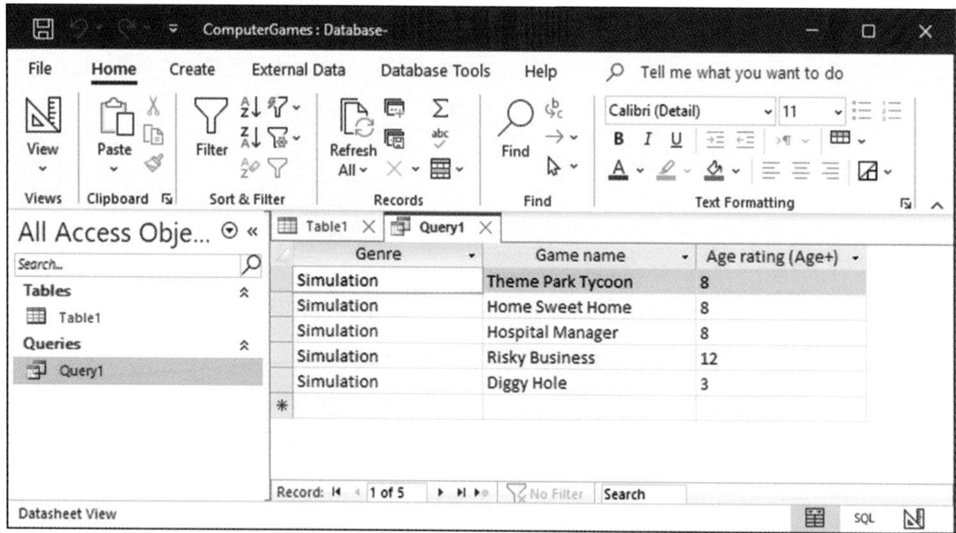

Figure 2.19: Query tab in 'Datasheet View', showing results

Practical task 2.6

You will need: a desktop computer, laptop or tablet with source file **2.3_computer_games.accdb**

Open the file 2.3_computer_games.accdb. You are going to create a query to find out which games in the database have an age rating for children over 10 years of age. The criteria that you will need to create this query is '>10' for the Age rating field.

Use the instructions given above to create a query.

1 Make all the fields appear in the query.
2 Add the criteria to the Age rating field.
3 View the results of the query.

Self-assessment

Look at the answer section or ask your teacher to tell you what the query results should be.

- Did you get the same result from your query?
- If you did, why do you think these are the only records that appear?
- If you didn't, can you see where you may have done something incorrect? Follow the instructions again carefully to check your query design is correct. Make sure that you have put the correct criteria in the criteria row.

To write this query on a piece of paper, you would write:

Age > 10

as it is the Age field that you are searching, and you want to know which games are for children over 10.

Unplugged activity 2.5

You will need: a pen and paper

Write down the field and the criteria for games in the computer games database that are:

- suitable for children under the age of 5
- suitable for children aged 8 or over
- puzzle games.

Practical task 2.7

You will need: a desktop computer, laptop or tablet with source file **2.3_computer_games.accdb**

Now create three queries using the criteria from Unplugged activity 2.5
Create separate queries for:

- games for children under 5
- games for children aged 8 or over
- puzzle games.

Peer-assessment

Working with a partner, look at the answer section or ask your teacher to tell you what the results should be for each query. Did you both get the same results from your queries?

If you did, why do you think these are the only records that appear?

If you didn't, can you see where you may have done something incorrect? Follow the instructions again carefully to check your query design is correct. Make sure that you have put the correct criteria in the criteria row and that you have included double quotation marks where you need to.

Do you and your partner find it easier and quicker to create queries now than when you started learning how to do it? Why or why not?

Show on your face how you feel about creating queries now. A happy face means you are confident and can even try out new types of query. A sad face means you need more help.

You have now learnt to create a query using greater than (>), less than (<) and equal to (=) applied to numbers. You can also use these symbols with letters to create criteria.

Using < and > with letters

You can use < and > when you are using letters too. You already know what alphabetical order is. The English language uses the Roman alphabet. Alphabetical order is:

A B C D E F G H I J K L M N O P Q R S T U V W X Y Z

Using < in a query will take you nearer to the beginning of the alphabet (A, B, C), and using > in a query will take you towards the end of the alphabet (X, Y, Z).

Remember: when you are searching using letters, you need to put double quotation marks around the letter, letters or words you are searching for.

For example, let's use the database with players' names.

Player number	Player name	Game name	Age rating	Genre
1	Mohammed Khan	Bill & Betty	12+	2D platform
2	Charlie Jones	Build Blocks	3+	arcade
3	Anisa Nababan	Ping Pong	3+	arcade
4	Mohammed Khan	Bill & Betty	12+	2D platform
5	Carla Estevez	Ping Pong	3+	arcade

Table 2.16: Database of computer games and players

The query, Player name < "D", would produce the results in Table 2.17.

Player number	Player Name	Game Name	Age rating	Genre
2	Charlie Jones	Build Blocks	3+	arcade
3	Anisa Nababan	Ping Pong	3+	arcade
5	Carla Estevez	Ping Pong	3+	arcade

Table 2.17: Results from query Player name < "D"

Because Charlie, Anisa and Carla's Player Name entry all start with letters that come *before* D.

Practical task 2.8

You will need: a desktop computer, laptop or tablet with source file **2.3_computer_games.accdb**

In the file 2.3_computer_games.accdb, you are going to create a query to find out which games have a name that begins with a letter that appears after Q in the alphabet.

Looking at the example in Practical task 2.7, can you work out what criteria you will need to use to create this query, and in which field?

Remember, the letter Q needs to be in quotation marks so that the database software will recognise it as text and not a number.

Now create your query.

1 Select the Game name field only to appear in the query.
2 Add the criteria.
3 View the results of the query.

You should see these eight records in the result:

Super Adventurer
The Great Race
Theme Park Tycoon
Work It Out
Train Ride
Risky Business
Word Crush
Zoomer

Table 2.18: Results for practical task

You should only see the names of the games in your results. To do this, make sure that you have only added the Game name field to the query design, or untick the show box for the other fields if you have added those.

Questions 2.4

1 What is a primary key?

2 What is the primary key in the computer games database?

3 Why is the Genre field not appropriate to be set as the primary key?

4 Why is the Game name field not appropriate to be set as the primary key?

5 Create a query to find out which games have a name that begins with one of the first three letters of the alphabet. Display the Game name field only.

   a Which results are in your query?

   b What criteria did you use for your query?

Practical task 2.9

You will need: a desktop computer, laptop or tablet with database software

Your head teacher has asked you to create a database about the people in your class.

Your first task is to collect some data about ten students in your class. You need to get:

- their name
- their age
- their height
- their eye colour
- number of pets.

In pairs, create a database that has a record for each of the students. If you do not know how to do this, ask your teacher to demonstrate how to create a table.

Are any fields in your database suitable to be the primary key? If not, you will need to make sure that you add a field that can be used as a primary key and set this as the primary key in the database software. Some database software, such as Microsoft Access, automatically adds a primary key field when you create a new database.

The head teacher wants you to create queries to find out:

- which students in the class are over 11 years old
- which students in the class have a height of 1.45 metres or less
- which students in the class have an eye colour that begins with the letters A to C
- which students in the class have two or more pets
- which students in the class have no pets.

Continued

Peer-assessment

Compare your query results with a partner's and see if they match. If you have got different results for any queries on each other's databases, discuss how you designed the query and work out where either of you may have been incorrect.

Summary checklist

- [ ] I can explain what is meant by a primary key.
- [ ] I can choose an appropriate field in a database to be the primary key.
- [ ] I can set a field in database software as the primary key.
- [ ] I can create a query to search a database using the criteria for 'greater than'.
- [ ] I can create a query to search a database using the criteria for 'less than'.
- [ ] I can create a query to search a database using the criteria for 'equal to'.

2.4 Data collection

In this topic you will:

- understand what an effective data capture form is
- understand the main mistakes that can be made when creating a data capture form
- understand what problems will occur if mistakes are made on a data capture form
- analyse an example of a data capture form to see what is effective and not effective about the form
- improve a data collection form that is not effective to make it more effective.

Key words

data capture form

effective

personal data

Getting started

What do you already know?

- You have most likely come across data capture forms of some kind. Forms are used to collect data in all sorts of areas of life, usually for a specific reason. Examples include:
  - signing up for a store loyalty card
  - taking out a subscription service for a product you use often
  - taking part in market research for a company whose products you buy, to help them understand their customers.
- There are many advantages and disadvantages to using a data capture form when collecting data.

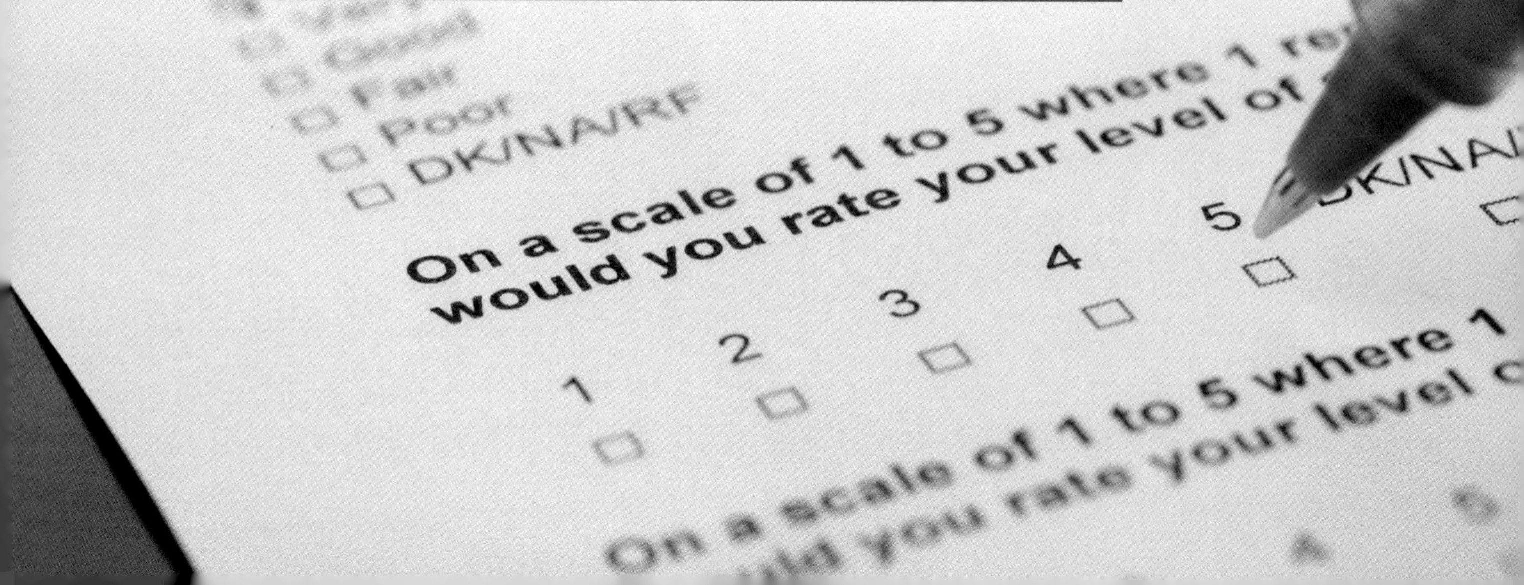

Continued

Now try this!

Imagine you are the owner of a cake shop. You want to find out a bit more information about the kind of cakes that your customers like. You would like to use a data capture form to get this information. Make a list of the advantages and disadvantages of using a data capture form to collect this data.

Figure 2.20: There is a lot of data in the world!

Did you know?

Every day we create approximately 2.5 quintillion bytes of data. This is a massive amount of data. Also, the volume of data we create doubles every two years. That's an *enormous* amount of data!

What makes a good data capture form?

We often find that we need to fill in forms with details about ourselves. Adults usually do this more than children, but you have probably filled in a form at some point.

Unplugged activity 2.6

You will need: a pen and paper

Think of a time when you completed a form. Talk with your partner about the form you filled in and write down answers to the following questions.

- Was it easy to fill in?
- Did you know what you needed to write in each section or how to answer each question? If not, why not?
- Write down some things that were good about the form and some things that weren't so good.

A **data capture form** is a form that is designed to collect data from a person. A data capture form needs to be **effective**. Something is effective if it is good at doing its job. The job of a data capture form is to collect useful, correct data from the person who is filling it in. But it is easy to make mistakes when creating a form, which can create problems with the data that is captured.

Some of the mistakes you might make when creating a data capture form are shown in Table 2.19.

When using data capture forms, you might need to ask for people's **personal data**. Personal data is any information that helps to identify a particular person, for example their name, address, phone number, date of birth or identification number. Many countries have laws that make sure organisations do not misuse personal data they collect and only collect it when they really need to. Make sure all the questions on your form are asking for information you actually need.

Therefore, important things to think of when creating an effective data capture form are:

- Is it clear what each question is asking?
- Is it clear what format the answer should be in?
- Are the spaces for written answers an appropriate size?
- Is it easy to see all the questions?
- Are the questions in an order that makes sense?
- Are all the questions asking for information I really need?

Mistake	Example	Problem it may cause
Questions are not asked in a logical order.	1 Select your top three pizza flavours from the list. (List of options...) 2 Do you like pizza?	People filling in the form might get confused or frustrated. If the form is confusing enough, this might make people select answers they would not usually give, leading to incorrect data being captured.
It is unclear how the answer should be given.	Date of birth:	If the answer to a question needs to be in a certain format, you need to say so in the question. Otherwise, the response may not be written in the way you want, and this could cause problems in the database, especially when searching. In the example, the question does not give a format for how date of birth should be written (for example DD/MM/YYYY). People from different countries give their date of birth in different ways. For example: • 21/11/2010 • 11/21/10 • 21st November, 2010 If all these formats end up in a database and then we search for people who are born on 02/01/2011, the results could list: • someone born on 2nd January, 2011, and • someone born on 1st February, 2011. If possible, always give answer options for people to select or boxes to enter specific types of data into, instead of letting people write their answer however they like. This helps to avoid errors.

(Continued)

Mistake	Example	Problem it may cause
The meaning of the question is unclear.	How many times do you use a phone?	Different people will think the question is asking different things, so not everyone will be answering the question you meant to ask. This example might mean 'How many times per day do you make a phone call?', 'How many times per day do you use any kind of phone for any purpose?' or 'How many times per month do you use your mobile phone for any purpose?'
The space given for the information is too small.	Address	In the example given, there is only one short line to write a person's address. Not giving enough space can cause problems, for example: • The answer could be squashed into the space, making it unclear to read. • The person might write their address somewhere else on the form and you will not see it. • The person might just write a small part of their address and not all of it.
The questions are not all clearly visible.	One single question on the back of the form when there isn't any text telling the person to turn the page.	If a question will not be easily seen, the person filling in the form may miss it. This could cause important information to be left out.
A valid answer option is left out of a list of multiple-choice options.	How many times a month do you eat pizza? • More than 10 times • 5–9 times • 2–4 times • Once	If all the possible answer options are not provided for a multiple-choice question, the person answering might skip that question because they cannot see any options they can tick. In the example, there is no option for someone who never eats pizza. Someone in this situation might skip the question, write their own extra answer or select one of the given options even though it is not true. All of these would cause problems when putting the data into a database and then analysing it.

Table 2.19: Mistakes made when creating a data capture form

Unplugged activity 2.7

You will need: a pen and paper

During the school holidays, Zara and her brothers join in an activity week that their school holds. They will be having lunch at the school. This is the form that their parents are asked to fill in.

ACTIVITY WEEK

Name: ....

Address: ....

Telephone number: ....

Date of birth: .... Age: ....

Allergies? ....

Number of children:

1 ☐
2 ☐
3 ☐

Figure 2.21: Activity week form

Zara's parents need to fill in the form before the activity week. Think about the effectiveness of this data collection form.

Continued

Write down two things that you think are good about the form. Share the two things you thought about with a partner.

- Did you think about the same two things?
- Do you agree the two things your partner thought of are good too?

Zara talks to Sofia about whether this was an effective form. They think about the problems that their parents might have when filling in this form.

Imagine you are having to fill in the form for your child. Would you know what to write for each section? Look carefully at how effective each request for information is. Can you see any issues? Think about the issues you can see, then share them with your partner.

How many more than Sofia can you think of?

How did you decide what would be and would not be effective?

For example, you may have asked yourself the question 'Is this question clearly written?'

Write two things down that you thought about.

Activity 2.5

You will need: a desktop computer, laptop or tablet with word-processing software or internet access for Google forms

You have discussed with your partner about what is effective and what is not effective about the data capture form. You are now going to improve the data capture form to make it better, based on what you discussed.

Using word-processing software or Google forms, create an improved version of the data capture form. Look at the information in Table 2.19 if you need help.

Continued

Peer-assessment

Ask a partner to imagine they are Zara's parent and to fill in your new form.

Explain to your partner what you have done to make the data capture form better. Tell them why you think your improvements make the form more effective.

Ask your partner:

- How did they feel about filling in your form?
- What did they find easy to fill in?
- Were there any parts that they still found difficult to fill in? If so, talk about how you could improve that area even further.

Stay safe!

Personal data such as your name, date of birth and address must be kept safe. Always be very careful who you give this information to. Personal data is very valuable, so people may try to trick you into giving it to them. If you are not sure whether you can trust a request for personal data, ask a parent or teacher.

Questions 2.5

1 What is a data capture form used for?

2 What are the important things to think about when creating a data capture form?

Summary checklist

- [ ] I can explain what an effective data capture form is.
- [ ] I can explain some common issues with data capture forms.
- [ ] I can analyse a data capture form to point out what is effective and what is not effective about the form.
- [ ] I can improve a data collection form that is not effective to make it more effective.

Project: Tennis club

Arun's school has decided to set up a tennis club and Farah, the school administrator, has asked if Arun and his friends would like to be in charge of running the club. The teachers and tennis coaches all think this is a good idea.

Task 1 Member fees spreadsheet

To take part in this club, the school pupils need to register as members and pay a subscription fee.

Arun has created the file **2.4_member_fees.xlsx**. This file contains the names of all the members and whether they have or have not yet paid their subscription fee.

Arun wants to be able to easily see who has not paid their subscription fee so that he can contact them. He needs to add some conditional formatting to the spreadsheet so that he can easily see who these members are when he opens the file.

Apply the conditional formatting to this file so that Arun can see who he needs to contact.

Continued

Task 2 Tournament model spreadsheet

Marcus wants the club to run a tennis tournament for charity. He has created a model in the file 2.5_tournament_model.xlsx that will allow the earnings and costs to be modelled for the event.

Marcus and Arun need to present the idea to the school, but they need to give the model to Farah first. Farah doesn't know what the model is for or how to use it. She wants Marcus and Arun to create a short guide explaining the purpose of the model and how to use it.

You can do this in whatever way you want to – for example, a presentation, a leaflet or a video.

Task 3 Club members database

Arun has a database of all the members' details for the club in the file 2.6_club_members.accdb. Marcus wants to create a list of people to play in different matches for the tournament.

For stages 7 to 9, students will play matches against others in their own year group. Create a query to provide a list that shows Marcus who will be in these three groups:

- members in Stage 7
- members in Stage 8
- members in Stage 9.

There will be two more groups for students in Stage 10 and above, but this time the students will be grouped by gender, not Stage. Create another query to provide this list for Marcus. It should show:

- female members in Stage 10 or above
- male members in Stage 10 or above.

Check your progress 2

1 State the purpose of conditional formatting. **[1]**

2 State what is meant by a condition in conditional formatting. **[1]**

3 A company has the following spreadsheet:

	A	B	C	D	E	F	G	H	I
1									
2	Indoor bookings		0			Maximum bookings		150	
3	Outdoor bookings		0						
4									
5	Total bookings		0						
6									

The company has applied conditional formatting to the spreadsheet.

a Choose the rule that would be applied to make the Total bookings value green if it is equal to the Maximum bookings value. Select the correct answer.

A If C5 = H2 then C5 is formatted green

B If C5 = H2 then H2 is formatted green

C If H2 = H2 then C5 is formatted green

D If C5 = C5 then H2 is formatted green **[1]**

b Choose the rule that would be applied to make the Total bookings value red if it is more than the Maximum bookings value. Select the correct answer.

A If C5 < H2 then C5 is formatted red

B If C5 > H2 then H2 is formatted red

C If C5 < H2 then H2 is formatted red

D If C5 > H2 then C5 is formatted red **[1]**

4 State what is meant by a computer model. **[1]**

5 Give the purpose of a simulator. **[1]**

6 Give *two* ways that a simulator could be used by an astronaut. **[2]**

7 A retailer has the following database:

Product ID	Product name	Colour	Supplier	Number in stock
P001	ballpoint pen	black	Pavithra Pens	25
P002	ballpoint pen	blue	Pavithra Pens	22
P003	ballpoint pen	red	Pavithra Pens	5
P004	ballpoint pen	green	Pavithra Pens	7
P005	HB pencil	n/a	Drawing Manufacturers	15
P006	eraser	white	Drawing Manufacturers	27
P007	ruler 15 cm	transparent	We Measure	12

a Identify which field in the database would be most appropriate as the primary key. Justify your choice. **[2]**

b The retailer wants a list of all the products that have fewer than 10 items in stock. Give the name of the field and the criteria that would need to be entered for that field to create a query to produce this list. **[2]**

c The retailer wants a list of all the products that have 20 or more items in stock. Give the name of the field and the criteria that would need to be entered for that field to create a query to produce this list. **[2]**

d The retailer wants a list of all the products that have a product name that begins with a letter in the second half of the alphabet (N–Z). Give the name of the field and the criteria that would need to be entered for that field to create a query to produce this list. **[2]**

3 Networks and digital communication

3.1 Accessing websites

In this topic you will:

- understand what a uniform resource locator (URL) is
- learn about the structure of a URL
- understand what an internet protocol (IP) address is
- learn about the role of a domain name server (DNS)
- understand how a DNS is used to find the matching IP address for a URL
- understand how a website is accessed when a user types a URL into a web browser
- learn how to check whether a website is secure.

Key words

digital certificate

domain name

domain name server (DNS)

encrypted

hypertext transfer protocol secure (https)

IP address (internet protocol address)

path

protocol

URL (uniform resource locator)

web browser

web server

Getting started

What do you already know?

- Devices such as computers, tablets and phones can all be connected to each other to create a network. Some networks have a central computer called a server.
- The largest computer network created is the internet. The internet is used to send data all over the world.

Continued

- A server is a piece of network hardware. It can be used to store data and perform one or more tasks. A server:

  1 receives a request from another computer in the network

  2 processes the request

  3 then finds the result.

  The server will either send the result back to the same computer, or it will send the result on to another computer.

- Websites are made up of data files that are stored on a server. We access these files using the internet.
- All devices on a network have an IP address. The IP address tells the network where data should be sent to – a bit like the address of your home that tells the postal workers where you live.

Now try this!

You are going to play a game of 'What am I?'

Your partner will write a key word or phrase about this topic on a sticky note. They will then stick the note to your forehead and you must guess what they have written.

1 Your teacher will give you a sticky note. Write down a key word or phrase that you can remember from your previous learning about networks. Do not let anyone else see what you wrote down.

2 Stick your sticky note to your partner's forehead. Your partner will stick their sticky note to your forehead. Make sure that your partner does not see what is on the note.

Continued

Whoever is oldest goes first. Ask questions about what is written on the sticky note on your head. Your partner can only answer 'yes' or 'no'. For example, Arun has 'server' written on his forehead, so he could ask:

- Is it a computer? Yes
- Is it a computer involved in the internet? Yes
- Is it a client? No
- Is it a server? Yes!

You have ten questions before you need to guess what is written on the note on your head.

Once you have done this, find another partner to switch your sticky notes with and play the game a second time.

What is a URL?

The proper name for a website address is a **uniform resource locator**, or **URL** for short. When you want to look at a web page, you open a **web browser** (software that displays web pages on your computer) and type a URL into the address bar. If you don't know which URL you need, you can search for the right one using a search engine.

A URL is made up of three main parts, these are:

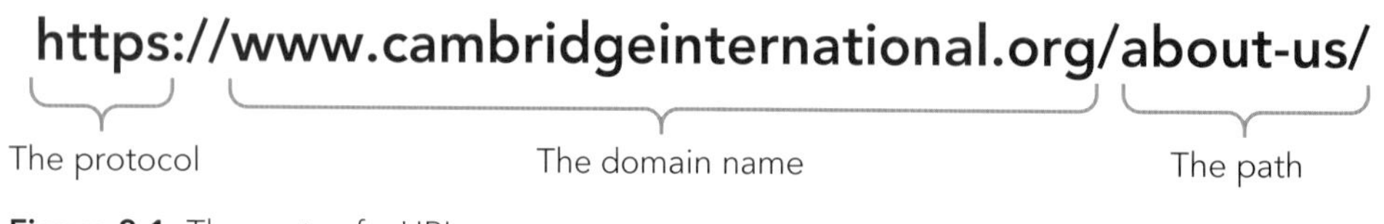

Figure 3.1: The parts of a URL

The protocol

The **protocol** is the first part of the URL. In computing, a protocol is the set of rules that computers use to communicate with each other. It is a bit like making sure that the computers are speaking the same language so that they understand each other.

In the example in Figure 3.1, the protocol is **https**. This is short for **hypertext transfer protocol secure**. This is used to send data between your computer and the **web server**, which is the computer where the website data is stored. You will learn more about the https protocol later in this topic.

The domain name

The **domain name** is the middle part of the URL. Each website has a unique domain name. It is often known as the website address. A domain name is the name of the web server that you type into a web browser's address bar to find the website. It is a text-based address.

In the example in Figure 3.1, the domain name is *www.cambridgeinternational.org*. This will tell the web server for the website of the Cambridge International webpage.

The path

The **path** is the last part of the URL. This will tell the computer which web page you want to look at on the website.

The path is the name of the file where the data for that particular web page is stored.

In the example in Figure 3.1, the path (or the webpage) *about-us* takes you to the webpage that is about the organisation.

What is an IP address?

An **IP address** is short for internet protocol address. An IP address is a label made up of numbers. Each device on a network has a unique label.

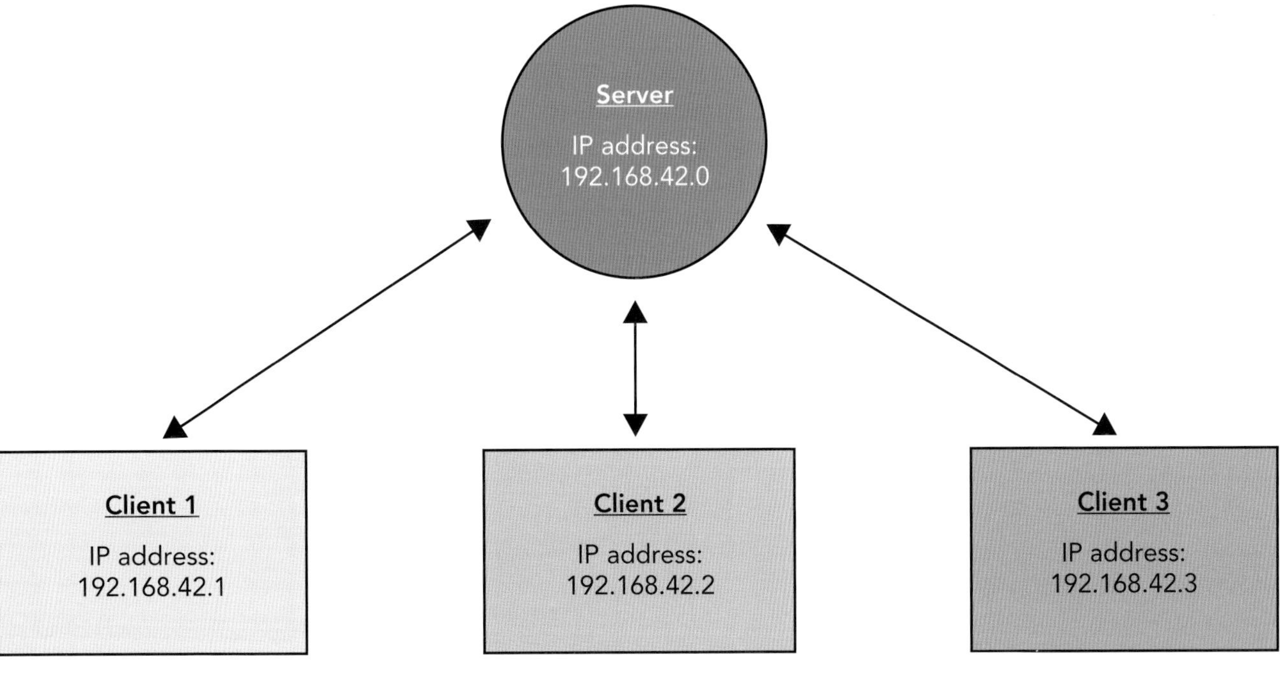

Figure 3.2: A network with four devices showing IP addresses

The relationship between URLs and IP addresses

Every URL has a matching IP address.

One way of thinking about the relationship between IP addresses and URLs is to think about how a phone stores people's phone numbers. Each number is stored with the person's name. For example:

Pedro 2691 2345

On most phones, you can find 'Pedro' and press dial, which will call your friend Pedro. You don't have to type in the whole phone number. However, you can also dial 2691 2345 to phone Pedro.

Figure 3.3: Calling a friend

In a similar way, the data for a website is stored on a web server. Each website has a URL (a name) and each web server has an IP address (a number). For example, the IP address for the website *www.cambridgeinternational.org* is 192.149.119.103.

However, an IP address is more like the number for a family's landline phone. If you dial it, any member of the family might pick up! This is because most web servers store lots of websites, not just one.

Did you know?

You can sometimes type the IP address of a website into your browser's address bar and it will open the website. However, this often doesn't work because either it is not clear which site at the IP address you want, or the security information for the site is not linked to the IP address, so you get a security warning. That's why we need domain names.

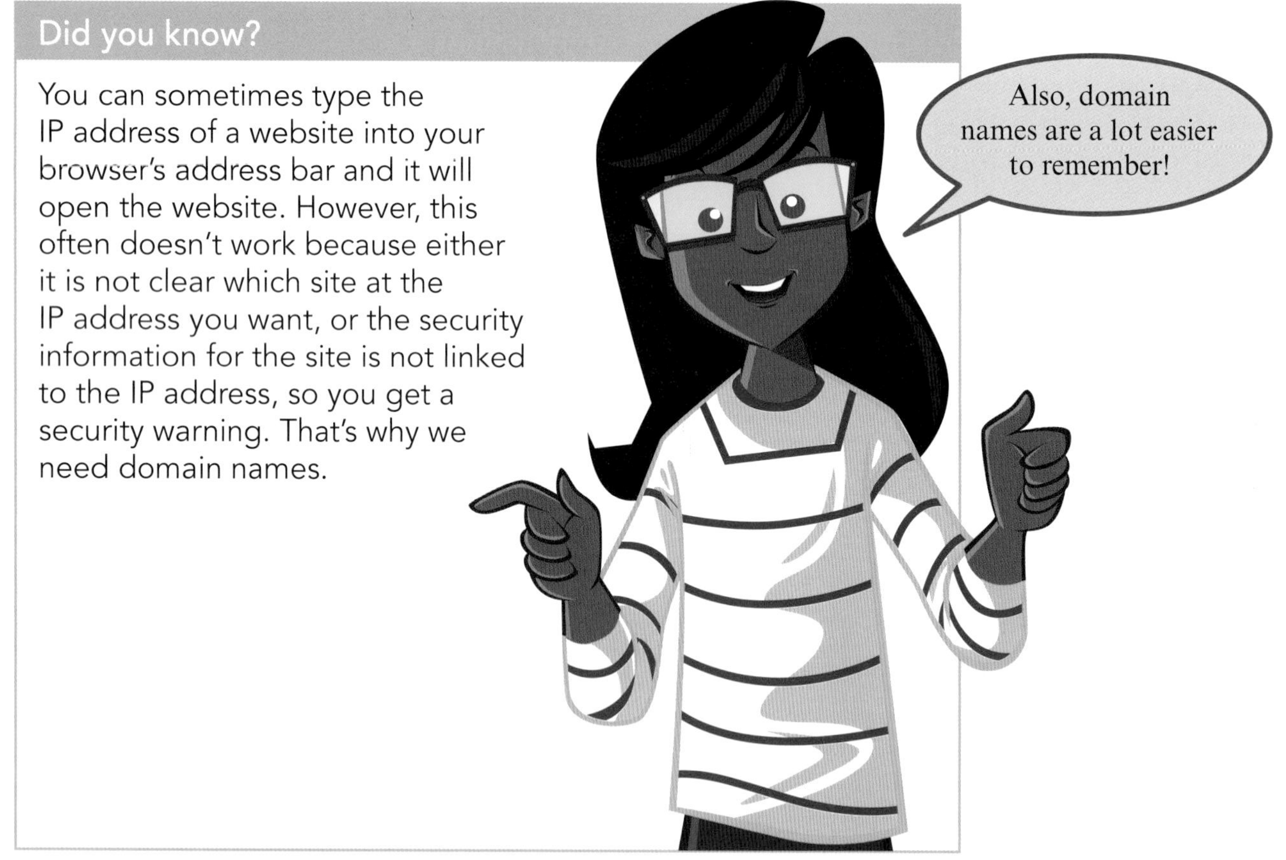

Questions 3.1

1 What do you call the piece of software that is used to display web pages?
2 How many parts does a URL have?
3 Which part of the URL is the file name for the web page?
4 Which part of the URL shows the rules the website uses for transmitting data?
5 What is a domain name?

What is a domain name server (DNS)?

To match the IP address to the URL, you need to use a **domain name server (DNS)**. A DNS is a special kind of server that stores a database of the domain name parts of URLs and their matching IP addresses. There are hundreds of DNSs that store all the domain names that have ever been created and their IP addresses.

How does a DNS work?

This is what happens when you search for a website:

1 You type a URL into a web browser.
2 The web browser sends the domain name section of the URL to the DNS.
3 The DNS searches through the database that is stored on the server to see if the domain name is in the database.
4 It will find the IP address that matches the domain name and sends the IP address back to your web browser.
5 When the web browser receives this IP address, it then sends a request to the web server at that IP address to request the data for the website stored on the web server.

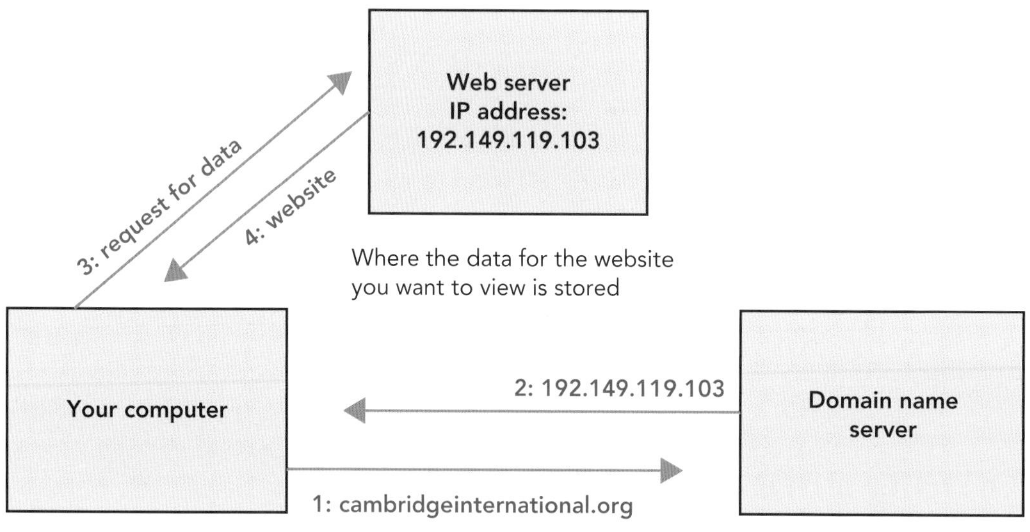

Figure 3.4: Data transfer when looking up a website

There are a lot of DNS all over the world. If the first DNS cannot find the domain name on its database, it will send the request to the next DNS to see if it can find it. This will keep happening until the domain name and matching IP address are found.

If the domain name is never found, then the final DNS that is searched will send a message back to the web browser stating that the website does not exist. This error message is called a 404 error.

Unplugged activity 3.1

You will need: some pens and paper, sticky tape, a clear space to move around in, hats (optional)

You and your classmates are going to act out the process shown in Figure 3.4.

Choose one student (or a small group of students) to be the computer requesting a website, one to be the DNS and one to be the web server. Any number of students can be 'the internet', running between the computers carrying data, or passing data along a line of students. Also, choose a narrator to say out loud what is going on as it happens and what needs to happen next.

Before you begin:

- Write labels on pieces of paper and stick them to hats (or another item of clothing) that the requesting computer, DNS and web server will wear to show who they are.
- Give the requesting computer a blank piece of paper and a pen so that they can write down the domain name of the website they want to see (to send to the DNS) and a request for data (to send to the web server).
- Write some pretend domain names and matching IP addresses on several pieces of paper and give them to the DNS to hold. When the DNS receives the domain name request, they should look through the pieces of paper to find the matching IP address and send it back to the computer.
- Draw a picture that looks like a website's home page or print out a screenshot of a website and give it to the web server (to send to the requesting computer).

Now get into the right places in the room and act out the process. It might take a few goes to get it right! Don't forget to say out loud what is going on as it happens.

Peer-assessment

Discuss as a class how you all did.

- Did everyone do what they were supposed to do?
- What worked well?
- Were there any aspects of the process that were hard to act out? If so, why?
- Were there any 404 errors?
- What would you do differently next time?
- Give yourselves a score of 1 out of 10 for your performance (1 is the lowest and 10 is the highest).

Questions 3.2

1 What is stored on a DNS?

2 Which software sends a request to the DNS?

3 What happens when the domain name cannot be found on any DNS?

How to check that a website is secure

A website needs to be secure so that the information you type into it is kept safe. Imagine you are buying your favourite treat from a website. You will want to know that your payment details are not going to be stolen or misused.

If the website is secure, your payment details should be safe. There are three main ways to check whether a website is secure. These are:

- look at the protocol
- look for the padlock symbol
- check to see if the website has a digital certificate.

Look at the protocol

If the website has the protocol *https*, then it is a secure website. If it is not a secure website, it will have the protocol *http*. The 's' stands for secure. This means that the data that is sent between your computer and the web server will be **encrypted**.

When data is encrypted, it is scrambled into a secret code. This code will make the data meaningless so it is safe to send. The web server will have a special key called a cipher, which will enable it to turn the code back into the original message. You will learn more about encryption and ciphers in Topic 3.3.

Look for the padlock symbol

Different web browsers have slightly different ways of showing you whether a website is secure, but all good browsers make this information clear. In most browsers, if you look at the left side of the address bar you should see a padlock symbol. If the website is secure the padlock will look like it is locked (closed). If the website is not secure there might be an unlocked padlock symbol or a warning triangle with the message 'Not secure'.

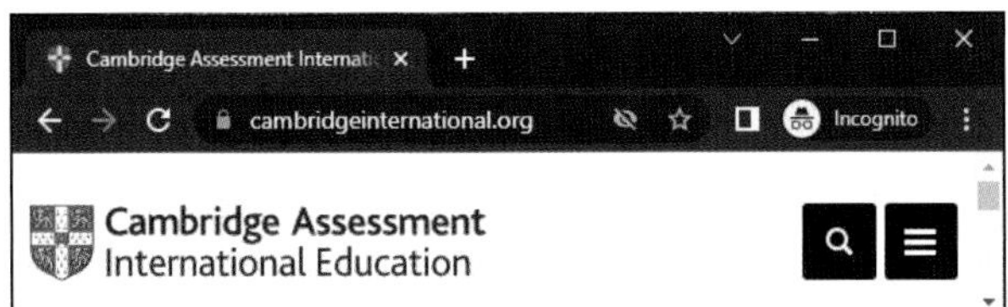

Figure 3.5: Secure website with locked padlock

Check to see if the website has a digital certificate

The owner of a website can request a special kind of **digital certificate** to show that the website is secure. The web browser will check to see if the digital certificate for a website is valid. You can view the result of this check by clicking on the padlock symbol. If the digital certificate is valid, you can choose to view it.

Figure 3.6: Cambridge International website's digital certificate

Stay safe!

Always check that a website is secure before submitting your personal details. These are things like your name, address, date of birth or payment details. If a connection is not secure and you enter personal information, there is more chance of your data being stolen or misused. Only use well-known sites that you and the adults around you trust.

Activity 3.1

You will need: a desktop computer, laptop or tablet with internet access and at least two different web browsers

You are going to find out how different web browsers show whether a website is secure or not. Some common web browsers are:

- Chrome
- Edge
- Firefox
- Opera
- Safari.

Your teacher will tell you which of these are installed on the device you are using, or you can find out by searching for them in the search bar on the device's desktop or apps menu.

Open one of the browsers and search for a well-known organisation – it could be a media or news company, a charity, a brand of clothing or a shopping website. Visit the official site of one of these organisations and look for the three signs the website is secure.

1. Is the website secure?
2. How does this browser display the protocol and padlock?
3. If the site is secure, can you work out how to view the digital security certificate?
4. If you have managed to find an insecure site (they can be hard to find!), visit a secure one and look at how the symbols in the address bar change.

   Now use a different browser and do the same again.
5. Are there any differences in the ways this browser shows a website's security level, compared with the first browser?

If the computer has more than two browsers installed, or you have access to a tablet device, see if you can find the three signs of website security on there too.

Summary checklist

- [ ] I can explain what a URL is.
- [ ] I can identify the three different parts of a URL.
- [ ] I can explain what an IP address is.
- [ ] I understand the role of a domain name server and know that it stores a database of domain names and their matching IP addresses.
- [ ] I can explain the process of how the web browser, the DNS and the web server are used to obtain the data for websites.
- [ ] I can explain three ways that I can check whether a website is secure.

3.2 Types of network

In this topic you will:

- learn about some of the characteristics of a wi-fi network
- know the different frequencies available on a wi-fi network, including their different ranges and speeds
- learn about some of the characteristics of a Bluetooth Wireless Technology network, including how devices are paired
- know the range and speed of a Bluetooth Wireless Technology network
- learn about the characteristics of a cellular network, including the use of cells and base stations
- understand the difference between 3G, 4G and 5G cellular networks.

Key words

base station

Bluetooth Wireless Technology network

cell

cellular network (mobile network)

cycle

frequency

pairing

router

wi-fi network

wireless access point (WAP)

wireless network interface card (WNIC)

Getting started

What do you already know?

- Devices can be connected using a wired or wireless connection. A wired network uses cables to connect devices to each other. A wireless connection uses radio waves.
- A type of wired connection is Ethernet. Ethernet is a secure, low cost, high-speed connection.
- Two types of wireless connection are wi-fi and a cellular network. They both transmit data using radio waves instead of wires or cables.

Continued

Now try this!

A company wants to create a network to connect the devices in their office so they can easily share data.

You are the IT manager, and you need to decide whether to create a wired network or a wireless network. Draw a diagram of both networks. Show the differences between a wired network that uses Ethernet and a wireless network that uses wi-fi.

Remember to think about how many devices you need for your diagram and what type of devices they are.

Network types

A network is a group of devices that are all connected to each other. Devices could be computers, printers, phones, tablets or any other device capable of sending or receiving data. Networks can also be connected to other networks. Networks allow us to share resources, exchange files or communicate with other people.

There are different ways of connecting devices together on a network. You can connect to a network by using cables, or you can connect by using wireless technology. On a wireless network, devices communicate using radio waves.

Radio waves

Radio waves are a type of electromagnetic radiation. This radiation moves up and down like ripples on a pond. The whole of a wave from the top of one wave to the top of the next is called a **cycle**. The wavelength is the distance between the top of each wave. It is the distance a wave takes to complete one cycle.

The **frequency** of a radio wave is how many cycles there are per second. The more cycles there are in a second, the higher the frequency.

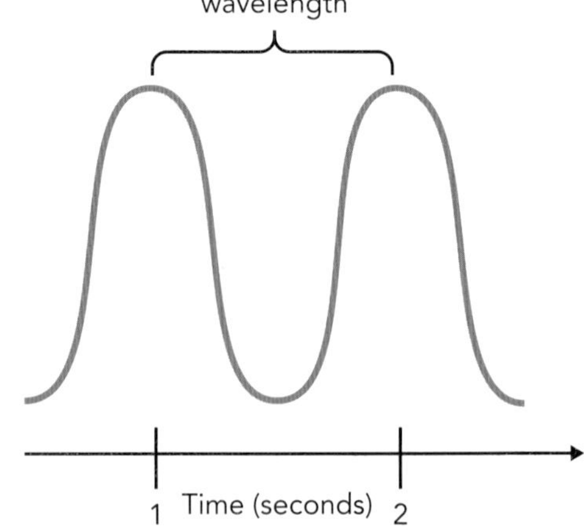

Figure 3.7: Wavelength

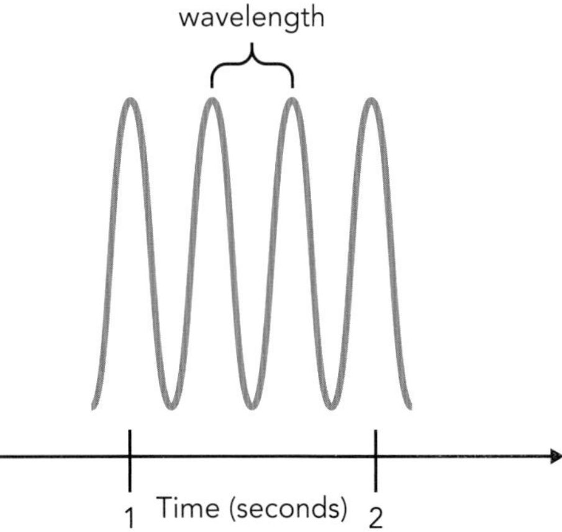

Figure 3.8: Higher frequency wavelength

Most radio waves have a frequency that is measured in gigahertz (GHz). 1 hertz means 1 cycle per second. 1 GHz is 1 billion (1 000 000 000) cycles per second.

There are three types of wireless technology you can use:

- wi-fi
- Bluetooth Wireless Technology
- cellular networks.

Wi-fi networks

A **wi-fi network** is a type of wireless network that uses radio waves to connect devices together. Each device is normally connected to a **wireless access point (WAP)**. A WAP is a small hardware device that allows other devices to connect wirelessly using radio waves to a wired network.

In most homes, the WAP is inside a **router**. A router is a hardware device that connects a network to the internet. If you want to connect a device to the wi-fi network, the device needs to have a piece of hardware called a **wireless network interface card (or controller) (WNIC)**. The WNIC allows the device to communicate over a wireless network.

Figure 3.9: Wireless network interface card (WNIC)

The radio waves that transmit data in a wireless network come from the WAP. The WNIC in your device will receive these radio waves and use them to connect to the network. The WNIC will then transmit data back to the WAP by sending out more radio waves.

The average range of a wireless network from the WAP is 50 metres (this means a device can be up to 50 metres away from the WAP and still be connected to the network). Wi-fi networks can transmit data at speeds of up to 1300 megabits per second (Mbps), although the average speed is about 200 Mbps.

Figure 3.10: Wireless router

Activity 3.2

You will need: a pen and paper, a desktop computer, laptop or tablet with word-processing software and internet access

The speed of the transmission of data when using wi-fi is measured in megabits per second (Mbps), but what does this mean?

Use the internet to research further information about this.

Make a leaflet explaining to a Stage 6 learner what Mbps means.

Peer-assessment

Compare your research about the speed of data transmission with that of a partner. Did you get the same information? Did they find out any information that you didn't find?

If you got different information, discuss what you both found and try to agree about what you think is the correct information.

Figure 3.11: Comparing research with a partner

Stay safe!

The internet can be a very useful tool for research. Make sure you stay safe when using it by using only trusted websites for your research.

Remember to check for the padlock symbol, 'https' and the digital certificate and avoid using sites that don't have these. If you are unsure about whether a website is trustworthy, ask your teacher or another trusted adult before you open it.

The radio waves used in a wi-fi network operate at two different frequencies: 2.4 GHz and 5 GHz.

- **Speed:** The 2.4 GHz frequency transmits data at a slower speed than the 5 GHz frequency. This means that downloads will happen faster using a 5 GHz frequency.

- **Coverage:** The 2.4 GHz frequency provides a larger area of coverage. This means that devices can be further away from the WAP when connecting to it.
- **Travel:** The 2.4 GHz frequency is much better at travelling through walls than the 5 GHz frequency. This is because radio waves at a higher frequency find it harder to go through solid objects.
- **Frequency:** Many devices in a house that have a wireless connection use the 2.4 GHz frequency. However, most routers let you switch frequency between 2.4 GHz and 5 GHz. Alternatively, you can set your router to transmit at both frequencies.

Figure 3.12: The wi-fi symbol

Figure 3.12 shows the wi-fi symbol. This symbol is used all over the world to show that a device can connect using wi-fi, or to show that a wi-fi connection is available in a particular place.

Did you know?

Wi-fi is a group of network protocols based on a set of standards called IEEE 802.11. The Wi-Fi Alliance is an organisation that tests equipment to make sure it meets these standards. In 1999 the technology was called 'IEEE 802.11b Direct Sequence', but the Alliance wanted to find a catchier name that people would remember. They asked a marketing company to help, and they came up with the name wi-fi.

Questions 3.3

1. What are the two different frequencies that radio waves can operate at in a wi-fi network?
2. What is the name of the component that a device needs to have built-in to connect to a wi-fi network?
3. Which wi-fi frequency is better at transmitting data through walls and why?

Bluetooth Wireless Technology networks

A **Bluetooth Wireless Technology network** is a type of wireless network that connects devices over short distances. You do not need a WAP or router to connect devices together. Bluetooth Wireless Technology is useful for connecting things like headphones or speakers to a phone, or a wireless mouse and keyboard to a computer.

Devices are connected using a method known as **pairing**. Pairing lets the two devices swap information with each other so they can communicate. Pairing is a bit like swapping telephone numbers. You only need to pair devices once, the first time you want to connect them. After they have been paired, they will remember each other like old friends.

To pair devices:

1 A user turns on Bluetooth Wireless Technology on each device.
2 The devices scan the area for other devices that have Bluetooth Wireless Technology turned on.
3 The user can then select the device they want to pair with and the devices are then paired.

Sometimes the user will need to enter a password or code to pair the devices. Once the devices are paired, they can use the Bluetooth Wireless Technology connection to send data to each other.

If you want to connect your device using Bluetooth Wireless Technology, the device will need to have a Bluetooth Wireless Technology transmitter built into it. It is also possible to use a Bluetooth Wireless Technology adapter to convert a device into one that can use Bluetooth Wireless Technology – adapters often connect via a USB port.

Like wi-fi, Bluetooth Wireless Technology uses radio waves to transmit data.

- **Speed:** Bluetooth Wireless Technology can transmit data at a speed of 25 Mbps.
- **Coverage:** Bluetooth Wireless Technology operates at a fixed 2.45 Ghz frequency. It uses less power than wi-fi and is designed to communicate over much shorter distances. Bluetooth Wireless Technology has a range of 10 metres.

There is a global symbol that shows that a device can communicate using Bluetooth Wireless Technology.

Did you know?

Bluetooth Wireless Technology is actually quite an old technology. It can be traced back as far as 1994, when Japp Haartsen, a Dutch electrical engineer, developed the foundations for the system that is now known as Bluetooth Wireless Technology.

Bluetooth was the code name given to the technology when it was being developed. It was named after King Harald 'Bluetooth' Gormsson, who is famous for uniting Denmark and Norway in the year 958. He had a dead tooth that was blue, so people gave him a nickname to match.

Originally, the technology was going to be called RadioWire. However, the company liked the name 'Bluetooth' more, so they kept it. The Bluetooth Wireless Technology logo is based on two ancient symbols: Hagall (ᚼ) and Bjarkan (ᛒ), Harald Bluetooth's initials.

Figure 3.13: The Bluetooth Wireless Technology logo and the symbols that make up its parts

Questions 3.4

1. What is it called when two devices connect to each other for the first time via Bluetooth Wireless Technology?
2. What is the range of a Bluetooth Wireless Technology connection?
3. What speed can data be transmitted at using a Bluetooth Wireless Technology connection?

Activity 3.3

You will need: a device with Bluetooth Wireless Technology capabilities, such as a desktop computer, laptop, tablet, smartphone, wireless 'Bluetooth' speaker, headphones, keyboard or other suitable device

You are going to try pairing two Bluetooth Wireless Technology devices together. Your teacher will divide the class into small groups and give each group two devices to pair. See if you can do this with as little help from your teacher as possible!

The basic steps are below, but the exact process will be different for different devices. If you don't know what to do or get stuck, search the internet for more precise instructions.

1. Make sure both devices have been charged up enough before you start.
2. Turn both devices on, then on the device that has a screen, turn Bluetooth Wireless Technology on. Often, devices without a screen turn Bluetooth Wireless Technology on when the device is turned on, but there may be a separate pairing button.
3. You then need to tell the desktop computer, laptop, tablet or smartphone to pair with the other device. You usually do this in the Settings menu.
4. When you think you are done, test whether the pairing has been successful. If you are pairing headphones or speakers, make sure the volume is turned up enough on both devices.

Wi-fi versus Bluetooth Wireless Technology

	2.4 GHz	5 GHz	Bluetooth Wireless Technology
Range	50 m indoors 300 m outdoors	15 m indoors 100 m outdoors	10 m indoors or outdoors
Speed	200 Mbps	1300 Mbps	25 Mbps
Ability to go through walls/objects	Good	Not as good as 2.4 GHz	Good within a short distance
Hardware needed in device	WNIC	WNIC	Bluetooth Wireless Technology transmitter (internal) *or* adapter (plug in)

Table 3.1: Comparing wi-fi and Bluetooth Wireless Technology

Cellular networks

A **cellular network** is the third type of wireless network that uses radio waves to transmit data. Wireless networks and Bluetooth Wireless Technology networks have very small ranges. A cellular network covers large geographical areas (areas of the Earth's surface). Mobile phones use a cellular network so that when you are driving long distances you can stay connected.

Geographical areas are divided up into smaller areas called **cells**. Within each of these cells there is a **base station**. This base station transmits radio signals that can be received by mobile telephones.

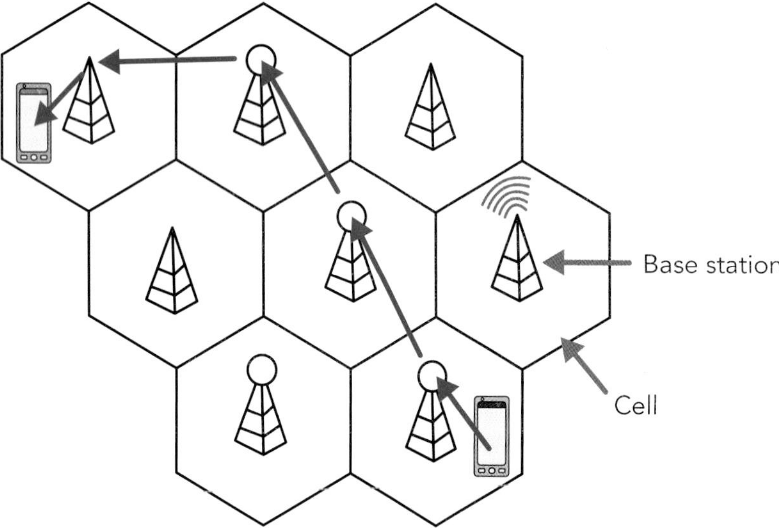

Figure 3.14: Showing how signals transmit from base station to base station between mobile phones

When you want to make a call with a mobile phone, you will normally be using a cellular network. You will be in one cell of the network when you make the call.

Base station

1. The radio signals from your phone travel to the base station that is within your cell.
2. The base station then works out which cell the phone you want to call is in.
3. The base station will then use radio waves to transmit signals from base station to base station, until the signal gets to the cell where the other phone is located.
4. The base station there will receive those signals and then transmit them to the right phone for the call to be made.

Have you ever made a call using your mobile phone while travelling in a car? You may have suddenly lost connection for a few seconds, then the call reconnected again. This is probably because you moved out of one cell into another, so your phone had to change which base station it was transmitting to.

Generations of cellular network

There are different versions of cellular network. The oldest and most well-known version is the 3G network (meaning third generation). The 4G and 5G networks are newer. The main difference between the three generations of cellular network is the speed at which they can transmit data.

You can see from the table that this difference has a huge effect on how long things take to download.

	3G	4G	5G
Year it was first used	2001	2009	2020
Average transmission speed	3 Mbps	20 Mbps	100+ Mbps, with max speeds of up to 10 Gbps (10,000 Mbps)
Approximate time taken to download a 2-hour movie	2 hours	6 minutes	3.6 seconds

Table 3.2: Comparisons of different versions of cellular network

Activity 3.4

You will need: some pens and paper, a desktop computer, laptop or tablet with internet access and with publishing or presentation software

Apart from transmission speed, there are other reasons why 5G transfers data so much more quickly than 4G or 3G. In addition, 5G is not only faster than 4G, it is better in other ways too.
Do some research on the internet to see if you can find out what those improvements are. Make notes during your research, then produce a poster or presentation to explain what 5G is, how it compares to 4G, how it works and what differences this will make for people who use it.

What strategy did you use for your research and poster/presentation?

How did you decide what was important to include in your poster?

Why did you choose to leave out the things you didn't include?

Do you think this was the right strategy to use for this task?

How would you improve the way you do this kind of task next time?

Summary checklist

- [ ] I can explain how a wi-fi network works, including the use of radio waves.
- [ ] I know the different frequencies available on a wi-fi network, including their different ranges and speeds.
- [ ] I can explain how a Bluetooth Wireless Technology network works, including how devices are paired.
- [ ] I know the range and speed of a Bluetooth Wireless Technology network.
- [ ] I can explain how a cellular network works, including the use of cells and base stations.
- [ ] I know the difference between 3G, 4G and 5G cellular networks.

3.3 Data transmission

In this topic you will:

- understand what an error in data is
- learn what can cause an error in data to occur
- understand what happens to data when it has been encrypted
- understand how encryption keeps data secure when it is transmitted from one device to another.

Key words

attenuation
binary
cipher
corruption
crosstalk
decrypt
hacking
identity fraud
identity theft
interference
surge

Getting started

What do you already know?

- Data is divided into small units called packets.
  Packets of data are transmitted from one device to another. Each packet could take a different route across the network from the sending device to the receiving device.
- Data is valuable so it must be kept safe and secure.
  If data is not kept safe and secure it may be lost or stolen and could be used for malicious (harmful) purposes, identity theft and fraud.
- Data can be encrypted to stop it being misused.
  An encryption algorithm (the steps of a method for encrypting data) is called a **cipher**. Two examples of ciphers are the Caesar Cipher and the Pigpen Cipher.

Continued

Now try this!

Create a new cipher for encrypting data. Decide whether your cipher will use letters or symbols. Then decide what steps will be in your cipher to encrypt the data. Write a short message to a friend and encrypt it using your cipher. Give your message and your cipher to your friend and see if they can decrypt your message.

What is an error in data?

An error is something that is wrong, like a mistake or an accidental change. Data can have errors in it, just like any other type of information. Data can sometimes get errors in it is if it becomes **corrupted** when it is being created, accessed, processed, transmitted (sent) or stored.

You may already know that computers only understand data that is in **binary**. Binary means 'made up of two things'. In computing, binary refers to the language of 1s and 0s that computers use to store data. For example, the number 55 in binary is 110111. Computers store all data as binary digits (called 'bits') and translate it into human languages and pictures so that we can understand it.

The binary number 110111 is transmitted from computer A to computer B. However, a problem in transmission causes the data to be changed during transmission. Can you spot where the error is?

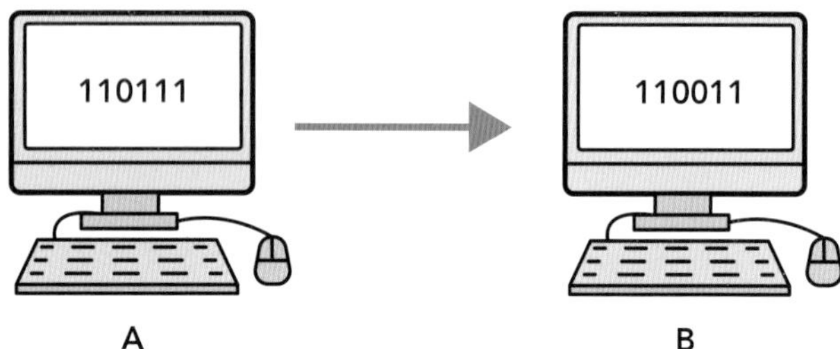

Figure 3.15: Error in transmission

You may have spotted that a 1 in the binary number 110111 (55) has been changed to a 0 in the binary number 110011 (which is 51). This has caused the data to be incorrect. This is one way that data can have an error.

Another way that data can have an error is if an issue in transmission causes some of the data to be lost.

$$110111 \rightarrow 10111$$

This time, an issue in transmission causes data to be lost. The first 1 of the binary for 55 was not transmitted and the binary value that Computer B received is 10111. This is actually the binary for the number 19. So the data has an error in it.

How do errors in data happen?

There are many reasons that errors in data can happen during transmission. Some of the main ones are:

- electricity surges
- interference in radio waves
- crosstalk.

Electricity surges

When data is transmitted from one device to another along a cable, it is sent using electricity. Sometimes, there can be **surges** in the electricity. A surge is when the voltage of the electricity supply suddenly increases. This can cause an error to occur in the data. A surge in electricity in a cable can disrupt the transmission of the data, which can cause some of the data to be accidentally changed or lost.

Radio-wave interference

Earlier in this unit, you learnt about different wireless connections that use radio waves to transmit data. This means that many devices in the same area are all transmitting and receiving radio waves at the same time. That's a lot of radio waves in the air!

Sometimes radio waves from one device can disrupt radio waves from another and cause errors in the data. This is called **interference**. Interference is when other radio waves get mixed up with the waves being transmitted.

One way to think about this issue is to imagine you are in a park and you are listening to a song on your device. Then the person sitting next to you plays a different song on their device at the same time. The sound that your ears receive is not the song your device is playing, but a mixture of two songs. In the same way, radio waves crashing into each other can mix up the messages being transmitted.

Figure 3.16: Radio waves that have been disrupted

Did you know?

Solid objects like walls can also cause problems with wireless data transmission, but this usually just makes the signal weaker rather than making it go wrong. This is not interference but attenuation. As you learnt in Topic 3.2, some radio waves can pass through objects more easily than others.

Crosstalk

Crosstalk is another thing that can cause errors during data transmission. A network can sometimes contain many devices. This can mean that there are lots of cables close together, all transmitting data from one device to another. Sometimes, the electrical energy in one cable can interfere with the electrical energy in another cable and create unwanted effects. This is called crosstalk. The ways cables are made can help to make sure crosstalk is kept to a minimum.

In later stages, you will learn about different error detection methods and how they can be used to check for errors in data when it has been transmitted.

Activity 3.5

You will need: a desktop computer, laptop or tablet with word-processing software and internet access

Use the internet to research one other issue that could cause errors in data to occur. Write an explanation of what you found out, then share this with a partner and discuss the issues you found.

- Did you and your partner find different issues in your research?
- How do you think you could stop these errors in data from happening?

Be prepared to tell your teacher what you have found out.

Self-assessment

Think about the research task and the explanation you wrote.

- Identify one thing that you think you did especially well.
- Identify one thing you could improve on next time you do a similar task.

Questions 3.5

1 What does it mean when there is an error in the data?

2 What is data corruption?

3 Can you give two ways that errors can happen during data transmission?

Encrypting data

We use the internet for a lot of things: email, looking up information, buying things, watching shows, listening to music and much more. This means that we send a lot of information about ourselves over the internet.

It is important that all this information is kept safe. Occasionally, people try to break into computer systems they are not supposed to access in order to steal data. This is a type of **hacking**. If hackers manage to get hold of your personal information, they could steal it to use for themselves – this is called **identity theft**.

They could then use your data to commit **identity fraud** by pretending to be you and buying things with your money.

Unplugged activity 3.2

You will need: a pen and paper

With a partner, write a list of all the different types of information you use on your computer or when you use the internet. For example, you may have your personal details (name and address), photographs of yourself, your parents' banking details if you bought something, and all of your passwords for the websites you use.

How many things can you list?

To discourage people from stealing data, it is often encrypted before it is transmitted from one device to another. Encryption can help keep data secure. If a hacker manages to find the data and steal it, they will not be able to understand or use it because it will be scrambled. This means hackers might not try to steal data in the first place.

In previous stages, you have learnt how to write and decode messages using ciphers such as the Caesar Cipher and the Pigpen Cipher. These are both methods of encryption. When the data is encrypted, it is scrambled and will look like a meaningless list of characters. For example:

WKLV LV ZULWWHQ XVLQJ WKH FDHVDU FLSKHU

Encrypted data will not make any sense if you try to read it. This is the aim of encryption. Encrypting data does not stop people stealing it, but it makes stolen data useless to those who steal it. It will be meaningless to anyone who is not able to **decrypt** (unscramble) it. Only the person with the cipher can decrypt the message.

Sending a message that is encrypted means that the data is safe. The data cannot be used in any way, including for malicious purposes such as identity fraud.

Stay safe!

Remember to always make sure that any website you use will encrypt your personal data before you send it across the internet. One way you can check that your data will be encrypted is by looking to see if the website starts with the protocol 'https' (not just 'http').

Did you know?

The Caesar Cipher is named after the Roman Emperor Julius Caesar. He used it to send secret messages to his military leaders. He used a shift of three letters, so A became D:

A	B	C	D	E	F	G	H	I	J	K	L	M	N	O	P	Q	R	S	T	U	V	W	X	Y	Z
D	E	F	G	H	I	J	K	L	M	N	O	P	Q	R	S	T	U	V	W	X	Y	Z	A	B	C

Unplugged activity 3.3

You will need: pens and paper

This text has been encrypted using the Caesar cipher. The first letter (the P) is an M when it is decrypted. What does the message say?

PB IDYRXULWH VXEMHFW LV FRPSXWLQJ!

Activity 3.6

You will need: a desktop computer, laptop or tablet with word-processing software and internet access

You are going to write a secret message for a friend, encrypt it and then send it to them. We can encrypt any word-processing document by protecting it with a password. Then, only people who know the password can open the document.

Continued

In Microsoft Word:

1. Open a new blank document and type your message.
2. Go to File > Info > Protect Document > Encrypt with Password.
3. Type a password. You will be asked to type this in twice.
4. Save the file and close it.
5. Test that the encryption has worked by opening the file again. The program should ask you to enter the password.
6. Email the file as an attachment to your friend.
7. Tell them the password using a different way of communicating, for example by speaking to them or sending them a text message.

If the computer you are using has different word-processing software, look up on the internet how to encrypt a document in that software, or see if you can work out how to do it by yourself.

Summary checklist

- [ ] I can explain what an error in data means.
- [ ] I can explain that electrical surges, interference and crosstalk are issues that can cause errors in data to occur.
- [ ] I can explain that encrypted data is data that has been scrambled so that anyone who does not have the cipher cannot understand it.
- [ ] I can explain that encryption makes data meaningless so this helps keep it safe. Even if it is stolen, it cannot be understood.

Project: School assembly

Sofia's class is going to lead an assembly on networks and digital communication to explain to the school what they have learnt in this unit.

They have been asked to explain how typing a URL into a browser makes data travel:

- from the school computer
- over the school network
- through the internet
- to the web server that holds the website's data.

Sofia wants to break the assembly down into three sections:

Task 1 How a website is accessed when a user types a URL into a web browser

Including:

- the parts of a URL
- how a DNS finds the matching IP address for a URL.

Task 2 How the data travels over networks

Including:

- how data travels over wired, wi-fi, cellular or Bluetooth Wireless Technology networks and the advantages of using each network type
- the fact that the data for one request may travel over more than one type of network.

Task 3 How we know that the data we are sending is kept secure and safe from errors

Including:

- what things keep our data safe and how we can check this
- why errors occur.

In a group of four, design that assembly. You need to consider how you will present the information.

You may want to give a presentation. However, you could also use different ways:

- You may also want to act out some information using your drama skills.
- You may decide to make a poster to present some of the information.
- Or you may have other ideas you want to use.

Check your progress 3

1 State the name of the text-based address for a website. [1]

2 Which of the following would help keep data safe when it is transmitted from one device to another? Select the correct answer. [1]

A Crosstalk

B Decryption

C Encryption

D Interference

3 The table contains three wireless network types and descriptions. There are two wireless network types and one description missing. Fill in the missing information.

	Wireless network type	Description	
a)		This network uses radio waves broadcast from a wireless access point (WAP) that operate at two main frequencies: 2.4 GHz and 5 GHz.	[1]
b)	cellular network		[2]
c)		This network uses pairing to connect devices and uses radio waves that operate at a frequency of 2.45 GHz to transmit data between them.	[1]

4 State the name of the hardware that stores the data for a website and sends it to the web browser when requested. [1]

5 Give *two* ways that a user can check whether a website is secure. [2]

6 Which of the following is not part of a URL? Select the correct answer. [1]

A Domain name

B IP address

C Path

D Protocol

7 Describe what a domain name server (DNS) does in three or four steps. [4]

4 Computer systems

4.1 Computer design

In this topic you will:

- learn how to evaluate a computer device or system
- identify the features of a computer device or system
- discuss the positive and negative features of a computer device or system.

Key words

critical thinking

evaluate

feature

user interface

Getting started

What do you already know?

- Hardware and software are combined to create a computer system.
- Parts of a computer system you can touch are called hardware. For example, a keyboard, a monitor or the motherboard and circuits inside the computer.
- Software is the programs that give instructions and data to the hardware, to tell the computer what to do.
- People decide which hardware and software they want by looking at its cost, speed and how it looks and feels to use.

Continued

Now try this!

Look at the following list:

Keyboard	**Spreadsheet**	**Headphones**
Word processor	**Monitor**	**Sound editor**
Mouse	**Database**	**Printer**
Speaker	**Video editor**	**Computer game**

Create a table like this:

Hardware	Software

For each item in the list, decide which column it belongs to and add it to that column in the table.

Evaluating the design of a computer device or system

You have looked at computer devices and systems in previous stages. When you are buying a computer device or system, you need to know that it will do the job that it is designed to do. To know this, you need to evaluate the design of it. Evaluating means getting an idea of the value of something by carefully looking at and thinking about it.

To evaluate an item, product, service or task, you can:

1 ask 'Does it do what it is supposed to do?' and 'Does it do what I want it to do?'

2 define its **features** (its different aspects and parts)

3 think about its positives and negatives

4 decide if the product or task has been made or done in the best way possible

5 look at what could be improved.

Evaluating involves **critical thinking**. This means using all the available facts and analysing them to judge how good or effective something is.

To evaluate the design of a computer device or system, you will look at its features and decide how good or useful they are. A feature is an individual part that makes up the whole design of a computer system. These features could include a large high-definition screen, a speaker, a hardwearing case, the case's colour and the **user interface** (the way user interacts with a device, for example by moving a mouse and clicking on images on a screen).

All these features are designed to be helpful to the user. Some of them may be more helpful than others. What do you find the most helpful feature on the computer that you regularly use?

Questions 4.1

1 What does a feature mean when talking about a computer system?

2 What are two features of a mobile phone?

3 How do you evaluate the design of a computer system?

Does it do what I want?

Before you look at the features of the computer device or system that you are evaluating, you need to ask two very important questions:

For example, there is no point buying a device to play a certain game if the graphics card in that device won't support the game.

Once you have answered these two questions, you need to evaluate the features of the computer device or system to work out how good those features are.

Defining the features of a computer system

Unplugged activity 4.1

You will need: a pen and paper

Work with a partner. Look at the following three devices:

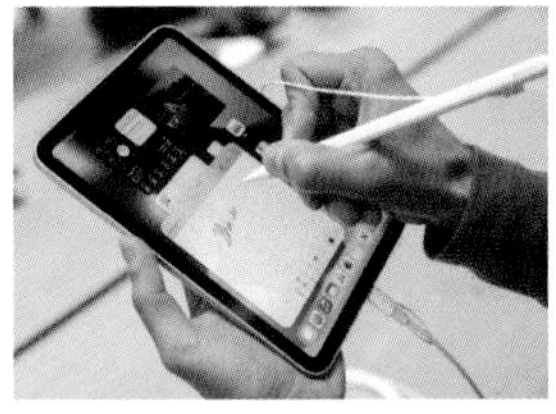

Figure 4.1: A tablet

Figure 4.2: A printer/copier

Figure 4.3: A laptop

Make a list of all the features you can see for each device. You could also add features to your list that you think the device might have. For example, for the laptop you might write that it is silver, has a large screen, has a keyboard, and so on.

These are things you can see. You might also add 'microphone' to your list, as you might think this is a feature that could be built into the laptop.

Have a discussion with your partner to compare the features. For example, you could discuss:

- Which has the largest screen?
- Which has the best colour?
- Which is the largest device?

The positives and negatives of the features of a computer system

During your discussion, you shared your thoughts with your partner about the features of each device. This is part of the process of evaluating the design of a computer device or system. The next step in evaluating is to think about the positives and the negatives of each of the features. This will help you decide if the device has been designed in the best way possible.

Unplugged activity 4.2

You will need: a pen and paper

Work with the same partner again. Look at the list of features that you made about each of the devices. Think about the discussion that you had with your partner when you compared the devices by thinking about a question such as 'Which has the largest screen?'

Now talk with your partner about the positives and negatives of each of the features you have listed. For example:

> Is it a positive or a negative that the laptop has a large screen?

You might think this is both positive and negative:

☺ It is positive because it means that the user can see things more clearly.

☹ It is negative because it will make the laptop larger and heavier to carry.

List all the positives and negatives of each of the features of the devices.

Self-assessment

How did you decide what was positive and what was negative about the features?

Were there any features where you and your partner thought differently?

Look at what could be improved

One thing that technology companies are always trying to do is improve the design of computer devices and systems. Many people want their devices to be as easy to use as possible. But they also want their device to be as advanced as possible in terms of technology. This can often be a difficult balance for technology companies to achieve. They spend a lot of time and money on trying to get this right for users.

Did you know?

Over $2 trillion is spent on buying technology each year, and this figure is always growing. This is a huge amount of money. It is one of the reasons why technology companies spend so much of their money on developing new and improved devices.

Activity 4.1

You will need: a device to evaluate, such as a desktop computer, laptop, tablet, smartphone, printer, keyboard or speakers, with word-processing software

You are going to use and evaluate a device. If you have used the device before, you may not have really thought much about its features or how it could be improved. Now is your chance to think critically about it. It would be best to evaluate a device you've never seen or used before, but if that is not possible, just pretend the device you are using is new.

Imagine that a technology company has sent you a prototype (early version) of a new device to test and to give your opinion on. The company has asked you to:

- identify its different features
- tell them whether each feature is positive, negative or both for you, and why
- give the product an overall score of 1 out of 10 for how well it does its job (1 is the lowest and 10 is the highest)
- suggest any improvements that you think would make the product better.

Test the device as thoroughly as possible, looking at and using every different feature, then write your report for the technology company.

Continued

Peer-assessment

Now evaluate your evaluations!

- Swap evaluation reports with a partner.
- Discuss with your partner what you think you have both done well.
- Write down two things that your partner has done well.
- What did you both find easy or hard about evaluating the device?
- Discuss with your partner what you both could improve upon. Write down one thing that your partner could improve about their evaluation.

Summary checklist

- [ ] I know how to evaluate a computer device or system.
- [ ] I can identify the features of a computer device or system.
- [ ] I can explain whether a feature is positive, negative or both.

4.2 Types of software

In this topic you will:

- learn how to describe the purpose of application software
- learn how to describe the purpose of system software
- understand the differences between how application software is used and how system software is used.

Key words

application software

maintain

manage

operating system

system software

utilities (utility software)

Getting started

What do you already know?

- Software performs an important role in a computer system. Without software, a user could not use the computer. There are two types of software: application software and system software.
- System software is the software that computers use to help them function (work). This includes the operating system, which controls and manages all the hardware and other software that the computer uses.
- Application software lets you do tasks on the computer. Examples include word-processing software to write your school assignments and the web browser you use to search the internet.

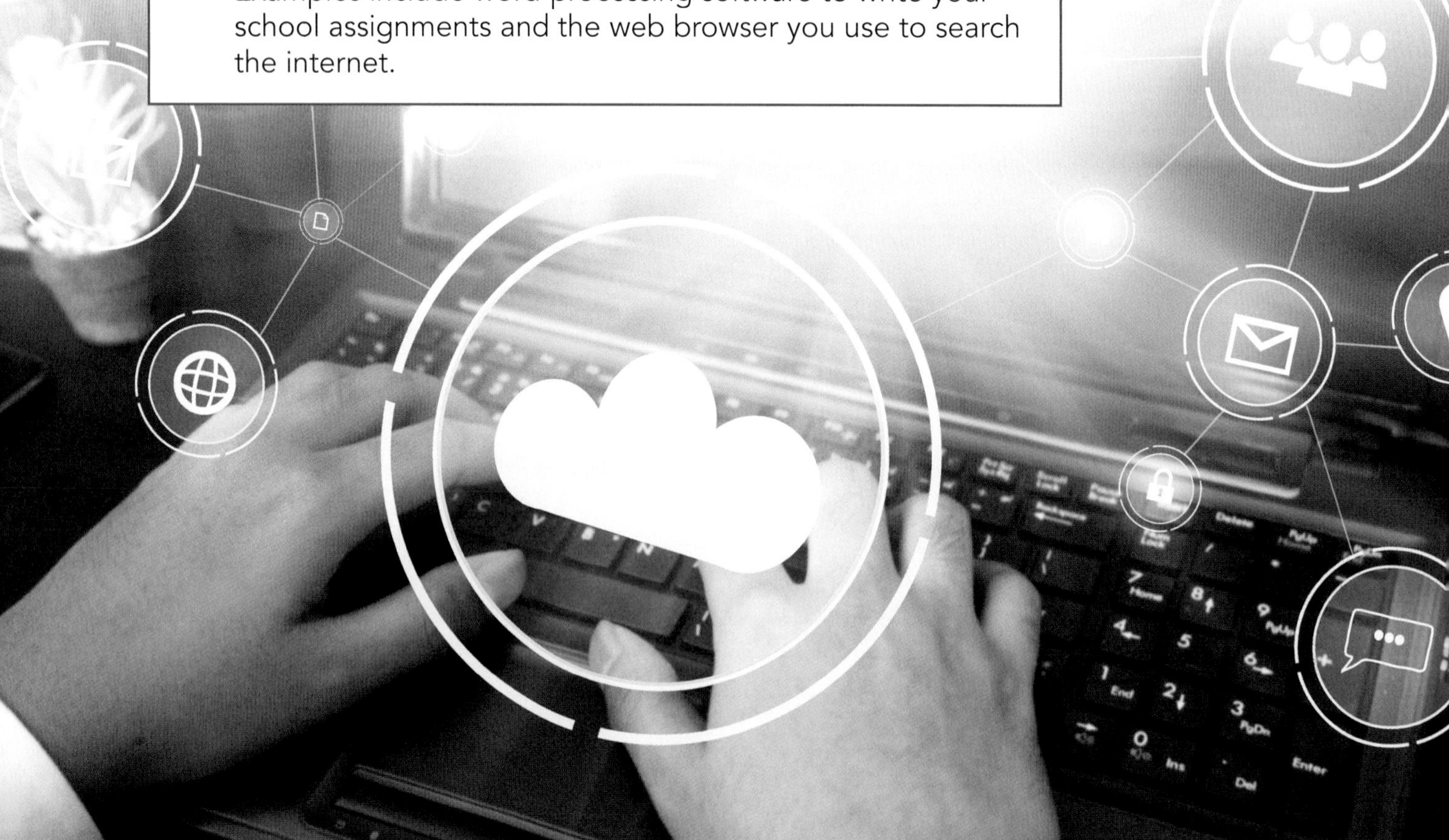

Continued

Now try this!

Write down ten examples of software that you have on your computer. For example, a word processor.

Now draw two ovals like this, with headings in them. Leave a good amount of space between the ovals.

Application software   System software

Create mind maps by adding each of your ten examples of software to the correct circle in the diagram. Try to make sure you include at least one example of each type of software. If you can't think of any examples of system software, see if a partner can help.

Application software

Application software is probably the kind of software you are most familiar with. It is the software you use to perform everyday tasks with your computer. When you email a friend, use a computer to do homework or do research on the internet, you are using application software.

Did you know?

Smartphone and tablet apps are application software – the word 'app' is short for 'application'. Application is another word we can use for a program or piece of software.

Stay safe!

Make sure that you only download apps from places and organisations you can trust. If you are not sure whether you can trust something, ask a teacher or another adult to check for you.

Questions 4.2

1 What are two examples of application software?

2 What is the purpose of application software?

System software

System software is software that enables the computer to work. System software makes it possible for the computer to run application software and **maintain** and **manage** the whole system. Maintaining means looking after something and keeping it in good condition. Managing means controlling the use of resources like power and space, making sure they are used in a way that makes sense.

System software does things like:

- finding viruses
- rearranging files on the hard drive
- backing up data (making a copy of it in case the original gets damaged or lost).

One important example of system software is the **operating system**. The operating system is a collection of programs that control and manage all the computer's software and hardware. The operating system allows the hardware to talk to all the other software. It also allows the user to interact with the computer and tell it what to do.

A lot of types of system software are built into the operating system. These include utilities – tools that help analyse and make the best use of computer resources. Examples include antivirus software, data compression tools and software for defragmenting (tidying up data stored on a disk so that space is used more efficiently).

Questions 4.3

1 What are two examples of system software?

2 What is the purpose of system software?

Unplugged activity 4.3

You will need: a pen and paper

Work in a group of three. You have just learnt that there are two types of software: application software and system software. Why is software split into these two different categories? Discuss in your group why this might be the case and what the benefits of this could be. Write down some notes or create a mind map of your ideas. You could use the headings 'Reasons' and 'Benefits'.

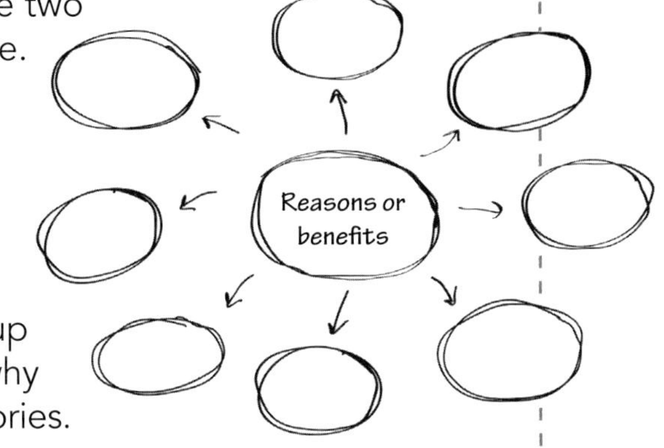

When you have had your group discussion, nominate a group speaker. Your teacher will ask your group speaker to share why your group thinks that software is split into these two categories.

Activity 4.2

You will need: a pen and paper, desktop computer, laptop or tablet

You will have interacted with the operating system on a few different devices, but you might never have used any of the utilities that are part of it. You are going to see if you can interact with and explore some utilities on a device.

If you are using a school device, you might not be able to change any settings because this is usually controlled by an IT administrator. You might still be able to view some of the settings and see what they do. Your teacher will tell you what you will be able to do.

In your device's app menu or search bar, try searching for one of the following:

- Security
- Antivirus
- Settings

Continued

If you can, explore the settings menus. Write down some notes about what you learn about the utilities on the device and what the user can change about them.

If the device will let you, see if you can change a small setting or make the system do something small and quick. For example, running a quick virus check or changing when the device goes to sleep. Be careful not to do anything that will take a long time or erase data, unless your teacher has said that this is OK. Ask your teacher before you ask the system to do anything you're not sure about.

When you have finished, use your notes to write a list of instructions someone could follow to change something on the system using the utility software.

Self-assessment

- Was it easy to work out how to interact with the system software? Why or why not?
- What did you learn?
- Is it easy to understand your instructions?
- How do you know?

Difference between application software and system software

Application software is most useful for the user.

System software is most useful for the computer.

The main differences between application software and system software are shown in Table 4.1.

Application software	System software
enables the user to do specific tasks	enables the system to function and provides the right conditions for application software to run
not essential for the system to run	essential for the system to run
only runs when the user asks it to	usually running when the computer/device is on, without any action from the user
user is aware of it running and uses it directly	runs in the background and the user is often not aware of it
does not interact directly with the hardware, but interacts with the system software	interacts closely with the hardware

Table 4.1: Differences between application software and system software

Activity 4.3

You will need: some pens and paper, a desktop computer, laptop or tablet with publishing or presentation software

Create an infographic to help students understand the difference between application software and system software.

In your graphic:

- State a few main differences. Include one that is not listed in Table 4.1.
- Explain why both types of software are needed.
- State some examples of each kind of software.

Peer-assessment

Divide into small groups and look at each other's infographics. Talk about each one in turn.

- Is the infographic easy to understand? Why or why not?
- What could be improved?
- Each person in the group should say which is their favourite infographic and why.

Summary checklist

- [ ] I can describe the purpose of application software and identify examples.
- [ ] I can describe the purpose of system software and identify examples.
- [ ] I can explain the difference between application software and system software.

4.3 Data representation

In this topic you will:

- learn that humans mainly use a denary number system
- learn that computers can only use a binary number system
- learn that humans understand analogue data but computers only understand digital data
- understand that digital data is binary data
- understand how binary digits can represent numbers, text, images and sounds so that computers can process and store them.

Key words

amplitude
ASCII
binary
bit
character
character set
colour depth
denary
digit
extended ASCII
frequency
pixel
place value
resolution
sample
sample rate
Unicode

Getting started

What do you already know?

- Digital data is data stored using the binary system. Binary data only has two values: 0 and 1.
- Analogue data is data that is made up of many different values.
- Humans understand analogue data, but computers can only understand digital data. All analogue data needs to be converted to digital data for a computer to be able to process it.

Now try this!

Look at the following numbers. Which ones could be binary numbers?

15	101	123	11	1000
61	010	456	01	111

Denary numbers

Most human societies today use the **denary** number system (also known as a decimal system or base-10). This means that the number system has ten **digits** (single numbers) that we can put together to represent all numbers. The digits are:

0 1 2 3 4 5 6 7 8 9

These can be combined to make any number, however large.
For example, 12, 107, 3571 or 98 979.

A digit's position in a number tells you what the value of that digit is. This is called **place value**. In 3571, the digit 7 is in the tens place, so its value is 70. If the 7 was in the hundreds place, its value would be 700.

The smallest place value is the ones, which are on the far right-hand side of the number. The positions get bigger as you add more columns to the left.

Place value	Thousands 1000	Hundreds 100	Tens 10	Ones 1
Digit (how many times the place value is in the number)	3	5	7	1

Table 4.2: Values of digits in a decimal number

So our example 3571 is three thousand, five hundred and seventy-one.

When we count, we start in the ones column and count 0 to 9.
Once we reach 9, we have run out of unique digits, so we put a 1 in the tens column and count 0 to 9 in the units column again.

10	1
(...)	(...)
	6
	7
	8
	9
1	0
1	1
1	2

Table 4.3: The tens column

For bigger numbers we need more columns. Because this is a base-10 number system, to get the next column to the left, you multiply the left-most column you already have by 10, as shown in the table below.

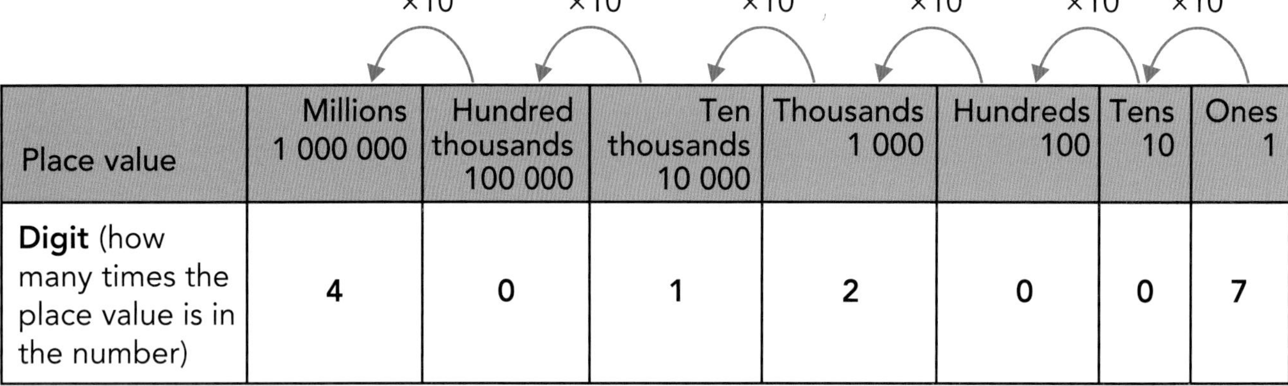

Place value	Millions 1 000 000	Hundred thousands 100 000	Ten thousands 10 000	Thousands 1 000	Hundreds 100	Tens 10	Ones 1
Digit (how many times the place value is in the number)	4	0	1	2	0	0	7

So the number in the table is four million, twelve thousand and seven, because it has four millions, one ten thousand, two thousands and seven ones.

Binary numbers

Computers use a binary number system. This is a base-2 system, which means that only two digits can be used to create numbers:

0 and 1

This time, you double (multiply by 2) the value of the left-most column to get each next place value column to the left. The smallest place value is 1.

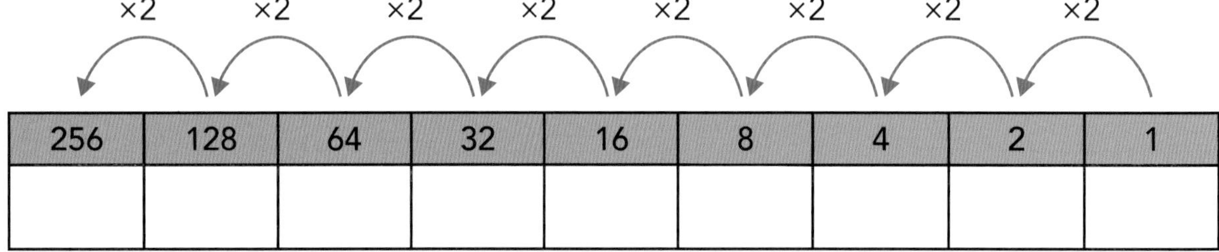

256	128	64	32	16	8	4	2	1

When we count in binary, we start in the units column and count 0 to 1. Once we reach 1, we have run out of unique digits, so we put a 1 in the twos column and count 0 to 1 in the units column again. We keep doing this until we reach 1 again and then we put a 1 in the fours column and count 0 to 1 again in the units and twos columns, and so on.

You can see in Table 4.4 how this works and what each binary number is in denary.

256	128	64	32	16	8	4	2	1	Denary
								0	0
								1	1
							1	0	2
							1	1	3
						1	0	0	4
						1	0	1	5
						1	1	0	6
						1	1	1	7
					1	0	0	0	8
					1	0	0	1	9
					1	0	1	0	10

Table 4.4: Denary and binary numbers

This is how numbers are coded into data that computers can understand. Whenever we type denary numbers into a computer, the computer converts them into binary so that it can store and process them.

Did you know?

Binary numbers were used in ancient Egypt. The binary number system we use today was invented by a mathematician called Gottfried Wilhelm Leibniz in approximately 1679. He invented it so that he could turn Yes/No statements into mathematical data.

Figure 4.4: Gottfried Wilhelm Leibniz

Why do computers use binary?

Computers use the binary system because they can only understand data that is made up of two different states (ways of being). Computers use electrical signals, which can either be high or low. High creates a value of 1 and low creates a value of 0. This means that all data must be converted to binary for a computer to be able to process it.

All of these can be converted to binary numbers and stored as computer data:

- denary numbers
- letters and symbols
- sounds
- images.

Questions 4.4

1 What is our human number system called?

2 What number system do computers use?

3 Using Table 4.4, can you work out what denary numbers these binary numbers are?

   a 1110

   b 11100

Binary representation of characters

The text we read and write is made up of lots of different **characters**. All the letters in the words in this sentence are characters. Can you name some other examples of characters?

In order to code text characters in binary, computers use **character sets**. These are standard sets of binary codes that represent each letter or symbol.

ASCII

One example of a character set is **ASCII**. This set uses 7 bits (binary digits) to code each of 128 different characters of the English language and the number characters 0 to 9.

Character	Binary code
A	1000001
B	1000010
C	1000011
D	1000100
E	1000101
F	1000110
a	1100001
b	1100010
c	1100011
d	1100100
e	1100101
f	1100110

Table 4.5: ASCII codes for upper-and lowercase letters A–F

Did you know?

ASCII was invented in the 1960s for early computers and for machines called teleprinters. These were a bit like typewriters – each character was printed by a little metal stamp that pressed ink onto paper. For this reason, they could only print a very limited set of characters. This is why ASCII only includes 128 different character codes.

ASCII is only useful for writing in English, so **Extended ASCII** was created. This character set uses 8 bits per character to represent 256 different characters. These extra characters include ones used in European languages such as French, German and Spanish.

Unicode

Unicode is the character set most websites use to encode text. It uses between 8 and 32 bits per character to represent over a million characters. Because it can encode so many characters, it can be used for text in a lot of different languages. The characters that use more bits take up more file space, but the advantage of Unicode is that many more characters can be encoded, even emojis! ☺

Activity 4.4

You will need: a desktop computer, laptop or tablet with internet access

Search the web for an ASCII to binary converter. Find one that will let you type in a message to see the binary code.

Type a short message to a partner, then send them the binary code and see if they can convert it back to text to see what the message says. You could award them extra points if they look up all the ASCII codes and decode the message without using a converter!

Binary representation of images

Converting numbers and text into binary code is relatively simple – only a few bits are needed for each number or character. So how do computers encode images, which are much more complex? How is a photograph that you take with a smartphone stored just using binary digits?

Once a digital camera captures the analogue image data, the computer (inside the camera or phone) breaks the image down into a lot of tiny little units of data called **pixels**.

Pixels

A pixel is the smallest possible part of an image. Each tiny little pixel has a single colour, and this colour has a matching binary value. Images are made up of thousands of pixels that are laid out in a grid.

Figure 4.5: The image on the right shows the pixels of a butterfly's wing

Each image also has data that tells the computer how many pixels wide and how many pixels high the image is. The data about the size and quality of the image is also known as the **resolution**. The more pixels an image has for its size, the higher the resolution will be and the clearer it will look. The resolution and the colour of each pixel is all encoded in binary data that a computer can process. Using this binary data, the computer can recreate the image on a screen for you to see.

A simple example of this process is to use an image that just has the colours black and white. In this image, the colour black has the binary value 1 and white has the binary value 0. The size of the image is 9 pixels wide by 8 pixels high. The binary data for the image is:

001111100 010000010 100101001 100000001 101000101 100111001 010000010 001111100

The pixels need to be laid out in a grid that is 9 pixels wide and 8 pixels high. The computer then makes each pixel black or white depending on whether the colour value for the pixel is 1 or 0.

If we complete this process in the same way that the computer would, starting with the top left pixel, we get this image:

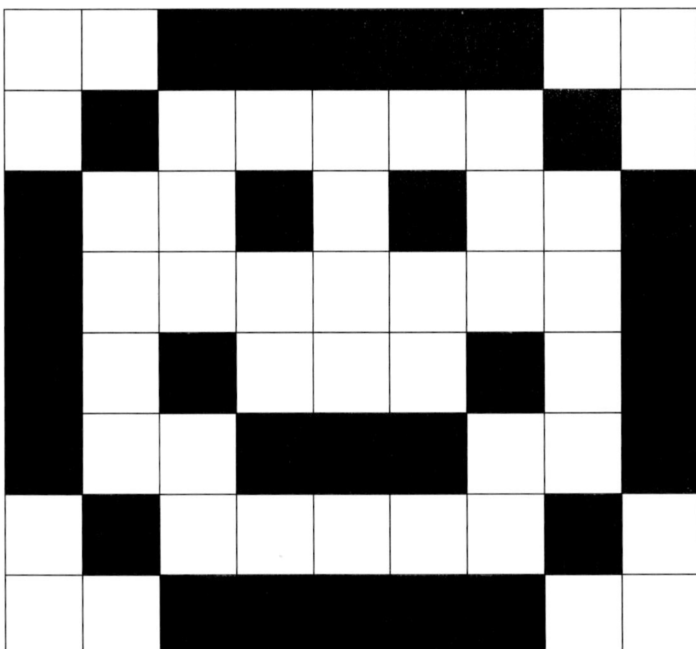

Figure 4.6: Creating a black and white pixelated image using binary data

Unplugged activity 4.4

You will need: a pen and paper

Have a go yourself! Draw a grid of 9 × 9 squares and use the binary data below to see if you can recreate the image.

011000110 100101001 100010001 100000001 100000001 010000010 001000100 000101000 000010000

Start with the pixel in the top left corner of the grid. The first value in the binary data is 0, so this pixel is white. Colour in black all the pixels that have the value 1. When you get to the end of a row, start at the left-hand side of the row underneath.

Coloured images

We have seen that if an image has just two colours (black and white), we only need one bit to code for each colour. If we want more colours, we need to use more bits per colour. The number of bits used to encode each colour is called the **bit** depth or **colour depth**. The higher the colour depth of an image, the more colours that can be used to create the image.

Bit depth	Possible combinations	Number of colours
1	0, 1	2
2	00, 01, 10, 11	4
3	000, 001, 010, 011, 100, 101, 110, 111	8

Table 4.6: Colour depths of images

Questions 4.5

Look at Figure 4.7.

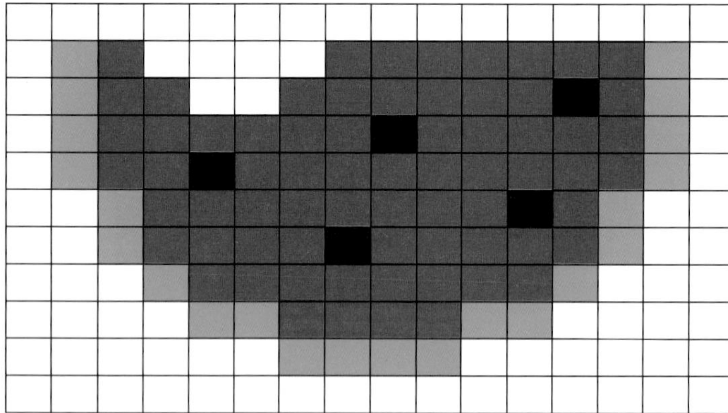

Figure 4.7: Image for questions

1 How many colours are there in this image?
2 What is the image's bit depth?
3 What does this tell us about the way the image is encoded?

Unplugged activity 4.5

You will need: some coloured pens or pencils and paper

You are going to write some binary code for a colour image with a bit depth of 2, then give it to a partner to decode. If you feel like more of a challenge, you could make an image with a bit depth of 3, but be aware that this could take a lot longer!

1 First, decide on a grid size – don't make it too large.
2 Decide what colours you will use and make sure you have chosen the right number.
3 Draw your image. Don't let your partner see!
4 Decide what the binary code for each colour will be and write these down to create a colour key.
5 Write the code for your image.
6 Give the code, colour key and grid size to a partner to see if they can recreate the image you drew.

Self-assessment

Did you find it easy or difficult to create the list of colour codes?

If you were asking a friend to make this list of data so that you could create their image, how would you explain the task?

Peer-assessment

When your partner has finished creating your image using the data you gave them, you can compare your two images. Did they get everything correct?

If they did, ask them if they found it easy or difficult to do.

If they didn't get everything correct, try and work out together where things have gone wrong. Did you give them the wrong data, or did they not follow it correctly?

Most images have a lot more than eight different colours in them. A bit depth of 8 is needed to create a reasonably realistic colour photograph. 8-bit depth images can use up to 256 different colours. Bit depths for high-quality photographs can go up to 24 or even 32, providing over 16 000 000 colours.

Figure 4.8: Comparison of different bit depths on the same photo: the 1-bit black and white section uses a technique called 'dithering' to give the effect of different shades of grey using only black and white

As you can see from Figure 4.8, the higher the bit depth, the higher the file size. This is because more bits are used to encode each colour, and therefore each image.

Activity 4.5

You will need: a desktop computer, laptop or tablet with image-editing software and internet access, photo files in various formats such as jpg, raw and tiff

Your teacher will give you access to some photo files to explore in an image editor.

Open one of the image files in the image-editing software. Then see if you can:

1. zoom in to see the pixels
2. find out the image's resolution
3. find out the bit depth
4. find out the image's file size. (It might be easier to do this in the window the file is saved in, rather than in the image editor.)

Now open an image in a different file format and do the same things again. Is the information different? Why do you think this is? Do some internet research to see if you can find out.

Binary representation of sounds

Sounds are another type of analogue data that can be encoded into binary and stored in digital form.

Sound is created when something vibrates and pushes and pulls the air around it. The thing vibrating could be a loudspeaker, a human voice or two hard objects knocking together. These vibrations create waves of air going up and down, back and forth, again and again, which reach our ears.

We can draw sound waves like this:

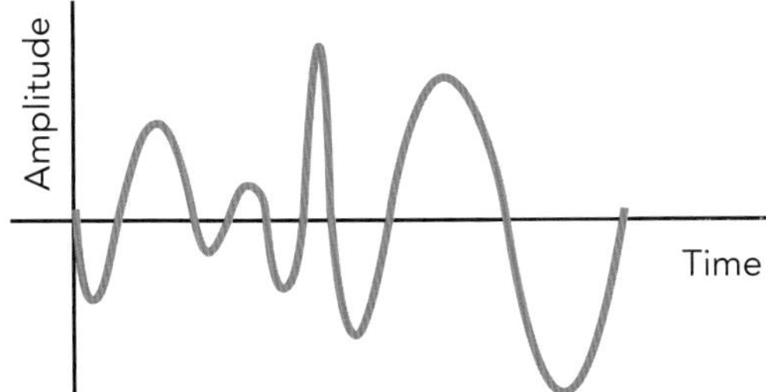

Figure 4.9: A sound wave

The height of each wave shows how loud the sound is. This is called the **amplitude**. A high curve means a louder sound, a lower one means a quieter sound. The width of the waves shows how high or low the pitch of the sound is. This is the **frequency**. If the curves look squashed together, the pitch is high. If the curves are wide and spaced out, the pitch is low.

To convert analogue sound into digital data, you need to capture it with a microphone and an analogue to digital converter (ADC).
The microphone converts the amplitude to electrical voltage. The ADC **samples** the voltage of the signal at regular points in time. This means measuring the voltage and recording the reading in binary.

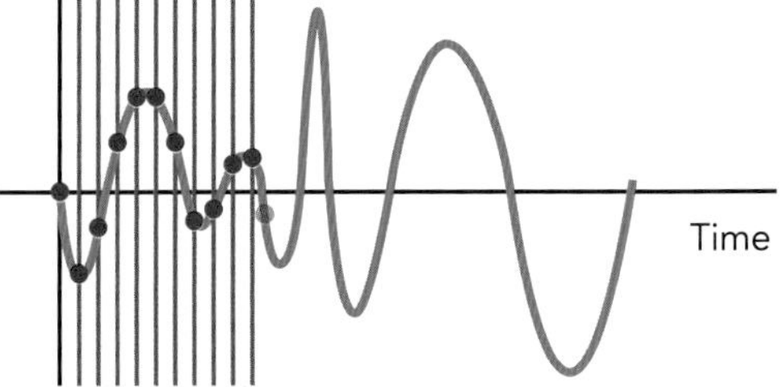

Figure 4.10: Sampling a sound wave

Sample rate

Samples need to be taken thousands of times per second for the digital version of the sound to be close to the original. Whenever a binary value is recorded, that value will represent the amplitude of the sound wave until the next value. The more often samples are taken (the higher the **sample rate**), the more detail of the original sound will be represented in the digital file.

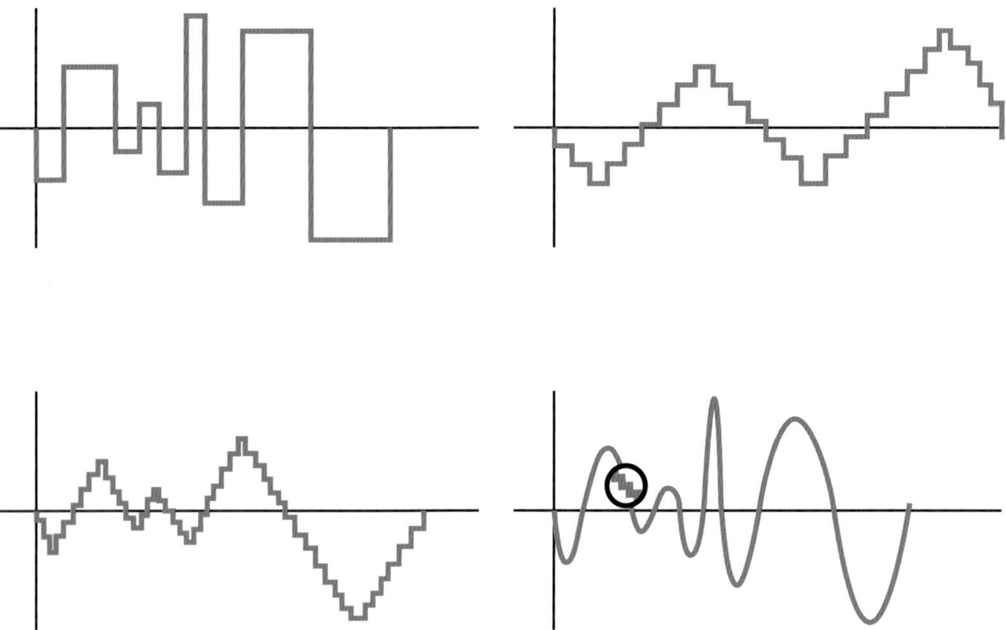

Figure 4.11: A sound wave with different sample rates

Different sample rates are used for different types of sound. For music, a high sample rate of 44 100 samples per second is often used. Sample rate is measured in hertz (Hz). (This is the same as the unit for the frequency of radio waves, which you learnt about in Topic 3.2.) 44 100 hertz is 44.1 kilohertz (kHz). For other types of sound, much lower sample rates of around 8 kHz can be used. Voice calls made over the internet can use sample rates this low.

Bit depth

Remember that with images, the bit depth (the number of bits used per pixel) affects how many colours can be represented. With sounds, the bit depth (the number of bits used per sample) affects how many different voltage values can be represented. The standard bit depth for CD-quality digital recordings is 16, giving 65 536 possible values. DVD recordings have a bit depth of 24, which gives over 16 million possible values.

Questions 4.6

1 How do you think sample rate affects the size of the digital sound file?

2 Why do you think a low sample rate can be used for voice calls, but a much higher one is needed for music?

Summary checklist

- [ ] I understand that humans mainly use a denary number system.
- [ ] I understand that computers can only use a binary number system.
- [ ] I understand that humans understand analogue data, but computers only understand digital data.
- [ ] I understand that digital data is binary data.
- [ ] I understand how binary digits can represent numbers, text, images and sounds so that computers can process and store them.

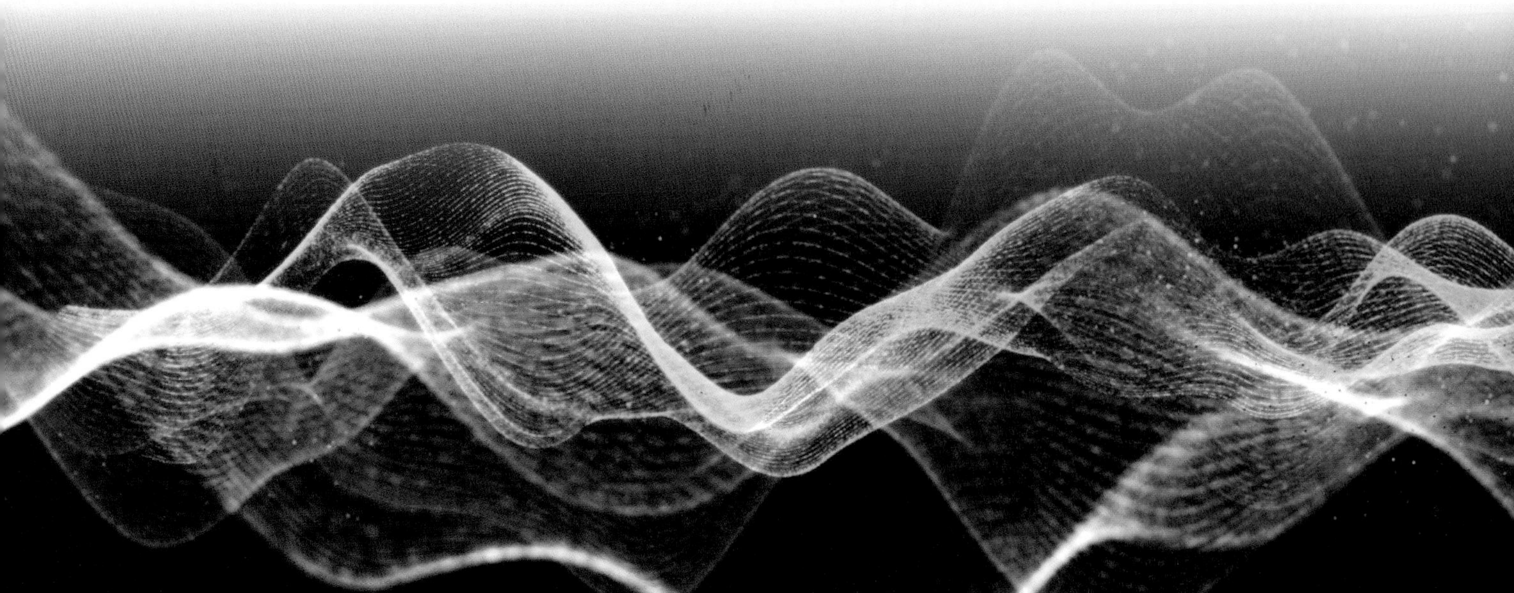

4.4 Logic gates

In this topic you will:

- learn what a logic gate is
- understand the role of a logic gate in a computer
- learn about the logic of a NOT gate
- learn about the logic of an AND gate
- learn about the logic of an OR gate.

Key words

Boolean data

logic gate

truth table

Getting started

What do you already know?

- All computer data goes through these steps:

  Input → Process → Output

  We give the computer the data (input), the computer processes it and then outputs it.
- The processor is the part in the computer that processes all data so that we can use the computer to do tasks.

Continued

Now try this!

Draw a picture that represents the input–process–output model to show how data is entered, processed and output in a computer system.

- Think about what hardware is used to input data into the computer.
- Draw the computer to show where the data is processed.
- Then think about and draw the hardware that will output the data.

About Boolean data

Earlier in this chapter you learnt that all data a computer deals with needs to be converted to binary. The computer does this because computers use electrical signals to process data. Electrical signals can only be high or low. Binary is a base-2 system, which means it can only use two digits to represent all data.

In Topic 1.2, you learnt about Boolean logic. **Boolean data** can only have *two* possible values: True or False. Boolean values are used for a variety of purposes.

Logic gates

The electricity that computers use to process data flows in and out of **logic gates**. A logic gate is a tiny piece of hardware that is used to control the flow of electricity. It is a bit like a switch. The logic gate tests an input binary value (0 or 1) and outputs a binary value that could be the same or different from the input value. The output depends on the kind of logic gate and what the input is.

Logic gates are extremely small in size. There are millions of logic gates inside the components in a computer system, especially in the processor.

Electricity flows into and out from a logic gate:

- The electricity flowing to the logic gate is known as the input.
- The electricity flowing from a logic gate is known as the output.

Each input into a logic gate can be 1 (high) or 0 (low). The output from the logic gate can also be a 1 or a 0.

Input–process–output

You know that computers take data, process the data and then output the result. In the same way, logic gates take input, process that input and then output the result.

1 Electricity flows into the logic gate.

2 The logic gate applies the rule of the logic gate to the input.

3 The logic gate outputs either a high or low flow of electricity.

You will learn about three logic gates in this topic:

- NOT gate
- OR gate
- AND gate

You learnt about how the Boolean operators work in Topic 1.2. Logic gates use these operators. The three gates are described below.

NOT gate

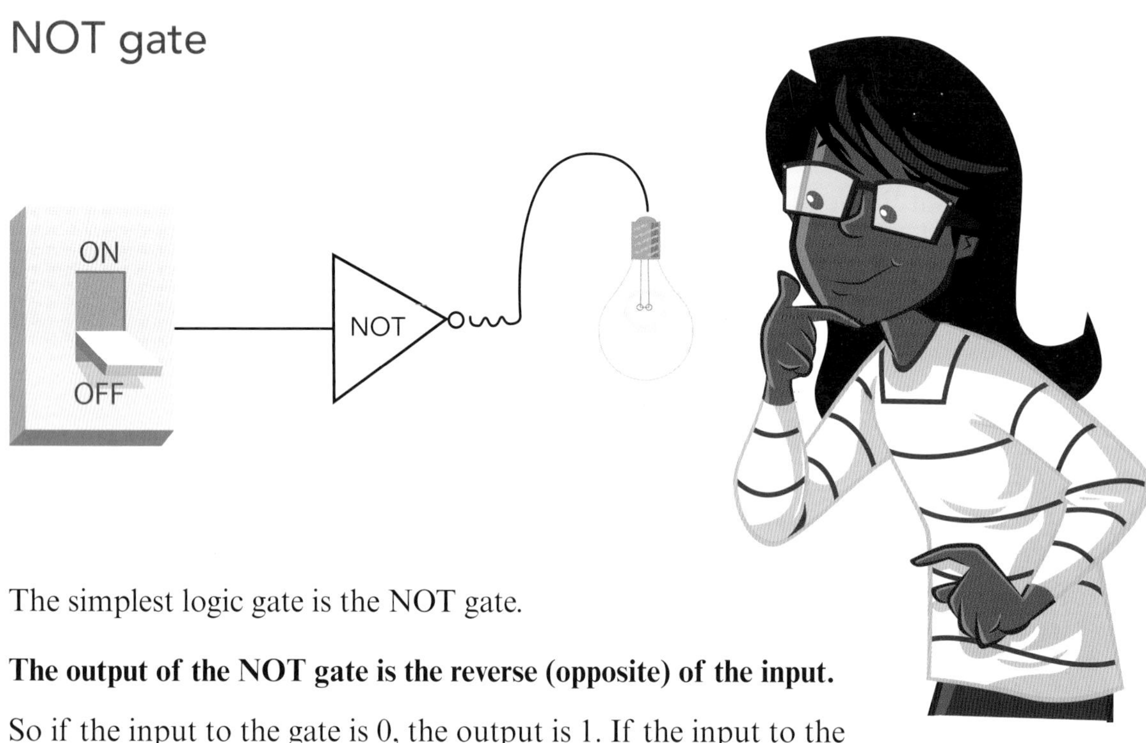

The simplest logic gate is the NOT gate.

The output of the NOT gate is the reverse (opposite) of the input.

So if the input to the gate is 0, the output is 1. If the input to the gate is 1, the output is 0.

NOT gate truth table

The logic of a logic gate can be clearly represented in a **truth table**. You saw something similar in Unit 1, where the results were given as True and False. Because computers work in binary, we use 1 or 0 for truth tables.

A truth table is a special table that is used to show:

- all the possible combinations of inputs for a logic gate
- the logic gate's output for each of these inputs.

You do not need to know how to complete a truth table yet, but they can help you to understand the logic.

The NOT gate has only one input, so there are only two possible combinations. This is a truth table for the NOT logic gate:

Input	Output
1	0
0	1

Table 4.7: Truth table for a NOT gate

Each logic gate also has a special symbol. The symbol for the NOT logic gate is:

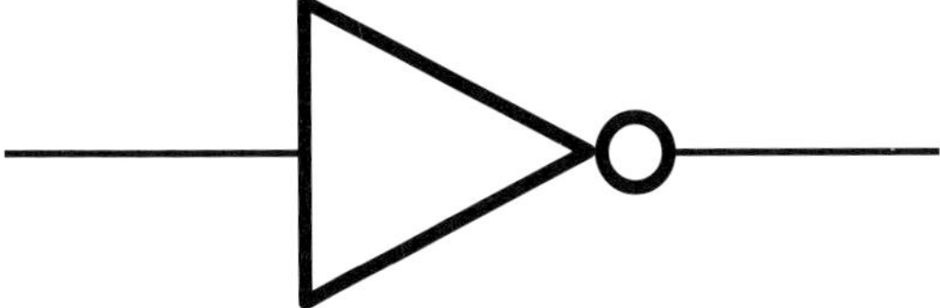

Figure 4.12: NOT gate

OR gate

A more complex logic gate is the OR gate. This logic gate can have more than one input. All logic gates only have one output.

The output of the OR gate is 1 if <u>either</u> or <u>both</u> of the inputs are 1.

Here's an example.

Marcus is hungry.

- If someone gives him one or two pieces of fruit, **he will have something to eat**.
- If nobody gives Marcus anything to eat, **he will not have anything to eat**.

Be careful! The logic gate isn't asking 'Will Marcus eat the apple OR the banana?' It is asking 'Will Marcus have something to eat?' Remember that an answer to a question to a logic gate can either be Yes or No. It can't be anything else.

OR gate truth table

As there are two inputs to the gate, there are four possible combinations for the electricity flowing through the logic gate. This is a truth table that shows the logic for the OR gate.

Input A	Input B	Output
0	0	0
0	1	1
1	0	1
1	1	1

Table 4.8: Truth table for an OR gate

If you look at the truth table, you can see that any time either or both of the inputs are 1, the output is 1. If both the inputs are 0, the output is 0 too.

The OR gate's symbol is:

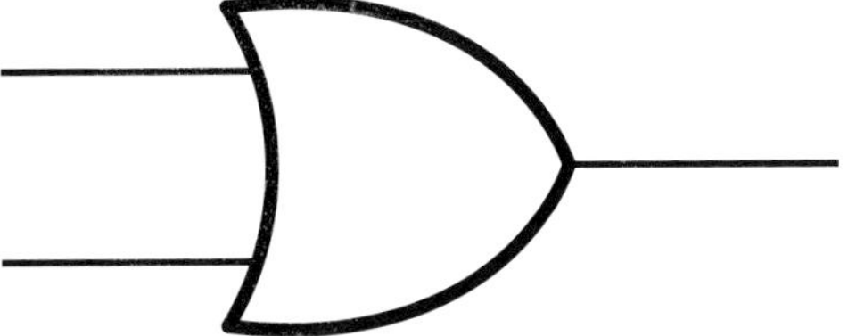

Figure 4.13: OR gate

AND gate

Let's look at one more logic gate: the AND gate. This logic gate has two inputs, but still only one output.

The output of the AND gate is 1 if both of the inputs are 1.

Zara and Sofia have arranged to play badminton together today at school during their lunch break. If they have both remembered to bring their sports kit to school, they will be able to play, but if one or both of them have forgotten their kit, neither of them will be able to play.

Can Zara and Sofia play badminton together?

- If neither Zara nor Sofia have their kit, they can't play. ✗
- If Zara has her kit but Sofia hasn't got hers, they can't play. ✗
- If Sofia has her kit but Zara hasn't got hers, they can't play. ✗
- If both Zara and Sofia have their kit, they can play. ✓

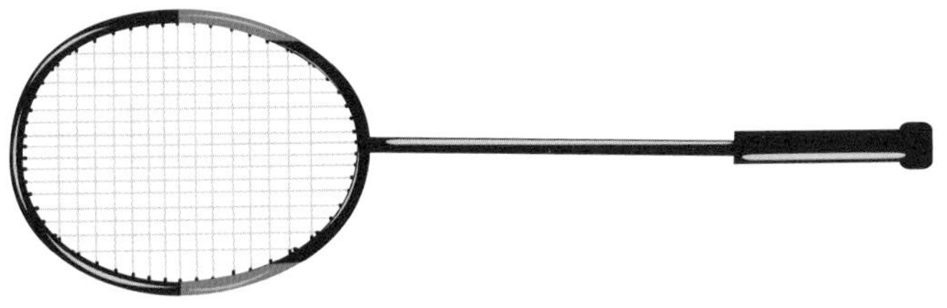

AND gate truth table

As there are two inputs to the gate, there are four possible combinations for the electricity flowing through the logic gate. This is a truth table that shows the logic for the AND gate.

Input A	Input B	Output
0	0	0
0	1	0
1	0	0
1	1	1

Table 4.9: Truth table for an AND gate

If you look at the truth table, you can see that the only time the output is 1 is if both the inputs are 1. If either or both of the inputs are 0, the output is 0.

The AND gate's symbol is:

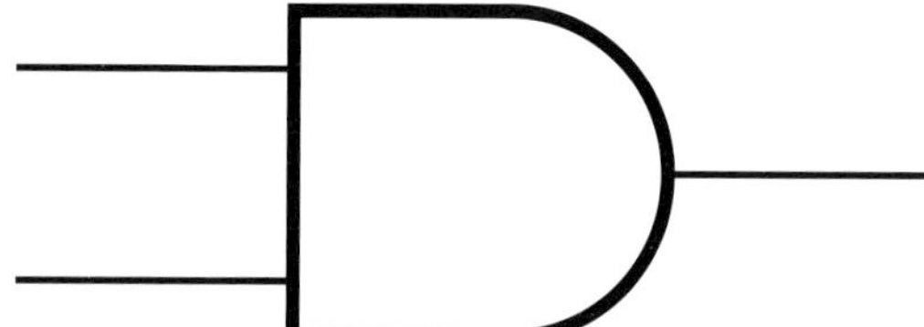

Figure 4.14: AND gate

Unplugged activity 4.6

You will need: a pen and paper

In the section about logic gates, real-life situations were used to help you understand how the logic gates behave. There are some more example situations below. Match each one with the logic gate that best explains how the inputs and outputs work in that situation.

Situation 1

A house has two doors that you can use to enter it: a front door and a back door. Both doors have a doorbell switch next to them. If at least one of the switches is pressed, the doorbell will ring.

Situation 2

A student gets up early if it is a weekday in school term time. If it is a weekday but not school term time, they can stay in bed. If it is school term time but not a weekday, they can stay in bed.

Situation 3

If it is above 20°C in the house, the heating is turned off. If it is below 20°C, the heating comes on.

When you have matched the gates with the situations, draw diagrams using the symbols for the logic gates and the different combinations of inputs and outputs.

Questions 4.7

1 What is a logic gate?

2 Name the three logic gates you have learnt about.

3 When the input is 1, the output is 0. Which logic gate is this?

4 When both of the inputs are 1, the output is 1. Which gates have this logic?

5 Is each of these statements true or false?

   a A logic gate is a piece of hardware.

   b All logic gates have at least two inputs.

   c A truth table shows all the possible combinations of inputs and outputs for a logic gate.

   d The actual inputs and outputs of real logic gates inside a computer are 1s and 0s.

Unplugged activity 4.7

You will need: a pen and paper

Write three more statements about logic gates. Make some of the statements true and some of the statements false. Swap your statements with a partner and complete each other's true or false activity.

Self-assessment

Did your partner give the correct answers for all the statements you wrote? Have you correctly decided whether each statement your partner wrote is true or false? What have you done to check this?

Summary checklist

- [ ] I can explain what a logic gate is.
- [ ] I can describe the role of a logic gate in a computer system.
- [ ] I can describe the rules for the NOT logic gate.
- [ ] I can describe the rules for the AND logic gate.
- [ ] I can describe the rules for the OR logic gate.

› 4.5 Automation and artificial intelligence

In this topic you will:

- learn that artificial intelligence (AI) allows computers to take information in from their surroundings, analyse it, make decisions about it and then produce an output based on this process
- understand that automation is when computers such as robots are programmed to carry out tasks without human input
- learn how automation is used in industries such as health, manufacturing and retail
- learn how AI is used in image recognition and computer games.

Key words

artificial intelligence (AI)

automated system

autonomous

cookies

Getting started

What do you already know?

- Robots are computers that can be programmed to control machines and other physical objects (things you can touch). Robots can be programmed to work autonomously (by themselves).
- Robots can be used in many different industries such as health, manufacturing (making things), delivery services and food production. It is helpful to use robots in these industries, as they can perform repetitive or dangerous tasks.
- AI is a simulation of human intelligence within a computer system.
- AI is used in software such as predictive text and speech-to-text.

Continued

Now try this!

You learnt about robots and AI in previous stages. What can you remember about robots and AI? Spend two minutes thinking about both of them.

Find a partner to work with. Spend five minutes talking to your partner about what you both remember about robots and AI. Make a list of all the knowledge you can remember.

Look at the list you have made. Agree with your partner which are the three things you think are most important to know, and underline them.

Using artificial intelligence

Figure 4.15: Robots programmed with AI

Artificial intelligence (AI) is a simulation of human intelligence within a computer system. A simple way to think about AI is that it is programming a computer to try and think like a human.

Like any other computer system, an AI system takes in data from its surroundings and processes this data to produce an output. The output will depend on how the AI processes the data and what decisions it makes when doing so. The difference between AI and a normal computer system is that AI has been programmed to be able to make decisions by itself, based on logic and reasoning, a bit like humans do.

AI can solve problems without being told how to solve each exact problem it comes across.

One way that AI can be used is to create an **autonomous** computer system. You may have previously learnt that robots can be programmed to be autonomous. If something is autonomous, it means that it can perform tasks without the need for human interaction. The system automatically takes in data – a human does not input the data. This data is then processed and an output is given. Giving computer systems the ability to work autonomously can be very useful in several different situations.

> **Did you know?**
>
> The first working AI was a computer program that could play a game of draughts (also known as checkers).
> A human could be one player and the computer was the other player. A British computer scientist called Christopher Strachey wrote it in 1951.

Automated systems in manufacturing

Automated systems are different from AI. Unlike AI, they can only make decisions using rules they were given beforehand. They can be programmed to automatically do specific actions again and again the same way every time, without humans needing to regularly input instructions. In the manufacturing industry, automated systems can be very useful for performing repetitive tasks quickly and accurately.

For example, in a factory that makes bottles of orange juice, an automated system can be used to fill each bottle and screw the lids on. Using an automated system for this means that every bottle gets exactly the same amount of juice and all the lids are screwed on tightly enough. This is much more difficult for a human to do. An automated system can also fill bottles all day every day. It does not need to take breaks or sleep like a human.

Figure 4.16: An automated bottling system

In the manufacturing industry, automated systems can also be very useful for performing tasks that could be dangerous for humans.

One place that automated systems are used is in the car manufacturing industry. Building cars involves moving large, heavy car parts and placing them very precisely. It would be a difficult and sometimes dangerous task for a human to lift these parts. Car doors and engines are very heavy. A human could badly injure themselves lifting and positioning parts like this many times a day. Other people nearby would also be in danger of heavy parts falling on them if someone dropped one.

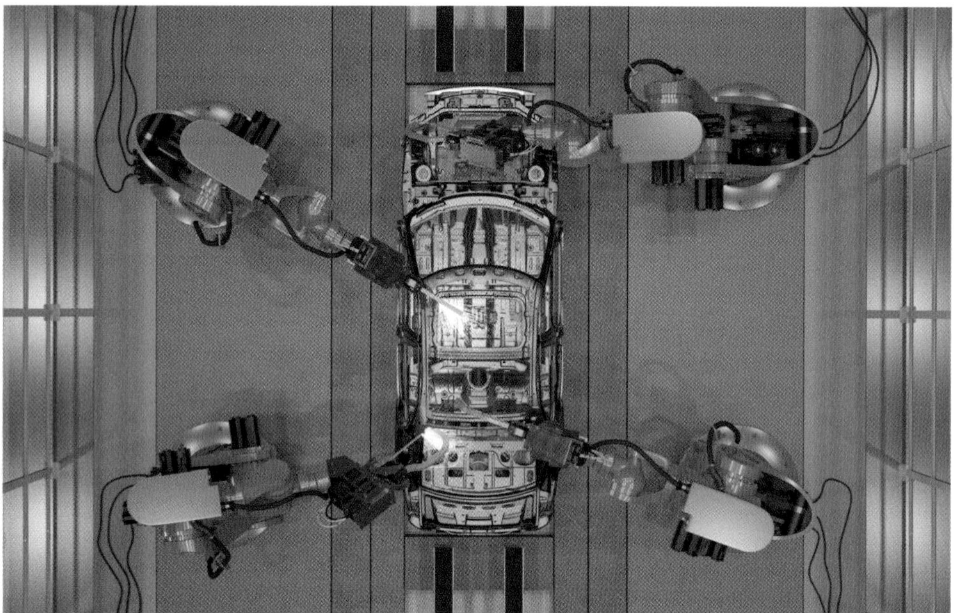

Figure 4.17: Robots building a car

Robots that are programmed to work autonomously can perform these tasks. A robot can be built to lift heavy car parts easily and safely, and place them accurately. This means that humans can keep a safe distance and stay out of danger.

Unplugged activity 4.8

You will need: a pen and paper

The owner of a small handmade chocolate company wants to increase the amount of chocolate they make so that they can sell it in a lot of different stores. They want to build a factory to make the chocolate.

Make a list of tasks that will need to be completed to make the chocolate. Decide whether a person or an automated system should do each task. Write down why you made each decision.

Automated systems in health

In healthcare, automated systems can be very useful for performing tasks at any time of the day. Hospitals can be very busy places and the doctors and nurses that work in them often have a very full schedule.

Many people who receive care in hospital need regular monitoring. For example, a person may need to have their oxygen levels and heart rate measured all the time if they are very ill. If a nurse had to monitor these and change the amount of oxygen given each time, this could be very time consuming.

An automated system can be used to check oxygen levels and heart rate. Then it could decrease or increase the amount of oxygen the patient has depending on the levels, and alert a nurse if the heart rate became too low or too high. This would free up the nurse's time to look after other people in the hospital. It would also mean that the person is monitored all through the night.

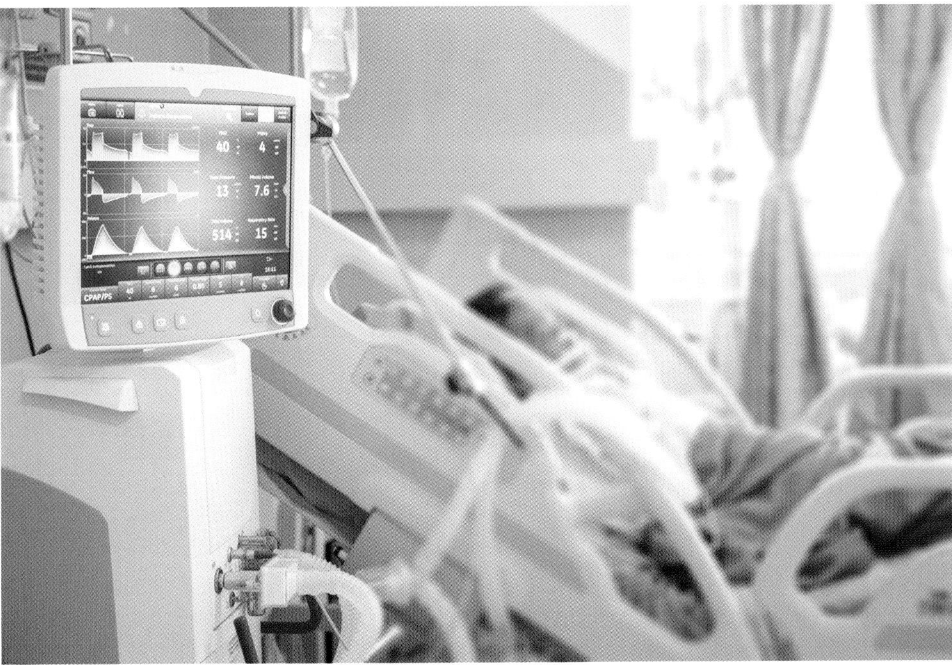

Figure 4.18: An automated system monitoring a patient's oxygen and other levels

In the healthcare industry, automated systems can also be used to perform tasks that may be risky. Radiation (for example X-rays and gamma rays) is used in some treatments in hospitals. Radiation can be harmful to people who do not need this treatment. An automated system can be used to monitor the levels of radiation in a room. It can be programmed to only allow entry to doctors and nurses when the radiation levels are low enough to be safe.

Unplugged activity 4.9

You will need: a pen and paper

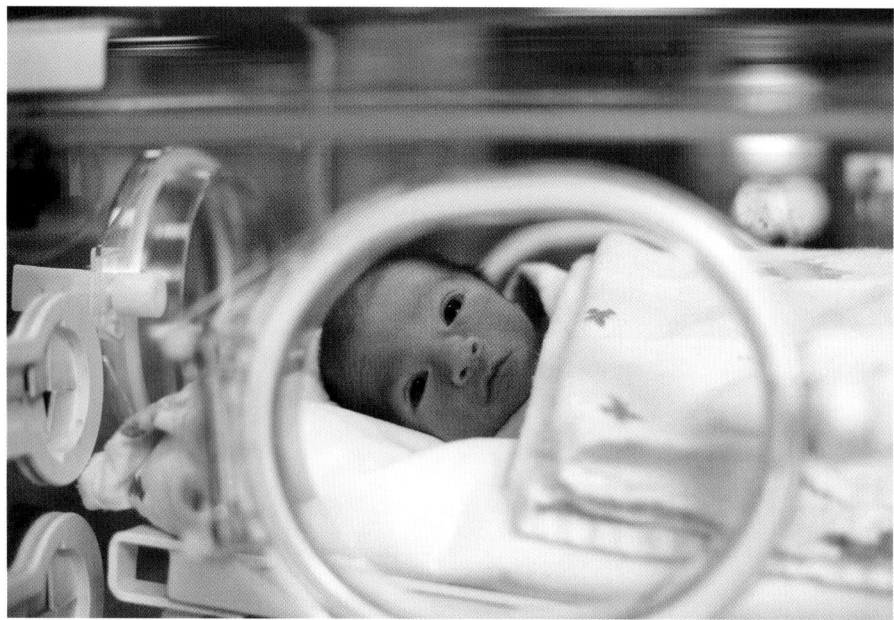

Figure 4.19: Baby in an incubator

Some babies need medical care as soon as they are born. As part of this care, they need to be kept at a constant temperature to make sure they grow and develop properly.

How could an automated system help with this? Find a partner and discuss your thoughts with them. What would the inputs and outputs be? Together, create a plan of how you would use an automated system to keep babies at a constant temperature, and explain how that would be helpful.

Join up with another pair and explain your plan to them.

Peer-assessment

Listen to the plan the other pair explained to you. Did you understand it?

- Say one thing you liked about their plan.
- Think of two questions you want to ask them about their plan.

When the other pair ask you their questions, take turns with your partner to answer one question each.

How did you decide what to include in your plan? After reading through the peer-assessment, what would you include next time that you didn't today?

Automated systems in retail

One of the most well-known automated systems in online retail is the use of **cookies** to show people adverts for things they will probably like.

Cookies are small data files that web servers send to a user's browser when they visit a website. The files identify the user and track what they do online. The collection of cookies on a user's computer helps to build up an idea of what that user likes. For example, if they have looked up information about their favourite movies, bought clothes from certain stores and viewed particular channels on social media, all this information will be recorded in cookies.

Retail companies can request access to view the data in these cookies. An automated system then analyses the data and selects adverts to show them based on what they have looked at before. This is called targeted advertising. Retailers use this to generate more sales.

AI in image recognition

You may have heard of, or even used, a web search tool that lets you use pictures as the search term instead of words. You can take a photo of something and the search tool will tell you what is in the picture. This can be very useful if you see a particular plant or insect and want to know what it is called. The search results will also tell you lots of other information about it.

This system uses AI. The AI analyses the image for information, then searches through a huge database of information to see if there is anything similar to the image. Based on what it finds, the AI will decide what it thinks the object is and provide the user with details about it.

Activity 4.6

You will need: a tablet or smartphone with image-recognition software and internet access

Figure 4.20: Image of a bee that your app could recognise

You are going to use an image-recognition app to perform a specific task. On your device, open the app your teacher tells you to use. Then see if you can use the app to do one of the following tasks.

- Identify a plant or creature and find out information about it.
- Find online stores where you can buy products found in the classroom.
- Translate text on an object or in a book into a different language.
- Find tips for questions in a textbook.

AI in computer games

In computer games, you often have one or more characters or vehicles you can control. There might be a few different things you can control about them, such as:

- the direction they move
- the speed at which they move
- other actions such as jumping.

In some computer games, there are other characters in the game moving around, but you are not controlling them. So what is controlling the direction, speed and other actions of these characters? These characters in the game are programmed with AI. The AI takes the actions you ask your character to do as input. It then uses this data to decide what the other characters will do.

Figure 4.21: A computer game

Activity 4.7

You will need: a pen and paper, a desktop computer, laptop or tablet with word-processing software and internet access

Deep Blue is a chess-playing supercomputer that uses AI to play chess. Use the internet to find out more about Deep Blue and how it uses AI. Make notes in a text document or on paper.

Peer-assessment

Find a partner to work with. Compare what you found out about Deep Blue. If you found out different information share what you found. If you found out the same information, see if you got that information from the same website. Did you both think that was a website you could trust?

Stay safe!

When you are using the internet for research, make sure you only use trustworthy websites. If you doubt that a website is reputable (has a good reputation), do not use it – find another website for your research.

A reputable website is normally written by a trusted and well-known source. It should have up-to-date information. Try to find out who wrote the information on the website and the date it was written.

Questions 4.8

1 What is artificial intelligence?

2 What is an automated system?

3 What are two ways that automated systems can be used in health?

4 How are automated systems used in retail?

Summary checklist

- [ ] I can explain that artificial intelligence (AI) allows computers to take information in from their surroundings, analyse it, make decisions about it and then produce an output based on this process.
- [ ] I can explain that automation is when computers such as robots are programmed to carry out tasks without human input.
- [ ] I can explain how automated systems are used in health, manufacturing and retail.
- [ ] I can explain how AI is used in image recognition.
- [ ] I can explain how AI is used in computer games.

Project: Go nuts!

Zara wants to be a computer game designer when she is older. She has joined the Computer Club at her school and is designing a new game. She has decided to create a booklet about her new game.

The booklet will be in three sections:

1. An introduction about computer games.
2. The main part about the game she is designing.
3. A small section about what device the game can be played on.

Task 1: The introduction

Write a paragraph introducing computer games. Include information about whether computer games are an example of application software or system software.

Task 2: The game

The main character will be a cheeky squirrel who needs to collect lots of acorns.

1. Design two other characters who will appear in the game.
2. Include simple images of each character, made up of pixels.
3. Include the list of data about the pixels in each character (see Topic 4.3 to remind yourself what is needed).
4. Plan the development of the AI for these characters. You will need to think about what actions these characters perform and how those actions are triggered. For example, if the main character steals an acorn, the other character runs after him.

Task 3: The device that the game can be played on

Computer games can be played on several different computer systems. These include personal computers (PC), games consoles, tablet devices and mobile phones.

Write a list showing which devices this game could be played on.

Choose three of these devices. Identify the features and state:

1. whether they are positive or negative for the task of playing computer games
2. why they are positive or negative for this task.

Include images of each device.

Finish by saying which device you would play this computer game on.

Check your progress 4

1 State which would be the most useful design feature for a mobile phone.

- lightweight
- large screen
- good quality speakers

Give reasons for your choice. [2]

2 Five statements are given about software.
Which ones are true? Select all of the correct answers.

A Software is the collection of instructions and data that tell a computer how to operate.

B Application software is designed to allow a computer to be maintained.

C The operating system is the main example of application software.

D Antivirus software is an example of system software.

E Without software, a user could not use the hardware in a computer to perform tasks. [3]

3 Draw lines to match each key term with its correct definition. [7]

Term	Definition
Denary	A continuous stream of data that is made up of many values
Binary	The quality of an image, which is related to the number of pixels it contains for its size
Analogue	A base-10 number system that is mainly used by humans
Digital	Binary data that is processed by a computer system
Pixel	A very small part of an image. Many of these are laid out in a grid to create the image.
Resolution	The number of bits that are used to create colours in an image
Colour depth	A base-2 number system that is used by computers

4 Marcus uses his digital camera to take a photograph of his friend.
Describe how an analogue image that Marcus photographs is converted to digital. [3]

5 Draw the symbol for:
- a the NOT logic gate [1]
- b the OR logic gate. [1]

6 Write the name of the correct logic gate for each of the following statements:
- a This gate only has a single input and output. [1]
- b If either of the inputs to this gate are 1, the output is 1. [1]
- c The only time the output for this logic gate is 1 is when both of the inputs are 1. [1]

> Glossary

Accelerometer: a sensor that detects movement 119

Amplitude: the loudness of a sound, shown by the height of the sound wave 259

Analyse: look carefully at data to work out what it means 147

AND: Boolean operator that has a true result when both conditions are true 34

Application software: programs that let us do tasks using a computer or mobile device, for example word-processing software, web browsers and games 243

Arithmetic operators: addition, subtraction, multiplication and division 68

Artificial intelligence (AI): a simulation of human intelligence within a computer system 272

ASCII: a character set (standard set of binary codes for text characters) that uses 7 bits per character to encode 128 different characters, and it only contains characters used in the English language 252

Assignment statement: a statement that stores data in a variable 68

Attenuation: wireless data transmission that becomes weaker when passing through objects like solid walls or over a long distance 228

Automated system: a computer or robotic system that is programmed to automatically do specific actions again and again the same way every time, without humans needing to regularly input instructions 273

Autonomous: able to work and make decisions without human input 273

Base station: a tower that transmits radio waves in a cellular (mobile) network; the area surrounding each base station is a cell 222

Binary: made up of the language of 1s and 0s computers use to store all data, the binary number system is a base-2 system that only has two different values 226

Bit: a binary digit (a 1 or 0), which the smallest possible unit of computer data 256

Block-based languages: a computer language such as Scratch where you drag blocks to create code 56

Bluetooth Wireless Technology network: a network in which two devices close to each other connect wirelessly using Bluetooth Wireless Technology 218

Boolean condition: a condition that can only be answered by true or false 33

Boolean data: a type of data with two possible values – true or false 263

Boolean logic: a set of rules that are used to test conditions, and the rules are applied to the inputs of a logic gate to create different outputs that are either true or false 34

Bug: a logic error in a program 106

Call: the way that an algorithm accesses a sub-routine 44

Casting: the way to change the data type of a value in Python 77

Cell (in a spreadsheet): a single box on a spreadsheet 147

Cell (mobile networks): an area of land surrounding a radio base station that transmits communications over a wireless cellular network 222

Cell reference: the column letter and row number of a cell in a spreadsheet, for example D4 165

Cellular network (mobile network): a network that transmits communications from one mobile device to another via land-based radio towers 222

Cipher: an encryption algorithm (the steps of a method for encrypting data) 225

Character: a letter, symbol, space or punctuation mark that can be typed on a keyboard, for example R o % ;) ? $ _ and * 252

Character set: a standard set of binary codes that represent each letter or symbol that can be typed on a keyboard 252

Colour depth: the number of bits (binary digits) that are used to create colours in an image 256

Comparison operators: >, <, >=, <= 31

Condition: a test that gives a true or false result 28, 148

Conditional formatting: formatting that is applied to a spreadsheet cell based on a condition that is given in a rule 148

Cookies: small data files sent between a web server and web browser to identify a web user and track their online activity 277

Corruption: errors that accidentally occur in computer data, causing changes or damage to the original data 226

Critical thinking: using all the available facts and analysing them to judge how good or effective something is 237

Crosstalk: interference in a data signal that can happen when electrical energy in one cable causes an unwanted effect in another cable 228

Cycle: the whole of a wave (such as a radio wave), measured from the top of one wave to the top of the next 214

Data capture form: a form that is designed to collect data from a person 192

Data flow: the arrows that show you how to move through the flowchart 10

Data type: the format that a data comes in 74

Database: a collection of data about the same topic or type of thing, arranged in tables, usually on a computer 177

Debug: the process of finding and correcting a bug 106

Decrypt: unscramble data to its original form so that it can be understood 230

Denary: a base-10 number system that is mainly used by humans, where base-10 means there can be ten different values in the number system (0, 1, 2, 3, 4, 5, 6, 7, 8 and 9) and these are used in different combinations to represent all possible numbers 249

Digit: one of the numerals (single numbers) from 0 to 9 249

Digital certificate: a data file that shows a website, device or user can be trusted, and that the internet connection is secure 211

Domain name: a text-based address for a web server, such as *example.com* 205

Domain name server (DNS): a piece of network hardware that stores a database of domain names (text-based web addresses) and their matching IP addresses (number-based web addresses) 207

Effective: something is good at doing its job 192

Editor: a special piece of software that lets you write code 57

Efficient: programs that run quicker or use less memory 43

Encrypted: scrambled into a code so that no one can understand it without the right password or equipment 210

Evaluate: to get an idea of the value of something by carefully looking at and thinking about it 84

Extended ASCII: a character set (standard set of binary codes for text characters) that uses 8 bits per character to encode 256 different characters, and it only contains characters used in English and some European languages 253

Feature: an aspect or part of a computer system or device 236

Field: a column in a database table, which contains information about one aspect of all the items in the database, such as colour, price or length 178

Flowchart: a diagram that shows a sequence of steps that should be followed 10

Formatting: the style that is applied to text or other aspects of a document, such as a cell in a spreadsheet 148

Formula: a simple calculation in a spreadsheet cell, for example =5-6 or =D4*G11 165

Frequency: the number of times something happens in a certain amount of time, for example radio/sound wave frequency tells us how many cycles there are per second, and a high frequency sound wave has a higher pitch 214, 259

Function: a built-in piece of code in a spreadsheet that saves us having to type a long formula to perform more complex calculations 165

Gravitational force: a measurement of acceleration caused by gravity 119

Hacking: using knowledge of computing to achieve a goal or overcome an obstacle, often by doing something unusual, and security hacking is when a person explores ways of getting into a computer system they are not authorised to access 229

Hypertext transfer protocol secure (https): a safe set of rules and standards that encrypts the data being transmitted, meaning there is less chance of someone stealing or misusing the data 204

Identifier: a name given to sub-routines and variables 44

Identity fraud: using someone else's personal details to pretend to be them or to buy things with their money 230

Identity theft: stealing someone else's personal details 229

IF, THEN, ELSE: the three parts of a selection statement 28

Initialising: setting a variable to a starting value 73

Input: for the user to enter data 10, 77

Interface: how you interact with the computer 84

Interference: disruption to a data signal caused by radio waves crashing into other radio waves 227

integrated development environments (IDE): an editor that allows you to run programs 57

IP address (Internet protocol address): a string of numbers that identifies each device that is connected to the internet, for example 192.0.2.1 205

LED (light-emitting diode): a light-emitting diode 113

Logic error: the program has the correct syntax, but there is an error that means the program doesn't do what it is supposed to do 104

Logic gate: a very small component in a computer system that controls the flow of electricity within the computer, and there are different types of logic gate including AND, OR and NOT 263

Maintain: to look after something and keep it in good condition 244

Manage (system software): to control the use of resources like power and space, making sure they are used in a way that makes sense 244

Mimic: to closely copy an event or process 168

Model: a computer file or program that represents a real-life system or process, where data is changed to see what happens 160

Modelling: changing values in a model to see what different outcomes are produced 162

NOT: Boolean operator that has a true result when the input condition is false 34

Operating system: a collection of programs that control and manage all the computer's software and hardware 244

OR: Boolean operator that has a true result when either condition is true 34

Outcome: the result or an effect of an action 161

Output: to display words and numbers to the user 10

Pairing: putting two things together, for example in networking, pairing refers to connecting two devices using a Bluetooth Wireless Technology connection 218

Path: the part of a text-based website address that is the file name for a web page 205

Pattern: a repeated design or sequence 41

Pattern recognition: looking at a design or sequence to identify a pattern 41

Personal data: data that helps to identify a particular person, for example their name, address, phone number, date of birth or identification number 192

Pixel: images are made up of thousands of pixels laid out in a grid, and one pixel is a tiny part of an image, which would look like a single-coloured square if you zoomed in 254

Place value: the value of a digit (how much it is worth), which we know from its position in a number, for example the place value of the 4 in the number 345 (three hundred and forty-five) is 40 249

Primary key: a field (column) in a database that contains a unique piece of data for each record (row), which makes sure that each record is different from all of the other records in at least one field 178

print: the Python statement that produces output 60

Process: to do a calculation or action 10

Project plan: plans that are used to decide what you are going to and when you are going to it 88

Protocol: a set of rules and standards that devices use when communicating 204

Prototype: an early version of an end product 84

Query: a request to search for or change particular data stored in a database, and it is written using criteria 181

Record: a single row in a table, which contains all the fields of information about one item in the database, for example the price, colour, length and number of a particular product in stock in a shop 178

Reserved word: a word that Python already uses 67

Resolution: the amount of detail that can be seen in an image, which is related to the number of pixels the image contains, and it can also mean how many pixels wide and how many pixels high an image is 255

Return: the command that tells a sub-routine to go back to the main code 44

Router: a hardware device that connects a network, for example in a house or office to the internet 215

Rule: an instruction that tells spreadsheet software to apply certain formatting to a cell when a certain condition is met 148

Sample rate: the number of times per second a sample is taken, measured in hertz (Hz) 260

Sampling: measuring a sound wave regularly and recording the reading using binary digits 260

Scenario: a description of a situation that might happen 162

Selection statement: used when a decision needs to be made in an algorithm 28

Simulator: a machine or computer program that gives a realistic imitation of a real-life system, such as an aeroplane, often used for training purposes 168

Software development: the process where you design, create and test a program 84

Spreadsheet: a document containing thousands of cells (boxes) arranged in rows and columns that can be used to store data and do calculations 147

Spreadsheet model: a representation of a real-life system or process that is created using spreadsheet software, so that data can be changed to see what happens 150

Statement: a sentence that provides the conditions of a rule when using conditional formatting 148

Sub-routine: a self-contained algorithm that can be used by other code 44

Surge: an unexpected sudden increase in electric voltage or current 227

Syntax: the grammar of the language, or the set of rules that have to be followed 56

Syntax errors: mistakes when the set of rules of the language aren't followed 56

System software: software, like an operating system, that computers use to help them function (work), run other software and manage and maintain the hardware 244

Systematically: working through a process one step at a time 106

Table: a structure made up of columns and rows that hold information, for example a database is made up of tables 178

Test plan: a formal way of recording testing 92

Text-based language: a computer language such as Python where you write statements 56

Truth table: a table that shows all the possible combinations of inputs for a logic gate and the output for each input 264

Unicode: the character set most websites use to encode text, and it uses between 8 and 32 bits per character to represent over a million characters 253

Unique: the only one of its kind, and nothing else is exactly the same 178

URL (Uniform resource locator): a text-based address for a website 204

User interface: the way in which a user interacts with a device, for example by moving a mouse and clicking on images on a screen 237

Utilities: tools that help analyse and make the best use of computer resources, like antivirus software, data compression tools and software for defragmenting 245

Variables: a named storage location where you can store data 13

Web browser: software that we use to visit and display web pages 204

Web server: a computer that stores the data and software to run websites 204

Wi-fi network: a wireless network that connects devices using radio waves 215

Wireless access point (WAP): a small hardware device that allows other devices to connect wirelessly to a wired network using radio waves 215

Wireless network interface card (or controller) (WNIC): the part of a computer's hardware that allows the device to connect to and communicate with a wireless network 215

> Acknowledgements

The authors and publishers acknowledge the following sources of copyright material and are grateful for the permissions granted. While every effort has been made, it has not always been possible to identify the sources of all the material used, or to trace all copyright holders. If any omissions are brought to our notice, we will be happy to include the appropriate acknowledgements on reprinting.

Thanks to the following for permission to reproduce images:

Cover Photo: AF-studio/GI

Unit 1: Olena_T/GI; Burke/GI; Cris Cantón/GI; Enot-poloskun/GI; Biblioteca Ambrosiana/GI; MirageC/GI; Erlon Silva-TRI Digital/GI; Kenny Williamson/GI; Melinda Podor/GI; Ina FassBender/GI; PeopleImages/GI; Degui Adil/GI; Shanina/GI; KristinaVelickovic/GI; RLT_Images/GI; Traffic_analyzer/GI; ATHVisions/GI; RobinOlimb/GI; PeterPencil/GI; Tovovan/GI; Jeff Spicer/GI; Gorica/GI; Justin Lewis/GI; Mikroman6/GI; Serdar415/GI; ONYXprj/GI; TravelCouples/GI; Tom Werner/GI; FangXiaNuo/GI; CandO_Designs/GI; JakeOlimb/GI; Daly and Newton/GI; Marina Andriychuk/GI; Yuichiro Chino/GI; MarsBars/GI; JDawnInk/GI; Paula Daniëlse/GI; Gary Chalker/GI; Riou/GI; Manusapon kasosod/GI; **Unit 2:** Jopstock/GI; Shannon Fagan/GI; Simon2579/GI; Hill Street Studios/GI; Doug van Kampen/GI; Ekapol/GI; CandO_Designs/GI; FluxFactory/GI; Peter Dazeley/GI; Macida/GI; Greg Pease/GI; Songsak rohprasit/GI; South China Morning Post/GI; Sergii Iaremenko/GI; Nadore/GI; Snorkulencija/GI; UroshPetrovic/GI; Ilya Rumyantsev/GI; Nomadnes/GI; Wokephoto17/GI; Caia Image/GI; Kasayizgi/GI; Yingyai Pumiwatana/GI; Yuichiro Chino/GI; Petko Ninov/GI; Carol Yepes/GI; **Unit 3:** Yuichiro Chino/GI; Roos Koole/GI; Matejmo/GI; AerialPerspective Images/GI; Fonikum/GI; AWSeebaran/GI; Kittichai Boonpong/GI; Cavan Images/GI; Avector/GI; The Bluetooth® word mark and logos are registered trademarks owned by Bluetooth SIG, Inc. and any use of such marks by Cambridge University Press & Assessment is under license. Other trademarks and trade names are those of their respective owners; Eyesfoto/GI; Busakorn Pongparnit/GI; Daniel Grizelj/GI; Catherine Falls Commercial/GI; Pobytov/GI; Pictore/GI; Yuichiro Chino/GI; SolStock/GI; **Unit 4:** Muriel de Seze/GI; Bloomberg/GI; Tascha Rassadornyindee/GI; Tvn Phph Prung Sakdi/GI; Morsa Images/GI; Sally Anscombe/GI; Busakorn Pongparnit/GI; Jeffrey Coolidge/GI; Rawpixel/GI; Nipitpon Singad/GI; Catherine Falls Commercial/GI; Hulton Archive/GI; Jackie Bale/GI; Karol Franks/GI; MR.Cole_Photographer/GI; Yuichiro Chino/GI; Indeccraft/GI; Yasser Chalid/GI; Andriy Onufriyenko/GI; SOPA Images/GI; Group4 Studio/GI; Xia yuan/GI; Imstepf Studios Llc/GI; Jackyenjoyphotography/GI; ER Productions Limited/GI; Paul Mödden/GI; Gremlin/GI; Floortje/GI; Martin Poole/Gi; Tim Robberts/GI.

Key GI= Getty Images.

Cover image by Pablo Gallego (Beehive Illustration)

Scratch is a project of the Scratch Foundation, in collaboration with the Lifelong Kindergarten Group at the MIT Media Lab. It is available for free at https://scratch.mit.edu

Micro: bit screenshots are used with thanks to the Micro: bit Educational Foundation

Screenshots from Microsoft software are used with permission from Microsoft.